Also by Mary E. Naples

Cult of the Captured Bride:
How Ancient Women Took Power

UNSUNG HEROES

WOMEN IN THE ANCIENT WORLD

MARY E. NAPLES

Unsung Heroes: Women in the Ancient World
Copyright © 2024 by Mary Naples

ISBN: 979-8-218-36419-9

EBook ISBN: 979-8-218-40459-8

To My Unsung hero, Tim
With love and gratitude.

TABLE OF CONTENTS

ANCIENT WOMEN IN HISTORY

ANCIENT WOMEN IN MYTHOLOGY

ANCIENT WOMEN IN COMMUNITY

TIMELINE FOR THE ANCIENT WORLD

BCE - Before Common Era
CE - Common Era
* Numerically equivalent to BC and AD

Greek Neolithic Age: c. 7000 BCE - 3200 BCE

Beginning of a settled human lifestyle. Known for the advent of agriculture for which women played key roles. Based on artifacts, most scholars believe that the feminine fertility festival of the Thesmophoria had its roots planted in Neolithic soil.

Bronze Age: 3000 BCE- 1500 BCE Minoan Era

Minoan Crete was the cultural mainspring of the Mediterranean until it was overpowered from the north by the (Indo-European) Mycenaean invasions in the 18th century BCE. Though their civilization eventually fell to the Mycenaeans, the Minoans had a strong influence on Mycenaean culture. To date, their writing system (Linear A) has not been decrypted.

Mycenaean Era (Late Bronze Age): 1800 BCE- 1100 BCE

The Mycenaeans were an advanced civilization with palatial states and urban centers. They traded extensively throughout the Mediterranean and were known for their engineering feats. With ruins ranked amongst the wonders of the prehistoric world, they built megaron type palaces, reinforced bridges, massive fortification walls, and beehive-shaped tombs.

Though they had a writing system (Linear B) it was primarily confined to inventories and everyday record keeping in this highly bureaucratic society. Because no narrative compositions exist from this time, they are considered pre or protohistoric. Called the "First Greeks" because they were the first to use the Indo-European (Greek) language.

They fostered an elite war-like culture and provoked the widespread suppression of goddess worship in Minoan Crete and on the Greek mainland replacing the indigenous mother earth goddesses with their thunderous and war-like male sky gods (eg. Zeus).

Greek Dark Age or **Sub-Mycenaean Period** (Late Bronze Age/ Early Iron Age): 1100-800 BCE

Known for the collapse of the Mycenaean citadels and palatial states likely due to natural disasters, invasions, and political/social unrest. A period with little or no cultural output and little contact with other societies. Though events in this period are thought to have greatly influenced the early Greeks during the Archaic Age, no written evidence exists from this era.

Ancient Greece (Iron Age): 800 BCE-31 BCE

Archaic Age: 800 BCE- 480 BCE

A period known for establishing the basic tenets of Greek civilization. The earliest surviving literature from the Greek world—Hesiod's *Works and Days* and Homer's The *Iliad*—were composed during the 8th century BCE.

Known for the creation of the *polis* (city-state) which laid down the groundwork for democracy. Architecturally, the first distinctively stone temples were built.

As sailors and explorers, colonization of nearby areas (e.g. Southern Italy and Sicily) began as early as the 8th century BCE primarily due to farmland shortage and overcrowding of the city-states.

Classical Age: 480 BCE - 323 BCE

Made significant contributions in the areas of philosophy, mathematics, astronomy, medicine, architecture, and the advent of Greek drama. Democratic rule was established in addition to more advanced warfare techniques.

Hellenistic Age: 323 BCE - 31 BCE

Marked a new wave in Greek colonization, Alexander and his successors established Greek monarchies throughout the east. This age begins with the death of Alexander the Great and ends with the death of his ultimate successor, Cleopatra VII, and the conquest of Egypt by Rome. The end of the Hellenistic Age marks the ascendance of the Roman Empire.

Ancient Rome: 753 BCE -27 BCE

753 BCE The mythical founding of Rome by the twins Romulus and Remus

625 BCE The official founding of Rome located in the areas of ancient Italy known as Etruria and Latium. A threat from the Etruscans led to the unification of Latium villages. Ruled by no fewer than six kings. Expanded and advanced militarily.

Roman Republic: 510 BCE - 31 BCE

Monarchy and kingship are replaced by upper class rule: namely senators and equestrians (knights). Continued to expand but soon descended into a period of civil wars. Shift to imperialism began in 60 BCE when Julius Caesar rose to power.

44 BCE: Assassination of Julius Caesar replaced by Octavian (his heir) who ruled alongside Marc Antony.

31 BCE: Battle of Actium. Octavian defeated Antony and Cleopatra marking Rome's conquest of Egypt and leaving Octavian as sole ruler of Rome.

Roman Empire: 27 BCE - 476 CE

27 BCE: Title of Augustus and princeps given to Octavian thereby granting him complete control of the state and ending the Roman republic. This marks the beginning of the principate and empire.

117 CE: Roman Empire reached its maximum size, spanning three continents: Asia Minor, North Africa, and most of Europe.

286 CE: Roman Empire split into Western and Eastern Empires each with its own emperor.

Persecution of Pagans

From 389-392 CE Roman Emperor Theodosius issued a series of decrees forbidding paganism of any form. even private religious rites were verboten.

The wholesale destruction and dismantling of temples and defacing of statuary occurred during this time.

In the Roman Forum the sacred fire was extinguished in the Temple of Vesta and the sisterhood of the Vestal Virgins was disbanded.

Less than 65 years later in 455 CE the Western Empire was sacked by the Vandals (a Germanic group) destroying much of the city. A hobbled Rome continued until 476 CE when the Western Roman Empire officially came to an end.

Eastern Roman Empire/Byzantine (capital in Constantinople): 286 CE-15th century CE

Distinguished as a Christian state with Greek as the official language. With the notable exception of religion, it was known for preserving the traditions of Ancient Greece and Rome. It survived until the 15th century CE when the Turks took control, changing the name of its capital from Constantinople to Istanbul.

Ancient Israel

17th century BCE: Abraham and patriarchs settle the land of Israel.

12th century BCE - 586 BCE: **Pre-exilic period.** The population appears to have been polytheistic as is marked by archaeological and literary evidence of Asherah worship.

586 BCE: Marks the fall of the Southern Kingdom of Judah, defined by the destruction of Jerusalem and the First Temple of Jerusalem ending the pre-exilic period. Most jews exiled.

538-142 BCE: **Second Temple Period.** During this time population became manifestly more monotheistic.

LIST OF ILLUSTRATIONS

1. An Egyptian portrait of a Ptolemaic queen, likely Cleopatra. c. 51 BCE-30 BCE. The Brooklyn Museum.

2. Granite head attributed to Caesarion. Found in the submerged sections of ancient Alexandria, 1st century BCE. Bibliotheca Alexandria Antiquities Museum, Egypt.

3. Statuette of Isis Nursing Horus. c. 664 BCE-332 BCE. The Metropolitan Art Museum, New York.

4. Egyptian limestone statue identified as Cleopatra and Marc Antony's twins Cleopatra Selene and Alexander Helios. c. 50-30 BCE. Wikimedia Commons.

5. Kleopatra Selene. Queen, Wife of Juba II, 25 BC-AD 24. Courtesy of Classical Numismatic Group.

6. Julia Caesaris Filia. c. 9 BCE. Wikimedia Commons.

7. Augustus of Prima Porta. c. 20 BCE. Wikimedia Commons.

8. (Vipsania) Agrippina the Elder. Marble Bust, c. 1st half of first century CE. Istanbul Archaeological Museum. Via Wikimedia commons.

9. Etching of Sejanus arrested and condemned to death. 18th century CE. By G. Mochetti after drawing by Bartolomeo Pinelli. Via Wikimedia Commons.

10. Nero and Agrippina the Younger depicted upon his ascension as emperor. c. 54-59 CE. Museum in Aphrodisias in Turkey. Via Wikimedia Commons.

25. Bronze statue of a Spartan woman, c. 500 bce. British museum. Via Wikimedia Commons.

26. Asherah Ivory Box. Minat al Bayda Ras. c. 1300 BCE. Via Wikimedia Commons.

27. Drawing of Kuntillet Ajrud. 9th century BCE. Via Wikimedia Commons.

28. Judaean female clay pillar figurines. 9th century to 586 BCE. Via Wikimedia Commons.

MAP OF THE MYCENAEAN PERIOD

c. 1700 BCE-1100 BCE

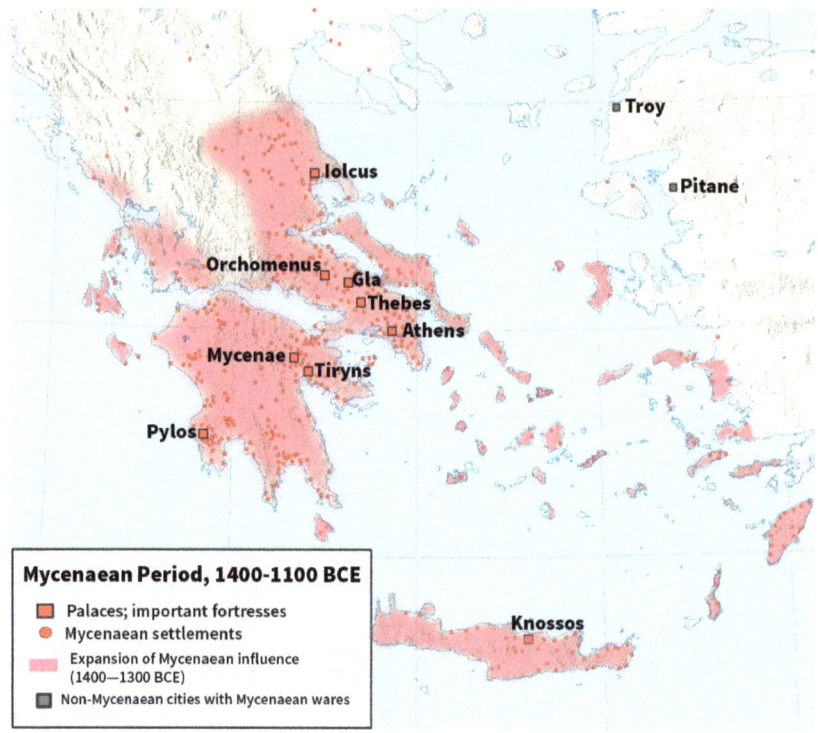

Courtesy: Wikimedia Commons

MAP OF THE GREEK WORLD

800 BCE- 31 BCE

Courtesy: Wikimedia Commons

MAP OF THE ROMAN EMPIRE

27 BCE-476 CE

Courtesy: Wikimedia Commons

PREFACE

I began writing about the ancient world while I was studying for a Master of Arts degree in Humanities with an emphasis in Women's Studies at Dominican University of California. While there, I discovered a fascination for learning about women in the ancient world. Frequently disregarded, women's stories have not only been buried by ancient chroniclers but oftentimes they are overlooked by modern historians as well.

The following is a compilation of articles written about women in the ancient world that were published by the online sites of *Classical Wisdom* or *Ancient Origins* over a period of ten years or so. All of my research is based on scholarship gleaned from various academic sources, including primary sources, whenever possible.

Please note that the articles may not correspond precisely to the categories in which they have been assigned. Frequently articles from Ancient Women in Community could just as easily be assigned to Ancient Women in Mythology or even Ancient Women in History. For example, I considered assigning Asherah, the lost Hebrew goddess, to Ancient Women in Mythology, after all, Asherah is a goddess not unlike Demeter—Greek goddess of the harvest. Instead, I placed the article in Ancient Women in Community since the focus is more about the anthropological context of her worship than it is about Asherah, the goddess herself.

As it happens in the ancient world, the boundaries between fact and fiction are not always clear-cut. Most experts agree that mythological women such as Clytemnestra, Helen, and to some degree Medea are composites of historical women with origins that may predate ancient Greece itself—as I note in the articles. In researching the ancient world, I have found that there is often a strong correlation between history and mythology. It has been argued that myths passed down through the ages spring from some form of cultural memory. As we peel back the mythological layers, vestiges of historical fact can be discerned with interpretations that are frequently supported by archaeological data,

With the exception of Asherah, and to some degree Cleopatra, the articles are predominantly from the Classical Greek and Roman worlds, though there are two articles from the the Byzantine era or the Eastern Roman Empire which is often considered a subset of the Classical World.

It is useful to consider that despite the voluminous scholarship that has been read, analyzed, and synthesized—when it comes to the ancient world, the only certainty is uncertainty; much about the realm of antiquity is open to interpretation.

Ancient Women in History

CHAPTER ONE

In Search of Cleopatra: The Early Years

Before apocryphally rolling out of the carpet and stepping into legend, Cleopatra (69 BCE-30 BCE) (see Figure 1) already had a storied past. The 21-year-old and her 13-year-old brother-husband Ptolemy XIII (62 BCE-47 BCE) ruled together for nearly two years before said brother, influenced by overly ambitious advisors, banished Cleopatra from Alexandria.

Prudently using her mastery of the Egyptian language—the first Ptolemy to do so in the nearly 300-year-old dynasty[1]—Cleopatra mounted an army to defeat Ptolemy. It was only shortly thereafter that she had the legendary encounter with Caesar. Yet most of what has been written about Cleopatra concerns her entanglement with ancient Rome—that is to say, it was written from a decidedly biased Roman perspective. Time and again, we hear about Cleopatra as the subversive siren from the East who seduced two of ancient Rome's greatest generals.

---

[1] The Ptolemies were Greek, besides Cleopata, none learned the language of the majority of their subjects— a Demotic form of Egyptian. In a sense the Ptolomies ruled over two Egypts— a Hellenistic kingdom with its capital in Alexandria—the cultural and scientific center of the world— and a native Egypt which accommodated the indigenous people with its religious capital in Memphis.

What could account for so much ire against the Egyptian queen? The truth is, in order to justify an unpopular civil war against his rival Marc Antony (83 BCE-30 BCE), Gaius Octavius "Octavian" (later Augustus—63 BCE-14 CE) launched first a propaganda campaign then a full-scale war against Egypt. He did so by painting Cleopatra as an Eastern harlot who seduced Antony with her depraved sorcery. This view soon took hold in the imaginations of the xenophobic and misogynist Romans. In his *Odes*, Horace calls her a "fatal monster," Sextus Propertius refers to her as the "whore queen" in *Elegies*, and in Lucan's *Poems* she is termed "Egypt's shame." What is never mentioned about the Egyptian queen is that she may not have had a drop of Egyptian blood. In fact, her lineage may have derived from a Macedonian Greek whose military accomplishments were the ambition of every Roman leader.

It is ironic that forasmuch as the Romans glorified Alexander the Great (356 BCE-323 BCE) they heaped an equivalent amount of disdain on Cleopatra, who was not only Alexander's political heir but may very well have been his biological heir[2] as well. Ptolemy I Soter (367 BCE-282 BCE), the founding member of the Ptolemaic dynasty, was one of Alexander's three most trusted Macedonian generals and by some accounts, his half-brother as well. While vilified in the Greek city-states, polygamy was practiced in the Greek kingdom of Macedonia, especially amongst the ruling class. Phillip II (386 BCE-336 BCE), Alexander's father, had several wives and many children, Ptolemy among them. Alexander even had a sister named Kleopatra, which in Greek means "glory of the father." Cleopatra was, in fact, a common name amongst queens in Ptolemaic Egypt. Alas, Cleopatra's link to Alexander continued after her demise; the Hellenistic period begins with the death of Alexander and ends with the death of Cleopatra.

---

2   Jane Draycott, *Cleopatra's Daughter: From Roman Prisoner to African Queen* (London: W.W. Norton, 2023), 170. Stacy Schiff, *Cleopatra: A Life* (New York: Back Bay Books, 2010), 20.

After Alexander's death, his empire was divided between his three generals, with Ptolemy winning the grand prize of Egypt. Alexandria, founded by Alexander in 331 BCE, had become Egypt's new Hellenistic capital. Because of the location of Alexandria's port—ideally situated between the burgeoning metropolis of Rome and the Orient—it became both an economic and intellectual mecca almost overnight. During its peak, Alexandria was the largest and most affluent city in the world. Upstart, backwater Rome paled in comparison to the glittering marble and jewel-encrusted splendor of Alexandria. Sparing no expense for their shining city by the bay, the early Ptolemies commissioned some of the most notable architecture of the ancient world—for example, the Lighthouse of Alexandria, one of the Seven Wonders of the Ancient World, was built on the island of Pharos adjacent to Alexandria. Under Ptolemy I the Great Library of Alexandria and its accompanying museum (*mouseion*-home of the muses) was built. Second to none in the Hellenized world, the transcendent Great Library and *Mouseion* attracted the best minds of the day, Cleopatra among them. Intellectually gifted with a talent for language—she was fluent in nine of them—she flourished in this rarified space.

Even her most ardent detractors begrudgingly praise Cleopatra for her considerable conversational and rhetoric skills. In his *Lives of Marcus Antonius*, Plutarch quips: "Plato speaks of four kinds of flattery, but Cleopatra knew a thousand." While her sweeping intellect and aptitude for languages likely came naturally, her erudition and rhetoric skills must have been learned. While the Greeks kept their daughters in a state of near ignorance, Ptolemaic girls were educated alongside their male counterparts. On account of sibling marriage, Ptolemaic girls stood just as good a chance at governing as their boys. Sibling marriage was a tradition the Ptolemies inherited from their Pharaonic forebears and was used to keep power in the clan by not weakening the Macedonian bloodline. It also helped prevent foreign powers from infiltrating Egypt.

While growing up, Cleopatra didn't have to look far to find authoritative female role models. Sibling marriage gave Ptolemaic women power they would never have had in ancient Greece. Sister-wives ruled right alongside their brother-husbands. Whereas women in ancient Greece were better seen (though rarely in public) than heard, Ptolemaic female rulers oversaw public works, built temples, mounted defense, and waged war. Egypt was also progressive for its time in gender relations. Unlike Greece, Egyptian women could arrange their own marriages and once married, did not have to defer to their husband's will. They could divorce, hold property, and inherit—all things beyond the reach of Greek women.

And it was not much better in Rome at the time. Roman women could not own or inherit property either. Moreover, they were restricted from being active in politics; in fact they could not even vote. Educated at a minimum, Roman women lived under the authority of a male; either their father, husband, or brothers who acted as their guardians throughout their lifetimes. Respected solely as wives and mothers, Roman women were defined by the men in their lives. Women who departed from the norm of the submissive matron were often ostracized from society at large.

While Egyptian women were liberated in comparison with their Greek and Roman counterparts, queens in Ptolemaic Egypt still needed a male co-regent. Though she ruled briefly alongside her father Ptolemy the XII until his death in 51 BCE, she and her ten-year-old brother Ptolemy XIII inherited the throne as co-regents. In co-regents, Cleopatra's options were limited: her 10-year-old brother, or her even younger seven-year-old brother. Married in name only, Cleopatra VII ruled for several years with Ptolemy XIII, until he—and his counsels—-had her ousted.

Why the ouster? Demonstrating the fortitude for which she would become renowned, she took charge in no time running roughshod over her younger brother/husband. Feeling slighted, the boy-king, Ptolemy XIII, and his ambitious advisors, led by the eunuch, Pothinus, forced Cleopatra out of Alexandria in 50 BCE.

Ultimately she decamped to Ascalon (today's southwestern Israel) where she amassed an army to take back the throne when a civil war broke out between Julius Caesar (100 BCE-44 BCE) and Gnaeus Pompeius Magnus or Pompey (106 BCE-48 BCE). Pompey had long been Egypt's benefactor, but after Caesar defeated him at Pharsalus, the boy-king and his advisors were quick to turn the tables on him. Expecting a warm welcome as he stepped ashore in Pelusium, Pompey was instead repeatedly stabbed while the gold-armored boy-king looked on.[3] For this heinous act, Ptolemy XIII lands in the ninth circle of Dante's *Inferno*, alongside Judas. Shortly thereafter, upon visiting Egypt, Caesar was presented with Pompey's decapitated head as a gift, which the boy-king thought the Roman dictator would appreciate. Caesar was repulsed and reportedly wept upon seeing the head of his adversary, who had once been a close friend and his former son-in-law.

Cleopatra's activities during this time are murky. Egyptian history was of little or no interest to Roman writers thus not much was recorded. In fact, until Egypt and Rome cross paths in a substantial way there is more unknown in Egypt than known. What is recorded, however, is that shortly after Caesar landed there, Cleopatra exhibited all the ingenuity for which she would become famous.

Did she first meet Caesar rolled up in a carpet, as Plutarch reports? The legend goes that while on a ship, Cleopatra slipped through Ptolemy's impenetrable blockade and hid in the boat of Apollodorus the Sicilian. We'll never know how he did it, but somehow while Cleopatra was wrapped in a carpet or blanket, Apollodorus strode past the probing eyes of countless sentinels who were on the lookout for the diminutive queen, finally presenting his precious

---

3   Gray-Fow, Michael. "What to do with Caesarion." *Greece & Rome* 61, no. 1 (2014): 38–67. http://www.jstor.org/stable/43297487.p.42.

cargo into the private quarters of the Roman general himself. There is much speculation about their first encounter. Ever the ladies' man, Caesar was likely immediately smitten by the charismatic and erudite Cleopatra, whom he promptly restored to the throne to rule alongside her errant brother as their father's will had dictated. When Ptolemy XIII found out he would once again be ruling alongside his older sister, he threw off his crown in a rage and ran out of the room in tears—displaying all of his 13 years of age.

Alas, poor Ptolemy! After his tantrum, he was not long for the world. He drowned during the prolonged Battle of Alexandria, which ensued shortly after Caesar reinstalled Cleopatra to the crown. Ptolemy XIV (61 BCE-44 BCE) soon followed XIII in co-regency, but once Cleopatra produced her (and Caesar's) male heir—Caesarion or Ptolemy XV (47 BCE-30 BCE)—Ptolemy XIV's time on the planet also ran out in short order. It should be noted that although the Ptolemies were known for many things in their nearly 300-year dynasty, familial harmony was not one of them. A long history of bloodlust follows the clan. Even Cleopatra's own father had her eldest sister, Berenice IV (77 BCE-55 BCE), executed for usurping the throne during his time away in Rome. Notorious for conspiring against her, Cleopatra's remaining three siblings were ultimately all put to rest during her reign.

Cast as a femme fatale by the victor's propagandists, to this day Cleopatra's astounding achievements are often overlooked. When she inherited the throne from her father, she inherited a heavily indebted Egypt that was a weak client of Rome. In the space of a few short years, by increasing agricultural output and extensive trade, she transformed Egypt's debt into surplus and regained the nation's status as a power player. Under her aegis, Egypt became a flourishing state once again. Alexandrians, long known for their revolts against her predecessors when times were lean (there were two such insurrections against her father) were sufficiently appeased —not one revolt took place during Cleopatra's 21-year reign.

Even with Rome hot on her heels, Cleopatra not only expanded Egypt's empire to the size it had under Alexander the Great, but she went beyond. Egypt under Cleopatra reached the size it had at its pinnacle 1,000 years earlier. She transformed the country into a world superpower. After her and Antony's crushing defeat at the Battle of Actium in 31 BCE, bountiful Egypt became the Roman province for which Octavian yearned. Yet for all the Roman ire against Cleopatra, Egyptians did not forget their regal queen whom even in life they revered as a deity. For hundreds of years after her death, she was still worshiped and even today is an icon recognized the world over.

Selected Reading for Cleopatra: The Early Years

Chauveau, Michel. *Cleopatra: Beyond the Myth*. Translated by David Lorton. Cornell: Cornell University Press, 1998.

Everitt, Anthony. *Augustus: The Life of Rome's First Emperor.* New York: Random House, 200.

Horace. *The Odes*. Edited by J. D. McClatchy. Princeton: Princeton University Press , 2020.

Gray-Fow, Michael. "What to do with Caesarion." *Greece & Rome* 61, no. 1 (2014): 38–67. http://www.jstor.org/stable/43297487.

Kleiner, Diana E. E. *Cleopatra and Rome*. Cambridge, MA: Belknap Press, 2005.

Lucan. *The Complete Works*. Translated by J. D. Duff. Strelbytskyy Multimedia Publishing, 2021.

Plutarchus, Lucius Mestrius. *Plutarch's Lives: Volume II—Life of Antony*. Translated by: Arthur Hugh Clough. New York: Modern Library, 2001.

Pomeroy, Sarah B. *Women in Hellenistic Egypt*. Detroit: Wayne State University Press, 1990.

Propertius, Sextus. *Elegies*. Translated by Vincent Katz. Princeton: Princeton University Press, 2016.

Roller, Duane. *Cleopatra: A Biography*. Oxford: Oxford University Press, 2011.

Schiff, Stacy. *Cleopatra: A Life*. London: Back Bay Books, 2011.

CHAPTER TWO

Cleopatra: The Goddess

Before she was a queen, she was a goddess. Born to the purple and weaned on pageantry, Cleopatra (69 BCE-30 BCE) ruled during a time when monarchy was divinity. Implicit in the belief in the sanctity of the royal line there was little distinction between the pharaohs and their gods; as a means of preserving the monarchy, it was imbued with sanctity. While an unpopular pharaoh could still be ousted from time to time, the dynasty would remain intact. The pharaoh or king was also a high priest. As such, it was believed he could communicate with other gods as well as the deceased.

While the king was the dominant ruler, the queen also wielded considerable strength—sometimes eclipsing that of her husband. This was due to the power inherent in the goddesses, who were often seen as more powerful than their male counterparts. It must be remembered that even in the Ptolemaic era (323 BCE-30 BCE), Egypt was an ancient kingdom whose deities were likely as old or older than their Greek counterparts. The most primal of them was the original mother goddess who endowed fertility on the region. Her beneficence was considered critical to the kingdom's well-being, so temples were erected and pageantry held in her honor. Largely illiterate, image was everything to the native Egyptians. Thus, playing the role of the goddess was tantamount to being one. Costumed in the full regalia of the deity with whom they identified, the goddess most identified with Egyptian queens was Isis the supreme mother goddess. Both wife and sister to the predominant deity Osiris, and mother to Horus, Isis—whose Egyptian name is *Aset*—began to appear in Egyptian texts as early as the Fifth Dynasty (2494 BCE-2345 BCE). She was the chief character in the Osiris resurrection myth in which Osiris, the King of Egypt, attends a party hosted by his evil brother, Seth. Seth lures Osiris into a narrow chest, locks him inside, and flings the chest into the Nile River. Isis is overcome with grief and over a period of years searches high and low for her husband. Finally, she finds his chest hidden within one of the pillars in the great palace of the King of Byblos (present-day Lebanon). A labyrinthine adventure ensues which culminates in Isis cutting the pillar to reveal the precious chest and then taking it back with her to Egypt in order to bury Osiris in his homeland.

Seth wasn't done with his brother, however. Somehow, in the Egyptian desert, he discovers Osiris lying in his coffin and hacks him into small pieces, scattering them everywhere. With the help of Anubis, the jackal-headed god, Isis was able to recover all of Osiris' body parts—all except for his penis, which, alas, the ever-greedy Nile fish consumed. Summoning her magical powers, Isis transformed herself into a bird and hovered over her husband's prone body, breathing her brand of magic into his inert form. Lo and behold, nine months later she bore Osiris a son, Horus.[4] Osiris withdrew into immortality to become king of the dead. As a good mother and an astonishing goddess, she guarded Horus from his evil uncle until he was old enough to demand his legacy.

In the legend, Osiris represents the eternity of deceased pharaohs, while Horus symbolizes his successors, the living kings ruling Egypt. Isis' agency drives the story. The men, if not outwardly evil like Seth, are relatively inert. After all, Osiris is dead for much of the myth and Horus isn't born until the end. Isis' powerful will and use

---

4   Some stories report that Isis conceives Horus on her own (parthenogenetically, without male input). After all, at this point Osiris was without a penis.

of magic saved the day. Not only did she give birth to Horus, she all but sired him as well. And it was Isis who kept Horus' legacy safe from the clutches of his evil Uncle Seth. Many scholars attribute the strong role that Isis played in the Egyptian pantheon to the relative freedom enjoyed by women in Egypt when compared to their feminine counterparts in Greece and Rome.

Over the centuries, Isis evolved into a more universal goddess connected not only to her native Egyptians but to Greeks and Romans as well due to her close resemblance to Grecian Demeter and Roman Ceres. She did so while retaining her primary maternal traits. In ancient Rome, the people adored Isis while the state was uneasy about the foreign cult; in the years 80 BCE, 58 BCE, 53 BCE, 50 BCE, 38 BCE, and 19 CE, temples were built in her honor, then torn down, then raised back up again by popular demand. Julius Caesar (100 BCE-44 BCE)—a man more than a little familiar with Egyptian goddesses—forbade the priesthood of Isis from entering Rome because it was Eastern thus considered decadent to the provincial Romans. Yet despite this, many Romans had Isis statuary in their household shrines and worshiped her alongside the Roman pantheon. Her cult symbol— that of a mother cradling her child— became known throughout the Graeco-Roman world and was the prototype for the early Christian Madonna and child.

Cleopatra helped perpetuate this iconography. Even at 14 years old, as her father's co-regent, young Cleopatra associated herself with Isis by incorporating the title *Nea Isis* or New Isis into her regal name. After giving birth to Caesarion (Little Caesar—Ptolemy XV, see Figure 2), Cleopatra became Isis personified. It must have seemed oddly synchronous that Isis' story so closely mirrored her own. Both were single mothers of sons whose fathers met violent ends and considered gods (after his assassination, Caesar was deified). Further, both Horus and Caesarion were heralded as sons of gods. Most Egyptians would have assumed that just as Cleopatra was the living Isis, Caesarion was the living Horus. The son of god in an age desperately seeking a savior, Caesarion symbolically linked East and West personifying a vision of world peace through global unification—the ultimate dream not only of his mother but of their forebear, Alexander the Great (356 BCE-323 BCE). Yet as important a role as Caesarion had, Cleopatra's was even more crucial.

Trumpeted as a deity from birth, is it possible that Cleopatra truly believed she was Isis? One thing is certain: she used metaphor and theatrics to her advantage. After Caesarion's birth, coins were issued featuring Cleopatra wearing the Isis diadem on one side and the image of Caesarion at his mother's breast on the other— a pose identical to the iconic pose of Isis and her suckling Horus (see Figure 3). At public events, Cleopatra played the part convincingly. Adorned in the ceremonial robes of Isis, donning a tripartite wig and vulture headdress with eyes outlined in black kohl and green malachite, she was the spitting image of the goddess. With little difference between the mortal queen and the eternal goddess in Egypt at that time, her pious subjects would have been reluctant to go against the queen's edicts.

While we can never know if her liturgical pageantry was devotional, politically expedient, or a combination of both, what we do know is that Cleopatra was a capable leader. From a weak client state, Cleopatra turned Egypt into a formidable force second only in power and clout to the Roman Empire. Moreover, throughout her twenty-one year rule, Cleopatra increased the size of the Egyptian empire to levels last seen at its zenith a millennium before. It was Egypt's growing influence—along with her ongoing relationship to Marc Antony (83 BCE-30 BCE)—that put Cleopatra in Rome's crosshairs.

After their defeat at the Battle of Actium, Cleopatra packed Caesarion off. As the biological son of Caesar, she knew his life was in grave danger. Plutarch claims that Cleopatra sent Caesarion to India, but that after her death Octavian lured the sixteen-year-old back to Alexandria where he had the youth killed. Ever the pragmatist, Octavian had been touting himself the adopted son of the divine

Caesar, hence "the son of god"—a term that would become quotidian during this time. The mere existence of Caesarion, the true son of Caesar i.e. god, was a direct threat to Octavian's leadership. There was only room for one son of god in the Roman Empire.

Characteristically, Cleopatra chose suicide over being paraded through the streets of Rome as part of Octavian's triumph. But even in death, she was worshiped. Egyptians formed a cult on her behalf whose iconography mixed with that of Isis, made it nearly impossible to tell one from the other. Egyptian gods were forbidden in the public square during the reign of Octavian, who had by then taken the name of Augustus. After his death in 14 CE, the cult symbol of the Cleopatra-Isis mother and child was soon embraced by the Romans. Ironically, while defeated by the Roman Empire, Cleopatra endures in the mother and child iconography that would eventually be adopted by the Christian cult and continues to this day.

The worship of Isis in Rome continued after the arrival of Christianity until Emperor Theodosius I issued a decree in 380 CE closing all pagan temples. Around this time, in 373 CE, the following inscription was found on a statue of the goddess queen at an Isis temple complex on the Egyptian island of Philae: "Overlaid the wooden figure of Cleopatra the god." This brief scrawl indicates that the cult of Cleopatra was still active until at least the 4th century CE. Is it possible that her religion continued beyond that date? In what is considered to be the grand finale of the Egyptian religion, the Cleopatra/Isis temple at Philae was forcibly closed in the 6th century CE by Byzantine emperor Justinian the Great (527 CE-565 CE). Closure by imperial edict suggests the temple was active until that time, which means that over 500 years after her death, Egyptians were still venerating their goddess queen. Celebrated as a goddess in life, and worshiped as one in death, Cleopatra achieved a level of immortality that remains to this day as she goes down as one of the most influential women in history. In legend, literature, and art, she is an icon that is as emblematic as the Madonna and child symbol which her worship helped propagate.

Selected Reading for Cleopatra the Goddess

Chauveau, Michel. *Cleopatra: Beyond the Myth*. Translated by David Lorton. Cornell: Cornell University Press, 1998.

Gray-Fow, Michael. "What to do with Caesarion." *Greece & Rome* 61, no. 1 (2014): 38–67. http://www.jstor.org/stable/43297487.

Kleiner, Diana E. E. *Cleopatra and Rome*. Cambridge, MA: Belknap Press, 2005.

Pomeroy, Sarah B. *Women in Hellenistic Egypt*. Detroit: Wayne State University Press, 1990.

Roller, Duane. *Cleopatra: A Biography.* Oxford: Oxford University Press, 2011.

Schiff, Stacy. *Cleopatra: A Life.* London: Back Bay Books, 2011.

Walker, Susan. *Cleopatra of Egypt: From History to Myth*. Princeton: Princeton University Press, 2001.

CHAPTER THREE

Cleopatra Selene: The Forgotten Queen

The only child of Cleopatra and Marc Antony's to reach adulthood, Queen Cleopatra Selene (40 BCE-5 BCE) of Mauretania was one of the most important women of the Augustan age— exceptional in and of itself considering the animus in Rome against her parents. According to archaeological and literary evidence, Cleopatra Selene had a reputation for being a powerful and formidable monarch—her mother's daughter through and through. At a mere fifteen years of age, she married King Juba II of Mauretania and they successfully ruled together for twenty years. The royal couple put the once-impoverished province on the map by turning Mauretania into a destination point throughout the Roman empire. On account of their resourcefulness Mauretania became a major exporter and home to one of the largest urban capitals (Caesarea) in the western part of the Roman Empire.

Her early life, however, was not always promising. After her vilified parents were caught in the crosshairs of the Roman fleet, she and her two brothers—her twin, Alexander Helios and younger brother Ptolemy Philadelphus—were unceremoniously dispatched to Rome so that they could play the starring role in Octavian's three-day-long triumph (29 BCE) celebrating his victory over their mother.

On the final day of festivities, the streets of Rome were drunk and riotous with delight. Always up for a party, hundreds of thousands of spectators were lined up in threes and fours to catch a glimpse of the three-mile-long procession winding its way through the capitol. As the clamorous procession rolled by Rome's mud and brick buildings, the rough and tumble streets were awash with the shimmering splendor of gold, silver, and ivory—swaggering plunder from Egypt's enormous reserves.

Spurred on by each other and goaded by the wine, the main exhibit the crowd was craning their necks to see was coming up at the rear. Since Cleopatra's suicide denied Rome the satisfaction of seeing her in shackles, the Romans had to settle for her likeness instead. Crudely outfitted with her signature asp in tow, the queen the Romans loved to hate was decked out in full effigy with her ten-year old twins manacled in chains of gold and flanked on either side of her. So that there was no question of whose children they were, the twins (see Figure 4) were dressed as the sun, Alexander (Helios) and the moon, Cleopatra (Selene).

Upon sight of the two innocents, a hush fell upon the jeering crowd. Even in their festive state, Romans were not without a heart. The children's state of mind, however, was another story. Less than a year before—hard on the heels of their parents' dramatic ends—their seventeen-year-old half brothers Caesarion, son of Cleopatra and Julius Caesar, and Marcus Antonius Antyllus, the eldest son and heir of Marc Antony, were summarily executed by Octavian's henchmen. As prisoners of war paraded in his triple triumph, they must have wondered what Octavian had in store for them. They had, after all, good cause to be pessimistic about their futures.

Their fall from grace is hard to imagine. Just some four years prior, they were hailed as potentates and worshiped as gods when they were the headliners in a different kind of spectacle. It was then that their parents summoned all of Alexandria to the six-hundred foot long marble colonnaded gymnasium— the largest structure in Alexandria— for a lavish extravaganza known as the Donations of Alexandria. In the grand finale, Antony and Cleopatra were seated on colossal thrones of gold dressed for all the world to see as their counterparts Dionysis/Osiris and Aphrodite/Isis. Costumed as their son Horus was the eldest of Cleopatra's progeny: the thirteen year old, Ptolemy XV Caesar or "Caesarion." Also elaborately dressed, the twins at six years of age and Ptolemy Philadelphus at two years make their first public appearance.

During the ceremony, Antony formally recognized Cleopatra as queen of Egypt, Cyprus, Libya and central Syria but the main event of the night—and one that might have sealed his fate— was the proclamation of Caesarion as son of the deified Julius Caesar thus the son of god. He was hailed as the king of kings and heir apparent to his mother's vast domain. Additionally, a diminutive Cleopatra Selene became queen of Crete and Cyrenaica (eastern Libya) and Alexander Helios became king of Armenia, Media, and Parthia. While the toddler Ptolemy Philadelphus was awarded the kingship of Syria, Phoenicia, and Cilicia.

More show than substance, the donations were a series of territorial gifts that Antony—acting on behalf of Rome—gave Cleopatra. Yet most of the territories were either already within her domain or under Roman control and fancifully within her reach. Although largely symbolic, the donations were one of the factors that would ultimately lead to a rupture in the precarious relationship between Antony and Octavian resulting in the final civil war of the Roman Republic—disguised as a war with Egypt. Within a few short years it would spell defeat for Antony and Cleopatra.

Following their loss at Actium and during Octavian's protracted approach to Alexandria, Cleopatra tried negotiating with him in order to salvage the kingship for Caesarion. However, Octavian remained non committal to her entreaties. As co-ruler and Caesar's son, Caesarion's life was most at risk, so she packed the seventeen-year-old to India with his tutor Rhondon—whose only claim to fame would be betrayal of his charge. Alas, Caesarion did not journey far before Octavian discovered his whereabouts and had him summarily executed. By killing Caesarion, Octavian ensured that the Roman Republic had only one son of Caesar. But he was not done. On that same day, Marc Antony's eldest son and heir, Marcus Antonius Antyllus was also put to death.

After the bloodletting, Octavian wanted to be seen as merciful. Thus, he put on a great show of sparing the lives of Antony and Cleopatra's three children, and appointed his benevolent sister Octavia to act as their guardian. Octavian knew what he was doing by having the children of his adversaries within reach. By keeping the former royals close at hand and incorporating them into his ever-burgeoning extended family, he was removing them from the grasp of the overly ambitious who might use them in a bid to overthrow his inaugural regime.

Worth noting, shortly after the death of her husband Marcellus in 40 BCE, Octavia had become Antony's fourth wife. The marriage was arranged in an attempt to repair the fractious relationship between Octavian and Marc Antony—the two remaining triumvirates. At the time of Antony's union to Octavia, Cleopatra gave birth to his twins; a fact she broadcast far and wide. While the marriage between Antony and Octavia produced two daughters—Antonia Major and Antonia Minor—in 36 BCE, Antony left Rome to command troops in Parthia and resumed his relationship with Cleopatra. His marriage to Octavia dissolved sometime thereafter.

Living on Palatine Hill next to her brother, the generous Octavia already played host to an extended family. In addition to her five children—her two daughters with Antony and her three children with her first husband: Marcellus, Marcella Major and Marcella Minor— she welcomed Iullus Antonius, the surviving son of Antony by his third wife Fulvia. Her burgeoning household also included an assortment of foreign royals such as Cleopatra Selene's future husband, Juba —the son of the late Juba I of Numidia—whose defeat by Julius Caesar in 40 BCE orphaned the two-year-old Juba. In fact, the children from the combined two neighboring households, including Octavian's only child Julia, and Livia's two sons, Tiberius and Drusus, would play significant roles in the Julio-Claudian dynastic landscape.

Even so, during an era when disease ran rampant, not everyone in the household survived. In ancient Rome, up to half of all children died within the first ten years of life; such would seem to be the case with both Cleopatra and Antony's sons. Orphaned at six years— Ptolemy Philadelphus is believed to have perished soon after the long sea voyage from Alexandria to Rome since only the twins are mentioned in Octavian's triumph. Likewise, since we never hear from him after the triumph, most experts now believe that an illness likely killed Cleopatra Selene's twin Alexander Helios, within a year or two of the triumph.

Nevertheless, the death that shook the up and coming first family to its core was the sudden passing of Octavia's nineteen-year-old son and heir apparent, Marcellus. The young Marcellus had proved himself on the battlefield and was hugely popular amongst the young and old alike throughout Rome. His marriage two years prior to Octavian's daughter, Julia, set him up as successor to Octavian. Virgil wrote movingly of Marcellus's passing in the *Aeneid*. Seutonius reports that Octavia fainted straight away upon hearing the poet's recital of the passage relating to Marcellus' death.

Fate, however, had other plans for Cleopatra Selene. Despite the amity against her parents in Rome, Cleopatra Selene appears to have thrived within the nascent Julio-Claudian clan. Navigating the sea change in venue and status, however, must have taken some adjustment.

Compared to the elaborate boulevards adorned with gold and marble in her hometown of Alexandria, Rome during the Late Republic was a drab provincial enclave with buildings largely made of mud and brick. Accounting for the venue was only half of it. Apart from the fact that Cleopatra Selene would likely have overheard her mother disparaged fairly regularly, she would also have been hard-pressed to avoid seeing poignant reminders of her former life scattered throughout Rome, not the least of which was a statue of Cleopatra herself at the Forum.[5]

Because Octavian's conquest of Cleopatra was the shining moment that gave his regime legitimacy, he took every opportunity to showcase it. The glittering spoils of Egypt would become ubiquitous throughout Rome. From mountains of gold and silver in the form of crowns, shields, and breastplates to gem-encrusted furniture, artwork, and sculpture—the emperor who would become known for transforming a Rome built from bricks into one built of marble did it largely on the largesse of Cleopatra. Cassius Dio would write that Cleopatra ensured that "the Roman Empire was enriched and its temples adorned."[6] From the conquest and annexation of Egypt, interest rates and property values rose exponentially in Rome.

Aside from the many distractions inherent in being Cleopatra's daughter, once again the family with whom she was associated was sovereign thus her education would have remained superlative. However, it must have come as something of a surprise that in addition to memorizing Homer, as a female she was expected to learn traditional domestic crafts such as spinning and weaving. Moreover, the women of the Julio-Claudian dynasty were tasked with making clothes for others in the household. These activities would have been leagues below Egyptian royal women's exalted

---

5   Stacy Schiff, *Cleopatra: A Life*, p 316 "Cleopatra's statue remained in the Forum. It was the least Octavian could do for the woman whose golden couches and jeweled pitchers financed his career."

6   Ibid.

status. In Ptolemaic Egypt—royal females were educated alongside their male counterparts. On account of sibling marriage— and more equity between the sexes —royal girls stood just as good a chance at governing as royal boys.

Weaving clothing was not the only adjustment she had to make. Cleopatra Selene had come from a kingdom where her mother reigned supreme to a state where women were not only restricted from holding public office, they were even restricted from voting. Unsurprisingly, the role models from the two disparate states were as divergent.

In Egypt, her most significant role model was her mother, who was both Egypt's queen and its most worshiped deity. After her parents' defeat, Cleopatra Selene's years with the larger-than-life Cleopatra and the power and pageantry surrounding her came to an abrupt end and she landed into the staid and conservative home of her stepmother, Octavia. The Egyptian queen's polar opposite, Octavia, was Rome's archetypal matron—submissive and dependent. As a counterweight to the flamboyant Cleopatra, Romans loved comparing the loyal Octavia, whom Antony left for the "Harlot Queen,"[7] whom they would come to fear. After her only son, Marcellus, died in 23 BCE, Octavia withdrew from society completely. It must have taken some fancy footwork for a young girl to reconcile these two disparate feminine types.

With all eyes on Cleopatra's daughter's every move, the Roman writers who found great joy in degrading the mother found no such delight with the daughter. Well-behaved and decorous, she provided no gossip for their rumor mill. In fact, nothing was written about Cleopatra Selene until she married her former housemate, Gaius Julius Juba. Though Octavia is credited for playing the role of matchmaker, even Octavian—now referred to as Augustus[8] —must

---

7   Pliny the Elder's description of Cleopatra in *Natural Histories* 9.58.1
8   In 27 BCE, as a means of promoting his authority, Octavian was awarded the

have seen the wisdom of the union. Coming from the inimitable Ptolemaic Dynasty, the marriage of Cleopatra Selene could pose a threat to Augustus' regime if she married outside the Julio-Claudian clan and perhaps pose an even greater risk if she married within the highly competitive clan —which was why the marriage to Juba— was nothing short of brilliant. Moreover, Juba— who had proven himself as an ally to Octavian—-shared many characteristics with Cleopatra Selene.

Not only did both hail from North Africa, but their parents had been Rome's adversaries who were vanquished by Roman armies and subsequently ended their lives. Both lost their homes, families, and cultures and were brought to Rome as prisoners of war to be paraded in triumphs. Despite their parents' vilification by the Romans, to his credit Octavian ensured the exiles were well-cared for and appropriately Romanized while living under his roof. Though nearly ten years separate Juba and Cleopatra Selene in age, it is easy to imagine the kinship that must have developed between the two exiles.

Aside from proving himself on crucial military missions, Juba had an intellect's curiosity and would become a prolific writer interested in history, geography, archaeology, and the arts. Pleased with the man Juba had become and certain of his loyalty, Augustus consigned Juba with ruling the enormous region of Mauretania[9] (present-day Algeria and Morocco) in North Africa as king at the youthful age of twenty-three. The region was a growing worry for Augustus after two former kingships went without leadership for several years. Hailing from neighboring Numida, Juba was a perfect candidate as its king. To find Mauretania's ideal queen, once again, Augustus did not have to look any further than his expansive household.

---

name Augustus (the exalted one) by the servile senate.

9   Ancient Mauretania includes central present-day Algeria westward to the Atlantic and northern Morocco to the Atlas Mountains.

Raised as a royal to rule as a royal, Cleopatra Selene was weaned at the foot of the master. As a Ptolemaic princess, she was Egypt's natural heir to the throne and continued to hold the title of queen of Libya. Descending from the Ptolemaic dynasty with its nearly three hundred years of sovereignty—not the least of which was her mother's celebrated reign in the region—Cleopatra Selene brought both credibility and stability to the newly minted monarchy. Moreover, she was the daughter of one of the most prominent and beloved Romans of the last generation, the General and Triumvir, Marc Antony—a man who was expected by many to become the sole ruler of the Late Roman Republic. In fact, as the only surviving child of the most powerful couple in the Hellenistic era, not only did Cleopatra Selene have more claim to the throne than Juba, she had more claim to the throne than any member of the Julio-Claudian brood. It is hard to imagine anyone more suited for the role of queen of Mauretania.

In 25 BCE, Cleopatra Selene was married to Juba, known to subsequent generations as Juba II. The royal couple could have chosen anywhere to reside within the huge swath of land that was Mauretania but they chose the coastal town of Iol as the capital because it was situated on the Mediterranean, providing easier access to Rome. Forthwith, they changed the name from Iol to Caesarea (today's Cherchell, Algeria) in honor of their benefactor, Caesar Augustus.

In the ancient world a queen was often considered nothing more than her husband's appendage. Unless she ruled independently, there were no set duties for which queens were responsible, thus the strength of the queenship was dependent on the sovereign. Effectively acting as co-ruler, Cleopatra Selene was respected throughout the Roman Empire and known for playing a significant role in her husband's administration.

One of Cleopatra Selene's first moves as queen was to bring in many prominent advisors and scholars from her mother's royal court to help the newly minted monarchs achieve their goals. Soon their court began to mirror her mother's in Alexandria. In fact, Caesarea would grow to become the largest urban capital in the western region of the Roman Empire; a multicultural hub celebrated as a center for arts and learning.

With Cleopatra Selene taking the lead, the couple embarked on a series of public work projects to transform their capital into a preeminent city. Taking their cue from Augustus who used Alexandria as his model when transforming Rome from a city of brick to one of marble.[10] Alexandria's influence on the newfound North African capital would have been apparent to anyone who visited Caesarea. Like Alexandria, their harbor was blessed with an adjoining island on which they built a lighthouse whose positioning near their newly built palace was not unlike the orientation of the Pharos Lighthouse—one of the seven wonders of the ancient world— from her mother's royal residence.

In another nod to Alexandria's shining example, they built a royal library that attracted scholars throughout the Roman Empire. Referred to as the "Scholar King," Juba was strongly influenced by Cleopatra Selene's Ptolemaic heritage. Some believe Cleopatra Selene may have contributed either in writing and/or research to the opus of Juba's scholarship. Other notable public work projects included a Roman Forum and a Greek Theater.

Aside from public work projects to beautify Caesarea, Mauretania gained recognition throughout the Mediterranean for its exports especially for its purple dye harvested from shellfish in Mauretania's "Purple Islands." [11] The famed purple dye was used in the production

---

10   Stacy Schiff, *Cleopatra: A Life*. p 318. "Alexandria deserves much credit for Rome's transformation from brick to marble."

11   Off the Mauretanian coast, Juba discovered the islands and created a

of purple stripes for Roman senatorial robes. As a result of all their efforts, Mauretania enjoyed great influence as a prosperous and well-regarded kingdom. Emblematic of this esteem was its coinage which held widespread respect across the empire. Moreover, it was within Cleopatra Selene's authority to issue coins herself. One such has her wearing a diadem with the Greek (significantly, not Latin) legend *Kleopatra Basilissa* (queen) on the obverse face and a crocodile on the reverse (see Figure 5).

Frequently, when Juba was away to quell incursions on the frontier Cleopatra Selene was left to supervise the day to day activities of their kingdom. As queen, she would have maintained frequent communication with a network of influential women around the Mediterranean, including the empress Livia and her foster mother Octavia— both considered members of a select group of three singular women who played a vital role in the founding of Augustan Rome.[12]

By all that is used to measure royal marriages, Juba and Selene appeared to have a successful one. After nearly two decades, it ended abruptly in 5 BCE when Cleopatra Selene died at thirty-five years of age. Ancient chroniclers are mute about how she died yet most modern historians believe that she likely succumbed to childbirth. Childbirth was a dangerous proposition in the ancient world. By some estimates, fully one-third of women died in childbirth. Not only was it dangerous for the mother, it was perilous for the newborn as well. In her seminal book about Cleopatra Selene, Roman historian and archaeologist Jane Draycott writes: "...when it came to such highly placed individuals, the death of a mother and child could be politically as well as personally catastrophic."[13] As it

---

dyeworks there that produced the famous purple.

12   Duane W. Roller, *The World of Juba II and Kleopatra Selene* (New York: Routledge Group, 2003), 90

13   Jane Draycott, *Cleopatra Selene: From Roman Prisoner to African Queen*, page 216.

was with Cleopatra Selene, the deaths of mothers and infants could signal the end of political dynasties.

She left one son, Ptolemy,[14] and at least one daughter, named Drusilla. However, regardless of how powerful their mother queens were, daughters could not succeed their fathers and were often married into other political dynasties. After his mother's death, Ptolemy would co-rule with his father until Juba's passing in 23 CE at which time Ptolemy became king.

The madness of Caligula put paid to the last vestiges of the Ptolemaic dynasty. In 40 CE on a visit to Rome, Caligula—his mother's great-nephew, hence Ptolemy's cousin—had Ptolemy assassinated. Ptolemy was likely a target for the paranoid emperor because of Mauretania's vast wealth.[15] Cleopatra and Antony's only surviving grandson was no more than 31 years of age. Ptolemy's sole child, a daughter named Drusilla, would marry into the Julio-Claudian clan. After Claudius succeeded Caligula, he exploited Ptolemy's lack of heirs to his advantage and took over the wealthy Mauretania, dividing it into the Roman provinces of Mauretania Caesariensis and Mauretania Tingitana.

Ironically, the only building that remains extant from their reign is the massive Royal Mausoleum of Mauretania in Caesarea. The enormous stone tomb, which measures sixty by sixty meters (209 by 209 feet) and rises to a height of forty meters (130 feet), was constructed by Juba in anticipation of a long and flourishing royal dynasty. Completed two years after Cleopatra Selene's passing it would never be fully occupied. Although the remains of Cleopatra

---

14 Perhaps significantly, he was named after her exalted family, not his. Was their goal to continue the Ptolemaic dynasty? An intriguing possibility that Draycott suggests in her book.

15 According to Suetonius, the emperor was jealous of his cousin because of the admiring looks Ptolemy received at the gladiatorial games wearing his "splendid purple cloak."

Selene along with Juba's and perhaps one or two of their children had once been interred in the tomb, it has long since been raided.

Cleopatra Selene's charisma, resourcefulness, keen intellect, and political acumen helped turn the once-impoverished province of Mauretania into a wealthy and prosperous client kingdom of the Roman Empire. Yet for all her achievements, she has been neglected by historians—eclipsed by her larger than life parents and male relatives. Even the manner of her death is unknown. Despite this disregard, she was revered by the local populace. Indicative of this high regard are coins bearing her portrait that were still in circulation within the region some decades after her death. Moreover, experts now claim that her impact may have had far reaching implications for centuries following her death as demonstrated by women's unusually high status in Caesarea.

Selected Reading for Cleopatra Selene

Draycott, Jane. *Cleopatra's Daughter: From Roman Prisoner to African Queen.* London: Liveright, 2023.

_____. "Dynastic Politics, Defeat, Decadence, and Dinding: Cleopatra Selene on the So-called 'Africa' Dish From the Villa Della Pisanella." *Papers of the British School at Rome* 80 (2012): 45-64. http://www.jstor.org/stable/41725316.

Gray-Fow, Michael. "What to do with Caesarion." *Cambridge University Press* 61, No. 1 (2014): 38-67. http://www.jstor.org/stable/43297487

Hickson, Frances V. "Augustus 'Triumphator' : Manipulation of the Triumphal Theme in the Political Program of Augustus." *Latomus* 50, no. 1 (1991): 124–38. http://www.jstor.org/stable/41535965.

Kleiner, Diana E. E., and Bridget Buxton. "Pledges of Empire: The Ara Pacis and the Donations of Rome." *American Journal of Archaeology* 112, no. 1 (2008): 57–89. http://www.jstor.org/stable/40037244.

Roller, Duane W. *The World of Juba II and Kleopatra Selene.* New York: Routledge Classical Monographs, 2003.

Schiff, Stacy. *Cleopatra: A Life.* New York: Back Bay Books, 2010.

Secundus, Gaius Plinius, "Pliny the Elder." *Natural Histories.* Translated by John F. Healey. New York: Penguin Classics, 1991.

Tronson, Adrian. "What the Poet Saw: Octavian's Triple Triumph, 29 BC, Jeremiah Markland's Conjectures at Propertius. 3.11.52–53." *Acta Classica* 42 (1999): 171–86. http://www.jstor.org/stable/24595069.

CHAPTER FOUR
The Banishment of Julia Augusti

*"I would certainly not describe as mercy,
what was actually the exhaustion of cruelty."*

Seneca from *In Mercy* refers to the deified Augustus

All of Rome was in an uproar. No one had imagined that even a cold fish like Augustus was capable of exiling his only biological child, Julia, to a barren and windswept island. "Let her be banished for life," he is recorded as saying about Julia's harsh exile. Banishment from Rome, however, was not enough. For her sins, the princess was exiled to the penal island of Pandateria (present-day Ventotene, off the Western coast of Italy). The real reasons for such harsh punishment—immorality was the given cause—are still debated. No men were allowed on the island aside from the guards who kept watch. Being deprived of male companionship would make for a more exacting punishment, so the thinking went. To that end, wine was forbidden in that stygian enclave. Food provisions were kept at a minimum. In other words, Julia was in prison.

This was a sea change from her former life. Adored within the palace and outside of it, Julia Augusti (39 BCE-14 CE) (see Figure 6) was charismatic, sophisticated, and renowned for her *joie de vivre*. When news of her exile hit the streets, people came out in droves for her. In an attempt to restore their adored princess lovingly referred to as "the merry widow," they packed the streets and held effigies calling for her release as they thronged the *curia*. Unmoved, Augustus responded: "Fire will sooner mix with water than that she shall be allowed to return." People threw fiery torches on the Tiber in a playful retort, but the emperor was not amused. "If you ever bring up this matter again," he told them, "may the gods afflict you with similar daughters or wives." While the protests eventually abated, the princess was not soon forgotten.

Once the apple of her father's eye, Augustus (see Figure 7) was so close to his daughter that he playfully used to call her "Juliola." Outspoken and independent-minded, she would often spar with her straight-laced Dad, inducing him to famously quip: "There are two wayward daughters that I have to put up with, the Roman commonwealth and Julia." Despite the back and forth, by all that is used to measure a father-daughter relationship in ancient Rome, theirs appeared adequate. So what could account for their sudden break?

Make no mistake, being labeled a woman of ill repute was reason enough to land Julia on the prison island during the authoritarian Augustan era. All the same, according to Roman Historian Suetonius, Augustus even debated putting his daughter to death. Considering the severity of her father's reaction to her disgrace, some believe that Julia's fall had to do with her involvement in a political intrigue to overthrow him. The question then becomes, why act against her better interests? Her two eldest sons were already adopted by Augustus and were primed for the throne.

First, some background. Julia has the unfortunate distinction of being the first in a long line of Julio-Claudian women forced into exile by the ruling males of their family with no trial or due process. In fact, with the exception of her granddaughter Drusilla (who died of fever as a young woman), all of Julia's female descendants were exiled; only Agrippina the Younger would survive her exile.[16]

On the day Julia Augusti was born her father—a mere Octavian back then—saw fit to divorce his second wife, her mother, Scribonia. As grounds for divorce in Rome, a husband could state that in addition to his wife being troublesome, she was also bad in bed; Octavian used both in his divorce decree. Some say he might have thought twice about deserting his wife if she had had the good sense to produce a son for him. Children in ancient Rome were their father's possessions, yet sources indicate that Octavian was in no rush to bring her into his home—as an infant daughter, she was not his first priority. Thus, Julia may have spent the first few years of life with her mother.

If Octavian was counting on a long line of heirs to carry on his imperial legacy with his second wife, Livia, he was mistaken. Like all successful monarchies—though Octavian decried it, his rule was effectively that—he needed heirs, and only males would do. While the first imperial couple may have had many favorable attributes, fertility was not among them.

Perhaps it was their shocking courtship the gods frowned upon. Indeed, the emperor—later known for his draconian marriage laws—had a rather tarnished record in that regard. With a pregnant wife at home, a married Octavian took up with the virtuous Livia while she was still married to her first husband, Tiberius Claudius Nero, and carrying their second child. This was scandalous behavior, even by the looser moral standards of the Roman Republic. Three days after giving birth to what would be her second and last child, Livia became Octavian's third, final, and most indelible wife. With two

---

16 Although Agrippina the Younger survived her exile, she did not survive her son's (Nero) reign. Nero was responsible for hiring assassins to kill his mother.

sons already born to the 20-year-old Livia, the newlyweds doubtless had high hopes for a long line of offspring.

But Octavian's new wife would produce no heirs—male or female—for him. Over the years it would become apparent that the humble Scribonia had succeeded where the imperious Livia had utterly failed. Thus the fate of the Julio-Claudian dynasty rested solely on the fertility of its female kin—three of whom played key roles in early dynasty-building.

Livia, with her two sons (Tiberius and Drusus) in tow, represented the interests of the Claudian contingency. The Claudians might have been royalty if monarchy were possible in the Republic. Moreover, Livia was a Claudian by birth as well as by marriage, raised in a family whose influence dates back to the foundation of the Roman Republic. Livia's first husband and the father of her two sons was also her cousin, which was typical in patrician families. Because the people preferred the Julian clan with Julius Caesar as their most noted exemplar, for public relations purposes, the blue-blooded nobility of Tiberius's double-Claudian heritage was made much of during his reign.

The Claudians may have been near sovereignty in Rome, but the Julians touched divinity. Their most recently deified son was Julius Caesar himself, whose divinity was proclaimed in 42 BCE. The ever-political Octavian made much of his being "the son of god" despite not being the son of Caesar—Octavian was adopted—nor the son of a god, at least not by our more exacting present-day standards. The Julians also claimed direct descent from Venus, the goddess of love and their patron goddess, whose son Aeneas was the legendary founder of Rome—vividly portrayed in Virgil's the *Aeneid*.

Representing the Julians, there is Octavian's elder sister, Octavia Minor (69 BCE-11 BCE). Considered a paragon of virtuous Roman womanhood, she was also quite fertile. She had five children in total: three with her first husband, Gaius Marcellus, and two with her second husband, Marc Antony (83 BCE- 30 BCE). The latter was a political marriage, and Octavian's idea. While still pregnant with her late husband's child, only months after he died, the ever-dutiful Octavia married Antony in a bid to patch up relations between him and Octavian. When Antony abandoned her in favor of Cleopatra, all of Rome was incensed.

This brings us back to Princess Julia. Because Octavia's children took second seat to Julia's future children, her marriage was politically loaded from the day she was born. As part of the treaty of Tarentum (present-day Taormina) between Octavian and Antony in 37 BCE, a two-year-old Julia was betrothed to Antony's eldest son and political heir, Marcus Antonious Antyllus. That changed abruptly when Octavian's foremost in law became his foremost enemy; after the Battle of Actium (31 BCE), he wasted no time in ending the seventeen-year-old's brief life. Octavian then planned to betroth Julia to Cotiso, King of Getae (present-day Bulgaria). Once again, plans (and allegiances) fell through. In fact, it would take 12 years for another marriage scheme to surface.

By then, Octavian-cum-Augustus (his handlers coined the term for him in 27 BCE) was the sole ruler of the Roman Empire and Julia's every move was closely monitored under the glacial and exacting eye of Livia, who played quintessential stepmother to the spirited child. In addition to her studies, Livia made sure Julia learned conservative and all-important feminine tasks such as weaving and spinning while her father ran the country. Classic helicopter parents, they only allowed those properly vetted (meaning, ruthlessly interrogated) to socialize with the sovereign's daughter. Some were sent packing after they failed the initial interview.

Such was the life of a princess. Then, at the ripe old age of 14, Julia was wed. Augustus had just the match for Julia: his beloved nephew Marcellus, the next best thing to a son. The 17-year-old's marriage to his first cousin Julia put him in line as heir and chief successor to the Republic. In setting up the match, Augustus had acted against the fierce protestations of Livia, who wanted *her* eldest son to marry Julia. Also 17 years old, the somber Tiberius—never a favorite of Augustus—paled in comparison to the charismatic and erudite Marcellus.

Livia did not have to protest for long, however. Poor Marcellus did not live to see his 21st birthday. After just two years of marriage to Julia, an epidemic swept through the Roman Empire that nearly killed Augustus and inflected Marcellus. Everyone expected the golden prince to make a full recovery. When he perished, it set off a period of mourning in Rome that resulted in some of the greatest poetry of the age. Both Virgil in the *Aeneid* and Propertius in *Elegies* wrote movingly of the prince's passing. The ancients tell us that after the death of her son, Octavia completely withdrew from society.

Now a widow at 16, Julia's feelings for her departed husband are unknown. Was Marcellus's death natural? Each time a dynastic successor for Augustus emerged, he met with an untimely end. Once Marcellus was laid to rest, there was talk that Livia had a hand in his death. It was her son, after all, who had the most to gain. Nevertheless, if Livia was responsible for Marcellus's demise, it was all for naught. Within a short year, Augustus betrothed his freshly-widowed daughter to his close friend and war hero, the mighty general and consul Marcus Vispanius Agrippa (63 BCE-12 BCE). Everything was set except for one small detail—Agrippa was already married. Augustus had himself arranged the union years ago with Marcellus's sister. This, naturally, didn't stop Augustus from pursuing the betrothal to Julia. Livia was livid. Once again, her son Tiberius was passed over—this time, by someone of humble and of *plebeian* origins, several rungs below the exalted Claudian line.

The political truth, however, was more complicated. With the support of his loyal legionnaires, if anyone could launch a successful armed insurrection against Augustus, it would be his beloved general. A central player in Rome's governance, Agrippa had been disappointed in Augustus's selection of Marcellus two years prior. Pertaining to Agrippa, Augustus's friend the poet Gaius Maecenas told him: "You have made him so great that he must either become your son-in-law or be slain."[17] Ever prudent, Augustus chose not to offend the man (or his legions) who all but won the Battle of Actium for him, so he made him son-in-law instead.

Once again a political toy, the 18-year-old Julia married Agrippa. The ancients do not comment on her feelings about being married to a man 25 years her senior. Often accompanying her husband on his campaigns abroad, in the nine years they were married she produced four children: two sons (Gaius and Lucius) and two daughters (Agrippina and Julia). She was pregnant with her fifth child (Agrippa Posthumus) when while on a military mission Agrippa contracted a fatal illness and died in 12 BCE.

Augustus, needing more fodder for his dynastic mill, formally adopted Julia's two eldest sons in 17 BCE, taking full possession of them lock, stock, and barrel. Adoption in ancient Rome was a complete and irrevocable affair in which the child officially became the adopted father's, with no formal ties to his biological parents. In this way, Julia was stripped of the principal functions of a *matrona* (married woman), unable to provide a loving home and early education to her sons, then aged eight and five. Yet again, the ancients are silent about her reaction to the appropriation of her sons. Taking Gaius and Lucius away from her was not the only autocratic item on Augustus' domestic agenda at the time, however, he had bigger fish to fry.

Augustus set forth a series of contentious marriage laws ostensibly designed to boost marriage and procreation amongst the patrician class in an attempt to revive the virtues and morality of the former Republic. He used his own daughter to promote the ideals of chastity

---

17   Cassius Dio, Book 54

upheld by the Julian Laws. In fact, for this reason, Julia was the first female to grace a Roman coin.[18] All was looking up for the princess, but the new laws were particularly constricting for women. While adultery was criminalized for both sexes, a married woman was considered guilty of adultery if she had sex with anyone except her husband. A married man, on the other hand, was guilty of adultery only if he had sex with a married woman. In other words, single women, slave girls, prostitutes, and concubines were up for grabs.[19]

Patriarchal to its core, the prime concern here was the assurance of paternity. Punishment for offenders was harsh; a father could kill his married daughter if she was caught *in flagrante delicto* with her lover. If found guilty, the newly divorced woman and her lover were handed harsh financial penalties and exiled. A cuckolded husband was obligated to divorce his wife immediately or be charged with pimping. Additionally, there were penalties for men who remained unmarried. Women who were divorced for other reasons were required to remarry within a year and a half if they were of child-bearing age. The only favorable element for married women was an exemption from male guardianship if they produced three or more children.

All in all, the new laws were deeply unpopular yet public demonstrations calling for their appeal fell on deaf ears. Make no mistake, it was not lost on anyone that the moralizing marriage laws were proscribed by a man whose marital record was itself deeply tainted. Moreover, the standard bearer for the new morality laws was quickly gaining a reputation as loose with her favors. Even while married to Agrippa, stories begin to emerge about Julia's infidelities. Macrobius's fifth-century CE work *Saturnalia* recounts many of Julia's witticisms originally recorded by Domitius Marsus, an Augustan poet privy to palace intrigue. When asked how her children all resembled Agrippa, she quipped: "Passengers are never

---

18   Annelise Freisenbruch, *Caesar's Wives* (London: Free Press, 2010), 53.
19   Ibid, 51.

allowed on board until the hold is full." The ancients tell us that Augustus had heard some of the rumors about his daughter, but because the children favored Agrippa, he chose not to believe them.

In this regard, the apple did not fall far from the tree. Augustus' indiscretions were legendary. While his scandalous courtship of Livia was common knowledge, it was hardly the only story going around. Antony, rather an expert on the subject, enumerated the affairs that Octavian engaged in since his marriage to Livia in a letter. Over the years, a name that appeared with frequency is that of Terentia or Terentilla, the wife of Augustus' "good friend," Maecenas.

"That he was an adulterer upon many occasions even his friends did not deny," Seutonius asserts. By seducing the wives of his adversaries, Augustus's seductions were for the good of the Roman state, he argues. Yet the orgy Augustus reportedly hosted on at least one occasion has no easy explanation. Livia's response was to look the other way. Some say that in his old age, she supplied him with fresh virgins for deflowering. While the reports may exaggerate, it is important to note that Romans frowned upon men driven by lust, deeming such activity feminized behavior. One thing was certain, however. If Augustus' marriage laws had been in place when they hooked up, he and Livia would have been exiled.

Julia was therefore playing a dangerous game. Irrespective of her feelings toward Agrippa, her life was rocked by his sudden death. If she had been any other woman living in Rome, a life of independence would have awaited her since marriage laws protected the mother of at least three children (*ius trium liberorum*) from having to remarry. But this was Julia. Obsessed with securing his dynastic line, Augustus had to make sure that his "own sons" (Julia's Gaius and Lucius) would succeed him after he died. With Julia widowed, any ambitious nobleman could potentially thwart his carefully-laid plans. Besides, at 27, Julia was still of child-bearing age. Yet again, Augustus swooped in to hand pick her next husband.

Thus, hard on the heels of the birth of her fifth child, Agrippa Posthumous, and still in mourning for her husband, the Princeps had his newly widowed daughter betrothed—this time to her step-brother Tiberius—one can only imagine Livia's delight. Finally, another Julio-Claudian union! Like Agrippa before him, there was just one small detail—Tiberius was married. In fact, Tiberius had been down this road with his step-father eight years before, when Augustus married him to Vispania Agrippina (Agrippa's eldest daughter with his first wife). Needless to say, the match was made for purely political reasons. Yet according to Suetonius, in 11 BCE Tiberius divorced Vispania *non sine magno angore animi* (with great mental anguish).

Unwittingly, Augustus had been responsible for a union that resulted in love. Upon their heartbreaking divorce, an inconsolable and pregnant Vispania lost their second child. Thus, the marriage of Julia and Tiberius had an inauspicious start. Raised in the Julio-Claudian palace more or less as brother and sister, rumor had it that the vivacious young Julia once had a crush on the solemn Tiberius. Those days, however, were long gone. Initially, they tried making a go of it, resulting in Julia's pregnancy. But theirs was not destined to be a happy union and the baby boy died in infancy. Shortly thereafter, injured fatally in a riding accident, Tiberius's beloved younger brother Drusus died. A man of somber temperament, Tiberius did not recover easily from so much loss.

The couple found it difficult to live under the same roof, much less in the same bed. Tiberius felt slighted that the tender-aged heir apparents—now his insolent stepsons—were increasingly promoted to consulships and distinguished priesthoods, while he, with an acclaimed military background, was relegated to diplomatic posts. When Augustus offered him the tribunician power in the East—much to his dismay and the consternation of Livia—Tiberius flatly refused, announcing he intended to "retire" from politics and move to the island of Rhodes where he would live for seven years studying philosophy. Julia did not accompany him. With a husband over 1,400 miles away, Julia was not content to stitch away the hours spinning and weaving like her role models Livia and Octavia. She ran with a sophisticated crowd that viewed extramarital activities with nonchalance. She must have known the risks, because she asked her father for a divorce. Augustus would hear none of it. An eligible princess would upset all his plans. With his successors waiting in the wings, the last thing Augustus wanted was someone jockeying for political power and potentially threatening the power of his "sons".

Julia was left with effectively no position in society. Even the cloistered Vestal Virgins had a more active social life than an unattached woman.[20] Social mores required the extroverted thirty-something Roman darling to live the life of a hermit. For her, it was impossible—a simple fact a more attentive father would have known.

He was, in fact, busy with other matters. In February of 2 BCE, Augustus celebrated his 25th anniversary of "restoring the republic" and was awarded the title of *Pater Patriae* (father of his country) amid much fanfare. He used the opportunity to promote his "sons," Gaius and Lucius, as legitimate political heirs, beginning a precedent for heritable rule. It should be noted that Tiberius was not his political heir. In fact, after Tiberius's self-exile to Rhodes, to a large extent, he was *persona non grata* at the palace and even considered a threat to the successors in the event of Augustus' death. In fact, whether or not Tiberius should be allowed to return to Rome at all was now determined by none other than Gaius, his 18-year-old stepson.

Six months later, propagandist extraordinaire Augustus threw another party to celebrate his reign. This time they were celebrating the inauguration of the Forum of Augustus, which housed the temple of the military god Mars Ultor. The edifice was dedicated to

---

20   Although Julia was married to Tiberius, because they were living separately, she was considered unmarried for all intents and purposes.

Roman nationalism and lined with statues of legendary Romans, highlighting the Julian clan with Aeneas, Romulus, *Divus Julius* (Divine Julius), and the headliner himself: Caesar Augustus. Romans were ostensibly celebrating 25 years of relative peace and uneven prosperity, a supposed golden era ushered in by Augustus. Yet it was Julia who stole the limelight that night. After the revels ended and the pageantry long faded, Augustus sent a letter denouncing his own daughter.

There are no details concerning Julia's detainment, but it likely happened in the dead of night. Beloved as she was, her arrest risked political unrest. Since she was the house of Augustus's first exile—though hardly its last—a system was not yet in place. Tiberius would employ squads of Praetorian Guards to fetch her daughter, Agrippina the Elder. There was nothing yet in place for Julia's case.

Some believe that it may have been Livia—the iron maiden herself— who summoned her in the middle of the night. Long an adversary of her headstrong stepdaughter, the omniscient and omnipresent Livia played no small role in Julia's abrupt downfall. Likely, the charges had been building up, though according to Augustus' letter to the Senate, he had just discovered that his married daughter had committed multiple adulteries. Adultery was not her only crime, however. Augustus ranted that she indulged in public depravity in the forum, "from the very rostra where he had proclaimed the *leges Juliae* (Julian marriage laws)." A public square was no place for a woman, the ancients noted. Rather suspiciously, her supposed depraved acts were only performed in the dead of night—a time when no respectable citizens could verify the story.

The most heinous and debauched acts have been attributed to her. Historians today consider them examples of misogynist hyperbole common in the ancient world. Many argue that the intensity of Augustus's wrath belied a more personal motive. In fact, accusing women of sexual license was often code for conspiratorial activity in ancient Rome. The five men with whom Julia was linked all came from notable patrician families, not least of which was Iullus Antonius, Antony's son with Fulvia raised by the benevolent Octavia. Even though Antonius would have been more or less raised right alongside the royal family, some ancients believed that he may have long harbored ambitions to avenge his father.

Augustus's anger could certainly be explained by the existence of a plot to depose him, in which case the real offense was not adultery but conspiring against the regime. If true, the son of his greatest enemy—linked to his daughter romantically—would have been enough to send him raging. About the liaison between Antonius and Julia, Seneca muses: "Once again a woman to be feared with an Antony." Julia's popularity with the people, coupled with the ceaselessly favorable impression of Marc Antony, could have made them a power couple. But did they, in fact, have designs on the throne? While it is easy to see why Antonius would, what would Julia have to gain? Both of her sons were being prepped for the throne. For eminent women in ancient Rome, some argue that adultery and conspiracy were one and the same thing. In view of this, marriage or, short of that, sexual commerce created vital alliances that Julia would need in order to negotiate the challenges surrounding her. Augustus, deaf to his daughter's pleas for a life of her own, chose to leave Julia in matrimonial limbo precisely because if remarried she was a danger to his regime. But as an (technically) unattached princess, all the men in her social circle were from prominent families, many of whom were likely power-hungry. It would have been a matter of time before she linked up to one of them. Exile to the barren and windswept Pandateria awaited Julia; Antonius was condemned to death.

Julia had one parent with her better interests at heart. In a show of support and undying love, Scribonia accompanied her daughter into exile. After five years of persistent public outcry for the return of their princess, Augustus made a move. When the boat came for her, if Julia thought she was finally returning home, she must have been greatly disappointed. She would spend the remaining 11 years of her life in Rhegium (the present-day city of Reggio Calabria in southern Italy). Over the years, Julia would live to see her three sons die before they reached 25 years of age. Accident and sudden illness officially claimed Gaius and Lucius within 18 months of each other. After Augustus died in 14 CE, her third son Agrippa Posthumous—then living in exile–was summarily executed by a centurion in the employ of the new emperor, Tiberius.

Julia fared no better with her daughter, Julia. Within 10 years of her exile, Julia the Younger was charged with adultery and exiled to a penal island where she gave birth to a child that Augustus ordered exposed. She would die in exile at age 48. As for her other daughter, Agrippina the Elder, her story made history.

Before we follow Agrippina down the annals of time, let's see how things ended for Julia. As the emperor's daughter, her world was even more constricted than that of the average Roman woman, her every move dictated by a despot's dynastic whims. After three loveless marriages and constant pressure to produce offspring for Augustus's imperial ambitions, Julia tried to take control of her life. The cards were stacked squarely against her, however. While she had reason enough to desire her father's ousting, without due process in a court of law, ancient and modern historians alike can only speculate about whether her exile was due to adultery, conspiracy, or a combination of both.

After Augustus died in 14 CE—at the advanced age of 77—the new emperor, Tiberius, exacted revenge on his former wife by stopping all food provisions to her isolated outpost. Shortly thereafter, Julia died of starvation. She was 52 years old.

Selected Reading for Julia Augusti

De La Bedoyere. *Domina: The Women Who Made Imperial Rome.* New Haven: Yale University Press, 2018.

Dio, Cassius. *Roman History: The Reign of Augustus.* New York: Penguin Classics: 1987.

Everitt, Anthony. Augustus: The Life of Rome's First Emperor. New York: Random House, 2006.

Fanthan, Elaine. *Julia Augusti: The Emperor's Daughter.* London: Routledge: 2006 .

Flower, Harriet I. *The Art of Forgetting: Disgrace & Oblivion in Roman Political Culture,* Chapel Hill: University of North Carolina Press, 2006.

Freisenbruch, Annelise. *Caesar's Wives: Sex, Power, and Politics in the Roman Empire.* London: Free Press, 2010.

Holland, Tom. *Dynasty: The Rise and Fall of the House of Caesar.* New York: Anchor Books, 2015.

Richlin, Amy. *Arguments with Silence.* Ann Arbor: University of Michigan Press, 2017.

Severy Beth. *Augustus and the Family at the Birth of the Roman Empire.* New York: Routledge, 2003.

Suetonius. *The Lives of the Twelve Caesars.* Translated by H. M. Bird. London: Wordsworth Classics, 1997.

Tacitus. The *Annals.* Translated by: J. C. Yardley. Oxford: University Press, 2008.

Williams, John. Augustus. New York: New York Review of Books, 2015.

Wood, Susan E. *Imperial Women: A Study in Public Images, 40 BC-AD 68.* Leiden, NV: Brill, 1998.

CHAPTER FIVE

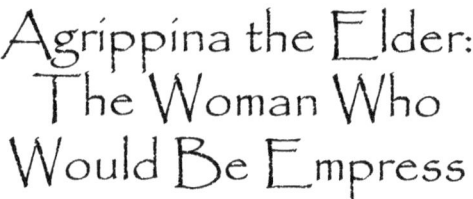

Long before her boat docked at the port of Brundisium in the winter of 19 CE, Vipsania Agrippina, more widely recognized as Agrippina the Elder (14 BCE- 33 CE) (see Figure 8), might have known that the mourners would come. Like a perfectly choreographed event—and many believe it was—the waterfront was packed elbow to elbow with people standing for hours or even days as they lined the city walls. The boldest of them were perched atop unstable rooftops, all to catch a glimpse of her. Adored and admired, she was beloved by her compatriots.

"The glory of a nation, they called her, the lone survivor of Augustus's bloodline,"[21] writes Tacitus in his *Annals*. Julia's daughter Agrippina was the sole biological grandchild[22] of the "Divine" Augustus.[23] More than just the beloved progeny of a god, however, Agrippina was one half the golden couple. Mourners flocked to assuage her grief for

---

21 Tacitus, *Annals* 3.4.

22 Her sister, Julia Minor (the Younger) was alive at this time but she was in exile on the oft-cited charge of adultery.

23 Like his adopted father (his Great Uncle) Julius, Augustus was deified upon his death.

her newly-passed husband, Rome's heir-apparent and a celebrated general, Germanicus Julius Caesar[24] (15 BCE-19 CE).

Germanicus was the biological nephew and adopted son of the ever-unpopular Emperor Tiberius (42 BCE-37 CE). Scion of the Julio-Claudian dynasty, Germanicus' charisma off the battlefield and his multiple successes on it likened him to another beloved war hero, Alexander the Great, who also died too young.

The very image of a grieving nation, a pale Agrippina made her way across the gangplank with two of her six children in tow, carrying the ashes from her freshly deceased husband, prompting a collective wail from the crowd. Men were crying, women were keening, and strangers to Germanicus wept as fervently as his friends.[25] People tore their hair, pounded their chests, and howled for all the world to hear. Their golden prince was dead!

The wave of grief that started at Brundisium shortly engulfed the whole empire. Two praetorian cohorts greeted Agrippina, lifting Germanicus's urn onto their shoulders while the funeral procession marched across the Italian peninsula, stopping at designated towns along the way. In a grand display of public bereavement, grieving Romans dressed according to their station; plebeians wore black, knights dressed in vibrant purple, and those in the upper stations wore dark togas. Coming far and wide to pay respects to their fallen prince, mourners flooded the streets and made their way to Rome, where they were met by consuls and senators as well as Germanicus's family members.

For all the pomp and circumstance surrounding Germanicus's funeral, one figure was conspicuously absent: Tiberius himself. That said, it was no secret that the relationship between the two men was often strained. A favorite of the Divine Augustus, Germanicus

---

24 In 9 BCE, the agnomen "Germanicus" was added to his full name when it was posthumously awarded to his father because of his victories in Germania.

25 Tacitus, *Annals* 2.75-3.6.

was made Tiberius's successor according to Augustus' will. That alone may have sealed his fate. In fact, Augustus initially wanted Germanicus to be his immediate successor but was persuaded into Tiberius by his wife, the conniving Livia. Since Augustus had no sons, he had adopted his stepson Tiberius, with the stipulation that Tiberius adopt Germanicus. Even though Tiberius's son Drusus was only a year younger than Germanicus, the proviso was that Germanicus be next in line for succession. Aloof and ill-at-ease, the unpopular Tiberius was uncomfortable in his role as emperor and felt threatened by Germanicus's rising fame. While Tiberius was apprehensive about Germanicus's military victories, he was even more worried about Agrippina.

As a general rule, Roman wives did not accompany their husbands on military expeditions. A staunch supporter of conservative values, Tiberius believed women should stay home to demonstrate wifely virtues such as spinning and weaving. Women from the Julio family were not known for their propriety, however—just look at Agrippina's mother, Julia. Indeed, Agrippina was born during just such a military expedition. Like mother like daughter, she insisted on accompanying her husband during a dangerous military exercise against mutinous forces in the Rhine in 14 CE. They were accompanied by their toddler son Gaius Julius Caesar Germanicus, affectionately dubbed "Caligula" for sporting miniature soldier's boots called *caligae.*

There were big problems on the field at the time. Unhappy with the tight-fisted Tiberius for not raising their wages, the soldiers called for a change in governance. Reports became increasingly alarming. In an attempt to quell the uprising, interceding senators had themselves become accosted. Even the popular Germanicus was unable to calm the mutinous soldiers. At a tense moment in the campaign, he insisted that Agrippina, along with tiny Caligula, withdraw from the skirmish. Initially, she would have none of it. The word 'retreat' was not in her lexicon.[26] Much back and forth ensued, with Agrippina ultimately acquiescing. As it turned out, the sight of their adored princess and her young son escaping from the very soldiers who were supposed to be defending them was a rebuke in and of itself. Shamed and crestfallen, the soldiers capitulated. Where military might and the state's authority had failed, Agrippina's presence had prevailed.

She was challenged again the following year. Returning to the Rhine, Germanicus and his troops were in hot pursuit of a German chieftain while a pregnant Agrippina stayed behind with the rest of the forces. When a rumor surfaced that the Romans were surrounded by Germans trying to cross the Rhine River into the Gaulish provinces, the soldiers' knee-jerk reaction was to dismantle the bridge as a means of cutting them off. Tearing down the bridge would have led to certain disaster, however, as Germanicus and some forces were still on the other side. Amidst the chaos and threat of warfare, Agrippina kept her head. Armed with ingenuity and the steel will that was her birthright, Agrippina stood at the foot of the bridge to distribute food and clothing to the returning soldiers. Looking for all the world like the sovereign she was, she greeted each soldier personally and thanked them for their service while they crossed the bridge she alone had saved.

If the people adored her before the military victories, they worshiped her after them. Across the Roman Empire, statues of Agrippina were erected in her honor. Even Tacitus calls her "a woman of great spirit," which is high praise from the historian. News of Agrippina's intervention on the battlefield was not well-received by Tiberius, however. Not only did he believe that the presence of a woman on the field feminized the valor of the soldiers, he was concerned about Agrippina's rising popularity. It exceeded that of his commanders!

---

26   Tacitus, *Annals* 1.40-44.

The truth is, if it had been left up to the officers, the bridge would surely have been demolished, spelling certain defeat for Germanicus.

The relationship between Tiberius and Agrippina had always been tense. Her stepfather as well as her adopted father-in-law, the dour Tiberius—Livia's firstborn from her marriage to Tiberius Claudius Nero—was ill-fatedly wed to the *bon vivant*, Julia, Augustus's only biological child. It was not a happy marriage, and Tiberius was ultimately responsible for Julia's death. One can only imagine the *animus* Agrippina must have felt toward him.

Meanwhile, Rome welcomed the conquering hero with a fete to celebrate Germanicus's growing family. Much to Tiberius's disdain, spectacle is what the golden couple did best, and the people adored them for it. One cold heartbeat away from becoming the first family, Romans from all walks of life thronged the streets to see the celebrity couple and their five children, Nero, Drusus, Agrippina, and Drusilla. The public's favorite was seated next to his father—four-year-old Caligula. They went into spasms of delight at the sight of him outfitted as a tiny soldier with his signature soldier's boots—Agrippina dressed him for maximum effect.

A short while later—at the zenith of Germanicus's popularity—Tiberius sent his heir designate into the eastern provinces under the proviso of breaking the client-king systems, that is to say, transforming ancient kingdoms into provinces. Accompanied by the ever-pregnant Agrippina and their favorite, Caligula, the almost-first family took in the culture of Athens, visiting ancient sites along the way. Agrippina gave birth to their last child, Julia Livilla, on the island of Lesbos. As a commander of the eastern provinces, Germanicus had the authority of an emperor. It may not have been a coincidence that when Germanicus was sent east, a new governor was installed in Syria whom many believe Tiberius deployed for the express purpose of spying on his heir apparent. A lifelong friend of the Tiberius's, Gnaeus Calpurnius Piso came from a distinguished

Roman family with strong ties to the Claudian line. Further, his wife, Munatia Plancina, was one of Livia's closest confidants. Piso was clearly not disposed to like Germanicus, hurling insults at him for visiting Athens and calling the Greeks "a decadent race."

Perhaps history would have taken a different course but for the benevolence of the golden prince. When Piso's flotilla was overcome by a storm, Germanicus generously sent out a party to save the governor. Saving his life did not improve Piso's behavior toward Germanicus, however. If anything, he grew more pugnacious. Things went from bad to worse when Germanicus returned to Syria from an excursion in Egypt only to discover that Piso had canceled all the orders he had made before his trip. Furious at the gross insubordination, Germanicus and the governor quarreled heatedly with Piso departing in "open enmity," reported Tacitus.

Soon after, Germanicus fell ill. From the outset, he was convinced that Piso and his wife had poisoned him. He wrote letters to his friends, telling them of his suspicions and calling for revenge. Upon news of Germanicus's untimely death, Piso and Plancina threw open the temples for celebration, flagrantly rejoicing his death, which added to growing suspicious that they were involved.

Germanicus' death left Agrippina's world in ruins. Overnight, her status changed from empress-in-waiting to Roman matron. According to Tacitus, Agrippina was "impatient for equality." A dying Germanicus begged her "to set aside her pride" and not anger anyone by competing for power, warning her "of the threat caused by Tiberius." Still, being the progeny of a deity does not lend itself easily to a lack of ambition. Beloved by the people, as the sole living grandchild of the Divine Augustus, Agrippina had no intention of retiring from public life. After all, her children were the future and the hope of the nation.

Devastated by the loss of her husband—yet unwilling to lose any time—Agrippina set sail for Rome on the wintry seas in January of 19 CE, with two missions in mind: retribution for Piso and his wife, and securing a place on the throne for her sons. By staging a funeral fit for a king, she was building public sentiment against his murderers while at the same time laying the groundwork for a change in succession.

Even before the funeral march, Roman tongues were wagging about Tiberius and Livia's potential involvement in Germanicus' death. Why had Tiberius sent Germanicus to the east just as he was installing Piso as governor of Syria? Further, when Plancina was in Rome, why were she and Livia always meeting behind closed doors? While Livia was a notorious schemer, was she really wicked enough to kill her own grandson? After all, Germanicus was the son of her second-born son Drusus, who had also died young. Tacitus claims that Germanicus, like his father before him, had republican instincts and would have "restored liberty to the people" had he become emperor. If that were the case, it is not difficult to see why ruling figures would have sought to quell his reign.

Tiberius did nothing to assuage fears that he was behind Germanicus's untimely death. In fact, he did the opposite. The emperor's absence from Germanicus's funeral was not only considered an affront to the prince's memory but evidence of Tiberius' culpability. Further angering the people, the emperor—in his hallmark frugality—conferred too few honors on the fallen prince in overseeing the burial he didn't attend. Tone-deaf as ever, Tiberius was impatient with the commemorations, displaying his petulance with the inconsolable mourners by urging them to go back to work.

Public outcry reached a fever pitch; according to Tacitus, things would have gotten out of control if Tiberius had not summoned Piso and Plancina to Rome for trial. Hesitant to further estrange his friends, the emperor deferred the case to the Senate. Meanwhile, Livia intervened on Plancina's behalf and got her pardoned. As for Piso, not even Tiberius had the gall to come to his rescue. Manic, the crowds were out for blood. Statues of Piso were toppled and smashed on the Gemonian Steps, where bodies of the condemned were tossed. All over Rome, posters appeared that cried "Give Us Back Germanicus." The writing was on the wall; Piso's fate was sealed. Beating them to it, he took his own life.

Eventually, a certain *détente* settled between Tiberius and Agrippina. Her children too young to rule, she resigned herself to Tiberius's son, Drusus, being named successor. Everything changed when Drusus, only 37, died after a brief illness. Within the year, one of Drusus's twin sons, Germanicus the Younger, also died. Alas, poor Tiberius, his successors—like those of Augustus—found it difficult to succeed him. His plans shattered, Tiberius went before the Senate to formally adopt Agrippina's two eldest sons, Nero Caesar and Drusus Caesar. "Adopt and guide these young men—these offspring of an incomparable bloodline."[27] Tiberius had planned for Drusus to act as a mentor to the boys since at 65 years old, he had neither the energy nor the enthusiasm for the endeavor. Drusus's death created a power vacuum that was quickly filled by an ambitious praetorian prefect, Lucius Aelius Sejanus. A favorite of Tiberius before Drusus died, Sejanus became increasingly indispensable to the emperor. Tiberius once referred to Sejanus as *socius labroum*, "my partner in my toil." Sejanus' ambitions, however, went far beyond that of a partner. He wanted the throne for himself.

It began slowly at first—mere whispers. With relations between Agrippina and Tiberius tepid at the best of times, it was easy. First, Sejanus suggested to Tiberius that Agrippina was overstepping when she asked priests to offer vows for the safety of her two eldest sons right alongside that of the emperor. Even though the priests denied that she did so, Tiberius cautioned the Senate to take the boys down a peg. Sejanus then told the emperor that a "faction of Agrippina" was threatening to divide the Roman state.

---

27 Tacitus, *The Annals:The Reigns of Tiberius,Claudius, and Nero*. Book 4, Chapter 8. Tr. J.C.Yardley.

While many now question the veracity of this claim, the truth is if anyone could raise an army against Tiberius, it would be Agrippina. The emperor began to tighten the noose around her inner circle. In 24 CE, Gaius Silius and his wife Sosia Galla were arrested. Close friends of Germanicus and Agrippina, Silius had rather indiscreetly bragged that if his forces had mutinied along with the others on the Rhine they would surely have overthrown Tiberius. Silius eventually committed suicide and Sosia went into exile.

Two years later, Agrippina's cousin and confidant, Claudia Pulchra, was accused of plotting against Tiberius. Like the charges against Silius and Sosia, there is no way of knowing if the accusations were true or not. Regardless, Agrippina's name was sullied by association, which Tacitus believed was the primary motive for the claims. Shortly thereafter, Agrippina confronted Tiberius. Infuriated, she raged at him for persecuting Augustus's progeny especially as she was "the true image" of Augustus, "a descendent of his heavenly blood." Unruffled, Tiberius responded with the dismissive Greek verse: "Because she did not rule did not mean she was being mistreated." The quote nonetheless revealed his fears about her thwarted desire to rule. According to Suetonius, Tiberius never spoke to her again.

In her late thirties by now, Agrippina sought to remarry. Tacitus, citing from her daughter's journal (now lost), said Agrippina requested permission from Tiberius to re-marry. A Roman widow—even a woman as powerful as Agrippina—had to get consent from the senior male in her family for remarriage.

The fact is, even as an unattached widow, Agrippina was a political threat to Tiberius. She was doubly so with a husband by her side. Tiberius could not risk her remarrying, but instead of flatly denying her, he chose the cowardly way out—he ignored her plea altogether. Under the "guidance" of Sejanus, Tiberius was becoming ever more paranoid. In fact, paranoia was Sejanus' specialty. He spread a rumor among Agrippina's inner circle of friends that the emperor was planning to poison her at his dinner table. Believing him capable of it, Agrippina refused to eat anything at his table. Initially stung, Tiberius then used her behavior to justify his severity with her. The noose was steadily tightening. Desperate for a reprieve from governance, Tiberius moved to Capri in 26 CE —quasi-permanently—leaving Sejanus in charge of everyday governance. As acting emperor and prefect, Sejanus now had the powerful Praetorian Guard at his disposal.

Initially, Augustus created the Praetorian Guard for his personal security, but it soon acquired a reputation for political intrigue. That it would one day be involved in plots against his progeny was probably the farthest thing from Augustus' mind. At the Sejanus' behest, officers spied on Agrippina and her son Nero. After taking copious notes of everything said and done in her household, nothing exceptional was found. That hardly mattered, of course. Masquerading as friends, Sejanus's operatives urged Agrippina and her son to move to Germany. Although their response is not known, Sejanus circulated the rumor that they were considering it. In his smear campaigns, Sejanus never needed proof to damage credibility.

Finally, in 28 CE, another close friend of Germanicus fell into one of Sejanus' traps and was accused of treason. A distinguished knight, Titius Sabinus had what he thought was an innocent conversation with one of his friends, Latiaris, who had been briefed beforehand by Sejanus. As instructed, Latiaris began by praising Germanicus and then expressed sympathy for his widow. Unlucky Sabinus walked right into it, agreeing with Latiaris's statements then went one step further by denouncing both Sejanus and even the emperor himself. Naturally, Sabinus's time on the planet would come to an abrupt end. Of this period, Tacitus wrote: "Never had the city known greater tension and paranoia." In an increasing climate of distrust and fear, Sejanus ruled by rumor and conjecture, pitting friends and family members one against one another. "People were tight-lipped even with their closest relatives," he reported. After the scandal, Tiberius sent a letter to the Senate thanking them for punishing Sabinus and making reference to various threats to his life aimed obliquely at both Agrippina and her son Nero.[28]

Agrippina might have been hard-pressed to believe that the only person saving her and her two eldest sons from a tragic fate was Livia herself, her mother's great nemesis. Agrippina's children were Livia's great-grandchildren, after all. But when Livia passed in 29 CE, things changed fast. No sooner had her body been relegated to the funeral pyre than a letter materialized accusing Nero Caesar of obscenity and homosexuality. Accusations of sexual transgressions were impossible to prove or disprove, which was a big reason they were so effective in smear campaigns. Besides besmirching Nero, Tiberius' letter denounced Agrippina as arrogant and insubordinate—no breach too petty.

Meanwhile, in the curia, the people made themselves heard, holding effigies and condemning the letter as a forgery. Edgy with the growing crowds, the Senate was confused. Was it a hoax? Why would Tiberius denounce his own family members? Even if it were real, the Senate was unsure what they were supposed to do about it. So they took a page out of Tiberius's playbook and ignored the letter altogether. Furious that his letter had been disregarded, the emperor sent the Senate another letter unequivocal in its wrath against his daughter-in-law and heir apparent. Back on track, the Senate condemned both Agrippina and her son as co-conspirators and then denounced Nero as an enemy of the state. Groveling, the Senate asked the most august emperor if these atrocious offenders should be put to death.

---

28 Not to be confused with the Emperor Nero Claudius Caesar Augustus Germanicus, who would be the nephew to Agrippina's son.

Tiberius had other plans for those two. They were bound, shackled, and put under heavy guard for transfer to two separate prison islands off the Tyrrhenian Sea. In a sinister nod to the past, Tiberius sent Agrippina to Pandateria, the island where her mother was confined before eventually starving to death. Again, the people took to the streets in protest. Never one to take the public's opinion to heart, Tiberius did what he did best—he ignored them.

Shortly thereafter, in another one of Sejanus' orchestrations, Agrippina's second son Drusus was condemned by the Senate on trumped-up charges and confined to a dungeon on the Palatine, where he would ultimately die when food was withheld. Meanwhile, in 31 CE, his older brother Nero was either executed or died of starvation while in confinement on the penal island of Pontia. The two heirs apparent thus eliminated, Sejanus must have been jumping for joy. He had effectively removed both obstacles in the way of succession and cleared the path for himself. Only Caligula was left. Living on an island retreat with his grandfather and adopted father Tiberius, the teenage Caligula was a difficult target for even a talented marksman like Sejanus. For the time being, he had to remain content with those whose lives he could more readily destroy.

By this time, Sejanus's power had steadily grown. Honors, decorations and even a consulship were stacking up for him; all over Rome, statues turned up depicting the ever-obedient Sejanus by the emperor's side. As Sejanus's influence grew in Rome, Tiberius's influence diminished. In the *Lives of the Twelve Caesars*, Suetonius writes that after Agrippina and her two eldest sons were condemned, Tiberius lived in such a heightened state of paranoia that "he never removed to any place but in fetters and in a covered litter, closely attended by soldiers." Apprehensive as he was, he was still emperor. Once Agrippina and her two eldest sons were out of the picture, Tiberius took a harder and closer look at his "partner in toil."

Tiberius may have used Sejanus all along, as Suetonius claims, in order to remove Agrippina's two eldest sons, thus paving the way for his grandson Tiberius Gemellus. Others held that it was a letter penned by Antonia the Younger, the mother of Livilla (Drusus' widow)—with whom Sejanus had long been enamored—that shook Tiberius out of his stupor. To Tiberius's horror, Antonia's letter implicated Sejanus (and Livilia) in his son Drusus's sudden passing.

It was time for Tiberius to act, and a trap was easily set for his ensnarer-in-chief. In addition to all the other powers conferred on him over the years, Sejanus was led to believe that he was being awarded the all-important tribunician power, a sure sign that he would be heir-designate. Hotly anticipated, he eagerly swallowed the bait. He arrived at the Senate chamber amid applause from the toadies and sycophants he had long cultivated there, but it did not take long before things began to go amiss. A letter from Tiberius was read on the Senate floor. It became increasingly incendiary toward his Prefect. Far from receiving the tribunician power, Sejanus was now on the receiving end of one heinous accusation after another. But this time the charges were all true.

Finally, he would get a taste of the punishment his nefarious activities had so long meted out to others. His so-called supporters who had fawningly rushed to his side only a few minutes earlier now scurried away like mice as the magistrates advanced to arrest Sejanus (see Figure 9). The end came swiftly—he was executed the following day. His lifeless body was thrown unceremoniously onto the Gemonian Steps where for three days it was abused and pummeled by those who had long despised him, which was just about everyone living in Rome. His remains were finally hurled into the Tiber, a burial reserved for only the most heinous and despicable of criminals.

If Agrippina had hoped that the downfall of Sejanus would help her situation, she was sorely mistaken. In contrast, after Sejanus left the scene, Tiberius became even more vocal and antagonistic against

Agrippina and her two eldest sons. He held fast to his petty grudges and grievances. Even the subsequent deaths of his adopted sons were not enough to calm him down.

By then, Agrippina had lived on the windswept and barren island of Pandateria for a few years. Never known for her forbearance, she was increasingly vocal about the grievous conditions there. In retribution, Tiberius ordered a centurion to beat her so brutally she lost an eye. Defiant until the end, Agrippina vowed to starve to death, but Tiberius had her force-fed. Finally, at 47 years old, on October 18 in 33 CE, the granddaughter of the Divine Augustus died of starvation. Tiberius boasted that he could have had his step-daughter and adopted daughter-in-law strangled or tossed on the Gemonian Steps. Priding himself on his leniency, he then declared the anniversary of her death (and Sejanus's two years prior) a national holiday and ordered an annual sacrifice be made to Jupiter each year in observance.

In a fitting *denouement*, Agrippina's only surviving son, Caligula, is rumored to have murdered Tiberius in 37 CE at his villa in Capri. By that time, the emperor was 78 and had served for 23 long, hard, and arduous years. Unsurprisingly, his death was greeted amid much fanfare amongst the Romans who were not only celebrating the death of their dour and utterly unlikeable emperor, but also reveling in the return of their long-lost hero, Germanicus, in the guise of his only surviving son. Although Tiberius did everything he could to prevent it, he was in fact succeeded by one of Agrippina's sons. In spite of the fact that his golden family was in tatters—or perhaps because of it—the people loved Caligula for no other reason than being the personification of their long-lost golden couple.

Once he ascended the throne, Caligula capitalized on the public's nostalgia for his family and made Agrippina the star of his campaign. With coins and statuary crafted in Agrippina's image the granddaughter of the Divine Augustus and mother to the extant emperor was made the centerpiece of the Julia-Claudian dynasty. Eventually, her legacy would span generations and include two emperors (a son and a grandson) and a daughter equally "impatient for equality" who was the driving force behind the reigns of her emperor husband (Claudius) and her emperor son (Nero). For centuries, Agrippina's indelible image of strength and fortitude was found throughout the empire, rendering her as famous in death as she had been in her abbreviated life.

Selected Reading for Agrippina the Elder

De La Bedoyere. *Domina: The Women Who Made Imperial Rome.* New Haven: Yale University Press, 2018.

Dio, Cassius. *Roman History: The Reign of Augustus.* New York: Penguin Classics: 1987.

Flower, Harriet I. *The Art of Forgetting: Disgrace & Oblivion in Roman Political Culture*, Chapel Hill: University of North Carolina Press, 2006.

Freisenbruch, Annelise. *Caesar's Wives: Sex, Power, and Politics in the Roman Empire.* London: Free Press, 2010.

Holland, Tom. *Dynasty: The Rise and Fall of the House of Caesar.* New York: Anchor Books, 2015.

Richlin, Amy. *Arguments with Silence.* Ann Arbor: University of Michigan Press, 2017.

David C. A. Shotter. "Agrippina the Elder: A Woman in a Man's World." *Historia: Zeitschrift Für Alte Geschichte* 49, no. 3 (2000): 341–57. http://www.jstor.org/stable/4436585.

Suetonius. *The Lives of the Twelve Caesars.* Translated by H. M. Bird. London: Wordsworth Classics, 1997.

Tacitus. *The Annals.* Translated by: J. C. Yardley. Oxford: University Press, 2008.

Wood, Susan E. *Imperial Women: A Study in Public Images, 40 BC-AD 68.* Leiden, NV: Brill, 1998.

CHAPTER SIX

The 'Crimes' of Agrippina the Younger

The ancient chroniclers would have us believe that Julia Agrippina the Minor better known as Agrippina the Younger (16 CE-59 CE) was a regicide, a perennial poisoner, a murderer, an incestophile, a seductress, and a detestable profligate. Indeed, some of her crimes were so heinous they would put a blush on the sallow cheeks of Lady Macbeth. But are the accusations true?

Agrippina was the great-granddaughter of the Divine Caesar Augustus (63 BCE-14 CE) and sister, wife, and mother of the three final Julio-Claudian emperors. The first ever living "Augusta," she was both an empress and a co-regent in her own right. In a time when ambitious women were considered beneath contempt, how could a woman who exercised power by proxy get fair treatment from the ancient historians? Who was Agrippina the Younger and why do stories of the depths of her depravity encircle her to this day?

To understand the accusations leveled against her, one must first understand the few sources we have about her: Tacitus (56 CE-120 CE), Suetonius (69 CE-122 CE), and Cassius Dio (155 CE-235 CE). These three historians wrote during the reigns of emperors who were hostile toward the Julio-Claudian clan anywhere from 50 to 200 years after she died. Otherwise put, to write positively about her was possibly to put their lives at risk.

Thus, the outrageous claims about Agrippina remain in some doubt. Historians in ancient Rome were expected to be biased and moralizing. More often than not, they were also deeply misogynistic. For example, unless women are demure and retiring, Tacitus—the most prolific of the three—seldom says a kind word about them in his 30-volume *Histories* and *Annals*. According to him, Claudius' marriage to Agrippina was a turning point in the nation's history. "From this moment the country was transformed," he wrote. "Complete obedience was accorded to a woman." He is also prone to reading his subject's minds.

Likewise, Suetonius' *Lives of the Caesars* relies on rumor for many of his narratives, seldom distinguishing word of mouth from actual facts. While equally hostile to women, Cassius Dio's *Roman History* also has a pronounced bias against the Julio-Claudian clan in particular.

Besides these three, another source that crops up from time to time is Pliny the Elder (23 CE-79 CE) who was more or less a contemporary of Agrippina. However, his interest was natural history as opposed to imperial intrigue, so unless it is a curious natural phenomenon (breech birth, double canine teeth, etc.), he seldom writes of Agrippina.

All this makes it difficult for us to get to know Agrippina, but understanding some of the distortions in the narratives spun by these ancient chroniclers may enable us to see her more clearly.

Excluded from the political arena, Roman women were a mere ornament for the men they represented and only considered praiseworthy when they were dutiful and modest. Agrippina the Younger may have been many things, but humble and obedient do not come to the forefront. In fact, many Julio-Claudian women were known for exercising considerable political influence, and their reputations suffered greatly for it.

Her mother Agrippina the Elder was a courageous woman who devoutly believed in her divine birthright to the throne. This sense of celestial entitlement was most assuredly passed on to her eldest daughter. She had strength, ambition, and fortitude; characteristics reviled in women were lauded in men. To describe these traits, the sources[29] peppered their writings with pejorative descriptions of Agrippina, such as *inpotentium muliebrem* (female imperiousness), *nimias spes* (excessive ambition), *potentia uxoria* (power of a wife) and *dominato regnum* (abuse of power).

But with the blood of the Divine Augustus coursing through her veins, who can blame her for being imperious? After all, survival within the Julio-Claudian family oftentimes meant kill or be killed. Agrippina was born at a dangerous time to an imperial dynasty at war with itself. Her family tree reads like the who's who of Julio-Claudian emperors.

On the Julian side, she was a direct descendent (great-granddaughter) of the Divine Caesar Augustus, a noble distinction of which only a handful could boast. The banished Julia—the only biological child of Augustus—was her grandmother.

On the Claudian side, she was Livia's great-granddaughter and daughter of the beloved heir-apparent and prominent general, Germanicus who died suspiciously at the tender age of 33. As we saw in the previous chapter, it has long been speculated that his uncle and adoptive father Emperor Tiberius (42 BCE-37 CE) had a hand in his demise. Next in line of succession was her mad brother Emperor Caligula (12 CE-41 CE) who, according to our questionable sources, was also her rumored lover. Finally, she was niece as well as fourth and final wife to her uncle Emperor Claudius (10 BCE-54 CE), her father's brother.

She was also mother—and rumored lover, yet again—to Lucius Domitius Ahenobarbus, better known as the ruthless ruler Nero (37

---

29   Tacitus, Suetonius, and Cassius Dio.

CE-68 CE) whose paranoid reign of terror completely wiped out the Julio-Claudian clan. Before things went from bad to worse there, she served for a time as his co-regent—an honor never before bestowed on a woman. It wouldn't happen again for another 100 years.

Instrumental in making her son emperor, Agrippina died by his hands a mere five years later. After a number of botched attempts at matricide, Nero ultimately succeeded when his hired henchmen bludgeoned her to death.

We have no records of her until the tender age of 13, when she was married to Gnaeus Domitius Ahenobarbus, her first cousin once removed, and 44 years old. The match was arranged by Tiberius, eager to marry her and her two sisters off to mediocre men of means so that their progeny could pose little or no threat to his dynastic plans. As unsavory as the age difference was between the couple—to say nothing of their being blood relations—it was not so unusual to marry off one's children based on political alliance in the patrician class.

Agrippina's family was in tatters when she married. With equal parts caution and paranoia, Tiberius had her mother and two eldest brothers banished from Rome and then later killed. Because he was too young to pose a threat to his regime, her youngest brother Caligula lived with Tiberius and was raised alongside Tiberius' natural grandson Gemellus, whose unhappy fate was sealed once Caligula became emperor.

After a 23-year-long reign, the death of Tiberius was celebrated. The party-like atmosphere resulted in a triumphal parade with their new Emperor Caligula leading the way. The Romans were not only celebrating Tiberius's demise but Caligula's ascension and the return of their long lost hero, Germanicus, in the guise of his only surviving son. When he first came into power, Caligula tried to right all the wrongs done to his family at the hands of Tiberius by heaping honors on both the living and deceased members of his immediate family.

No honors were more significant than those he lavished on his deceased mother and his three living sisters. Agrippina and her sisters Julia Drusilla and Julia Livilla were not only offered the rights of the Vestal Virgins but their names were included in the state prayer and in the oath that the Consuls used to introduce motions in the Senate. Every oath of office read: "I will not hold myself or my children dearer than the emperor Gaius and his sisters."

Caligula also had his sisters' faces placed on coins, a powerful propaganda tool used by emperors since Augustus. Agrippina and her sisters have the distinction of being the first living women ever to be identified on a Roman coin.[30]

Rumors began circulating about Caligula having incestuous relations with his sisters. Was it true? Perhaps more to the point, given the proclivity of incest charges against powerful figures, how common was incest in Rome? While illegal and abhorred, the accusation was a common form of political invective. Since it was impossible to prove or disprove, the mere suggestion tainted the accused—a powerful weapon indeed.

During all the hoopla over her brother's ascension to the throne, Agrippina became pregnant. Life was looking up for the eldest daughter of the revered Germanicus. Finally, her family was sovereign and the world lay at her feet.

Then Nero was born. Unsurprisingly, his beginning was an inauspicious one. In what Romans considered an evil portent, he was born breech. Intriguingly, we learn of his hazardous birth from Agrippina herself! Sadly, her memoirs are lost to us, but now and again we can hear her whispering in the records of the ancients.[31]

---

30   While their grandmother, Julia, had the distinction of being the first living woman identified on a Roman coin, the images of the three sisters were the first instance of multiple women gracing a coin.

31   In his *Annals* 4.53, Tacitus used Agrippina the Younger's memoirs to highlight certain events. One such was when her mother had to ask Tiberius (her

The portent soon bore itself out. Right after Nero's birth, things began to sour for the family. Caligula fell ill sometime in 38 CE and was so ill that no one saw him for months. Rumors spread about who was next in line of succession. His favorite sister, Drusilla, died during this interval. Some believe Caligula may have lost his senses as a result. Once recovered, he began to do the bizarre things for which he would become notorious—such as accusing his remaining two sisters of conspiring against him.

With the threat that he had "swords as well as islands" at his disposal, Agrippina and her sister Livilla were banished from Rome like their mother and grandmother before them. At the age of 26, Agrippina traded her tranquil life with her husband and four-year-old son for the wind-swept and barren island of Pontia (today's Ponza).

Within five years of sending his sisters into exile, Caligula was assassinated and succeeded by his Uncle Claudius, then in his 50s. No one expected Claudius to live long—in fact, no one ever expected much from him at all. Agrippina returned home a widow. In short order, Claudius found husband number two for her: Gauis Crispus Passienus, another mediocre older man of means. Several years later, Agrippina's second husband died, leaving her the primary heir to his substantial fortune.

At the time, Romans expressed sympathy for the twice-widowed princess, yet historians who wrote with the benefit of hindsight—several hundred years after she died—have suggested that Agrippina poisoned him. They said the timing was too perfect for him to have died naturally. Like incest, poisoning in the Roman world was difficult to prove or disprove. After all, people die from natural causes all the time.

---

guardian) for permission to remarry after Germanicus had died. His answer came in the form of his leaving the room. Agrippina's memoirs are tragically lost to us.

It was after Agrippina's second husband died that Claudius's marriage to Messalina disintegrated. Allegations of Messalina's philandering abounded during their 10-year union. Several decades older than his wife, Claudius—certainly not monogamous himself—was said to have looked the other way to his wife's many indiscretions. Then something truly scandalous happened. While Claudius was away on a trip, Messalina openly married her lover and declared him emperor.

To this day, historians are at a loss to explain that foolhardy maneuver. Claudius belied his reputation as a doddering old man and acted swiftly, ordering his Praetorian Guard to force Messalina into suicide. Regardless, Claudius's image was damaged by the scandal. Who better to revive the throne than a fourth wife with purple Julian blood?

While some sources say Agrippina tried to seduce Claudius, their union was mutually beneficial. By marrying Agrippina, Claudius not only gained the lineage of Augustus but also of his beloved brother, Germanicus. Agrippina's bloodline was paramount for the non-charismatic and often-infirm Claudius whose reign had just been tainted by disgrace. Besides, she was fertile, and could potentially produce more sons for him. For Agrippina, at long last, a husband worthy of her pedigree! There was only one small issue—he was her uncle.

Claudius and his aides tried to get around that technicality by asserting the uncle-niece union was not truly incestuous because other countries[32] condoned it. After much back and forth with lawmakers, the Senate passed a statute making uncle-niece marriages legal. Surprisingly, this law remained in effect for over 300 years in Rome.

---

32 Avunculate marriage (between uncle and niece) was not uncommon (and sometimes preferred) amongst the ruling dynasties in many countries including: Egypt, the Seleucid Empire, and ancient Israel and Judah.

Once married, the chroniclers reported that Agrippina made sure to get her son in the line of succession by having him betrothed at the age of 10 to Claudius' daughter Octavia. In fact, Claudius was as eager as Agrippina to further unite the two families. He officially adopted her son, who shed his old name and became how he is known best—Nero Claudius Drusus Germanicus Caesar.

Agrippina manipulated Claudius into adopting Nero, according to the ancients, but the truth is more complicated. Ensuring a smooth succession for the infirm emperor was a real concern: Nero was four years older than Claudius's biological son, Britannicus. This may have been an important factor in Claudius' choice of Agrippina as wife. If anything should happen to the ailing Claudius, Nero—critical to both the Julian and Claudian bloodline—could assume the crown earlier than his stepbrother.

When Claudius adopted Nero, he bestowed Agrippina with the honorific title of Augusta, which held powers akin to being named empress. Although Messalina had lobbied fiercely for the title, Agrippina has the distinction of being the first living woman (Livia had the honor conferred upon her only in death) to be an Augusta. In another first, Claudius celebrated their union in a coin called the *jugate* showing Agrippina's profile alongside that of Claudius suggesting their parity. For every accolade and honor bestowed upon her, however, historical sources double down on vitriol and insinuation.

They describe Claudius as passive, easily manipulated by a morally corrupt wife running roughshod over him. Evidently, Claudius sat by twiddling his thumbs while Agrippina settled old scores vis-a-vis poisoning, banishment or other brutality. Even old rivals for Claudius' hand were put to death by the fearsome Agrippina when she "vented her spleen."[33] She was accused of having affairs with a number of Claudius' freedmen as well as the philosopher Seneca,

---

33   Tacitus, *Annals*, Book 13, Chapter 13,

whom she had restored from exile to tutor her son. With no end to the "depths of her moral degradation," ancient sources claimed Agrippina used her sexuality as a means of promoting her political agenda. Although denounced for nefarious activities in both domestic as well as foreign policy, the truth is Agrippina was an effective partner in advocating Claudius's policies across the board.

One straightforward way to evaluate her leadership is to compare Claudius' reign before her (41 CE- 49 CE) and after her (49 CE- 54 CE). In his first eight years as emperor, Claudius executed nearly 35 senators and 200-300 equestrians.[34] Interestingly, in the five years after Agrippina became empress—despite tales of her murderous campaigns—the number of executions dwindled to a mere handful.

Besides executions, another aspect of a successful administration is stability or lack thereof. Just how stable was Rome? Before Agrippina, factions within the senate had tried to overthrow Claudius twice. After Agrippina, Claudius had nothing but good relations with the senate and other power brokers like the Praetorian Guard, whose loyalty to Germanicus easily transferred to his eldest daughter. Many historians[35] now believe that Agrippina's influence as a relationship builder and diplomat within the regime was considerable.

Agrippina was single-minded in her mission to get Nero on the throne and often characterized as the evil stepmother who would stop at nothing to promote Nero's interests ahead of those of Britannicus. "Let him kill me, just let him rule," she was rumored to have said about Nero. She would not have succeeded in advancing her son if not for the age difference between the two boys, however. Image was everything in ancient Rome, and the four years between 13 and nine were considerable. A lanky 13-year-old with a deepening voice comes off considerably more mature than a wide-eyed nine-year-old.

---

34   Equestrians are known in our modern vernacular as knights.
35   Barrett, Anthony, A. *Agrippina*; Southon, Emma, *Agrippina: Empress*.

Truth be told, Agrippina was not the only person who had high hopes for Nero's future. Claudius himself moved up the rites of maturation for Nero so he received his *toga virilis* at 13 instead of the usual 14 years of age. Enthusiastically endorsing Nero's coming into adulthood, Claudius made Nero a Consul-Designate, arranged for him to speak in front of the senate and appointed him prefect of the city of Rome. He even allowed Nero to host his own games, a move designed to make him look like a victor in a military triumph. Claudius and Agrippina had both witnessed bloody and erratic regime changes—ensuring a smooth succession was their primary goal.

The propaganda campaign was a huge success. People adored young Nero and looked up to him as a man. As for Britannicus—besides being the son of the shamed Messalina, he was only a child. So when Claudius died in 54 CE, Nero—at age 16—was made the youngest-ever emperor.

First, however, a quick note about Claudius' death. According to ancient sources, toward the end of his life, Claudius made no bones about regretting both his ill-fated marriages and the wrongs done to his natural son, Britannicus. Fearing a divorce and the rise of Britannicus, Agrippina reportedly ensured Claudius' time on the planet was shortened by enlisting the help of Locusta, a notorious poisoner who appears repeatedly in the Julio-Claudian psycho-dramas. Poison was applied on "particularly succulent mushrooms"—Claudius' favorite food—but it was insufficient. The emperor merely took ill to his bed.

Agrippina then hired another accomplice to more promptly dispatch the emperor, according to the chroniclers—a reputable doctor by the name of Gaius Stertinius Xenophon. "Xenophon, it is thought, put down his throat a feather smeared with fast-acting poison," reports Tacitus. But sickly Claudius often took to his bed. It is therefore not surprising that Agrippina would summon a doctor to administer to him.

Even Tacitus himself seems uncertain about the doctor's use of a poisoned feather in the emperor's death. Impossible to prove but effective in ruining a reputation, Agrippina has long stood accused of poisoning Claudius on the flimsiest of evidence.

But questions remain. After an emperor's death, his will was to be read in public. Yet, Claudius' will was never released. Unless she had something to hide, why wouldn't Agrippina release the will, ask the ancients? If the will named Britannicus heir, it would set up another claim to the throne—which is the last thing she would want.

There was some delay in announcing Claudius' death as Agrippina was busy setting the stage to prepare Nero for the role of a lifetime. Crowds assembled outside the palace to hear news of Claudius' health while the Praetorian Guard assembled to welcome and protect their new emperor. Finally, the palace gates opened, and out stepped fresh-faced, 16-year-old Nero. By his side was Sextus Afranius Burrus, the Praetorian Prefect, a former tutor, and now advisor to the new emperor. At Burrus' nod, the Praetorians hailed Nero "*Imperator!*" [36] Soon after, the senate proclaimed Nero emperor and awarded him the necessary powers. No one protested—Agrippina got the seamless succession for which she had worked so hard. Within a few short hours, she went from being the wife of an emperor to the mother of one.

For all intents and purposes, now she was in charge. After Nero was made emperor, Agrippina made sure he visited both the senate and the Praetorian Guard, where his first imperial password was *optimam matrum,* or best mother. Then she orchestrated a funeral for Claudius on par with that of Augustus. Her goal was to have Claudius

---

36   Annelise Freisenbruch, *Caesar's Wives* (London: Free Press, 2010), 120.

deified and his elaborate five-day long funeral helped facilitate this. Deifying Claudius also elevated her status considerably.

She was now the wife of a god and chief priestess in his cult where she had—at long last—an official public role. She was given two *lictors*, or bodyguards—Livia only had one—and a German guard.[37] When mother and son appeared in public together (see Figure 10), which was often, he would walk beside the litter in which she was carried, making it look for all the world to see that it was she, not he, who was regent.

So as to no longer rely on second-hand accounts, Agrippina invited the senate to convene in the palace in order to eavesdrop on their debates from behind a curtain. In another first for coin design, the first coins issued under Nero were of mother and son facing each other, underscoring their parity.

About Young Nero, Tacitus laments: "What hope is there in a child led by a woman?" Historians say that Nero couldn't give a fig about governing—which sadly never changed much in his lifetime. He was a musician, an actor, and a poet. Unlike his mother, he had no interest in the intricacies of politics. So initially he let her run the show and everything was fine—until he fell in love.

By this time, Nero had been unhappily married to Octavia for at least a few years. Although politically well-matched, they were ill-suited in every other way. It was no secret that they loathed each other.[38] So when his heart was captured by Acte—a Greek ex-slave on the palace staff—Seneca, now co-advisor (along with Burrus) to Nero, helped him hide the relationship from his mother.

---

37 Composed of Germanic soldiers, the German guards were known to be fierce and personal bodyguards for the Roman Emperors of the Julio-Claudian dynasty.

38 Tacitus, Annals, Book 14, 60-4.

Agrippina found out about the affair before long and predictably went into a fury. "A handmaid for a daughter-in-law!" she cried, demanding that Nero return to his matrimonial bed where—it was hoped—they would produce the all-important Julio-Claudian heir.

Alas, that was not to be. For perhaps the first time ever, Nero defied his mother. After all, he was the emperor. Not only did he openly flaunt his affair with Acte, but he began to grow closer to his advisors, who were often at loggerheads with Agrippina. Thus began a clash of wills between his advisors and his mother, with the teenage Nero calling the shots. If she were angry about the affair with Acte, however, she must have been *enraged* by what followed.

Nero dismissed one of Agrippina's most stalwart confidants, Pallas, from court. Her right-hand man, Pallas had been a key financial advisor throughout Claudius' reign. His name comes up time and again as more a friend and a confidant than just an advisor for Agrippina. Nero, however, wanted to clean house and choose his own people. Upon discovering Pallas's dismissal, an infuriated Agrippina cried: "I gave you the empire!"

She even threatened to pull her support of Nero and champion Brittanicus, poor thing.

To be caught in a tug-of-war between Agrippina and Nero—a worse fate cannot be imagined. Nothing could prepare her for what happened next. Over dinner one night, Britannicus fell ill and died— right there at the table. Agrippina went white with fear. Never bosom buddies, Britannicus grew up with her son. Could Nero really poison his stepbrother with such disregard? Little did she know, this was just the beginning. Nero would later claim that Britannicus suffered from epilepsy and died from a seizure. Some historians today believe that it was epilepsy, not poisoning, that killed Brittanicus.

Once again, however, the timing of his death was flawless. Britannicus was just about to receive his *toga virilis*—the ceremony that would usher in his manhood—and Agrippina was making overtures in his direction. He was just coming into his own. The famed Locusta's name gets bandied about regarding his death. Characteristic of something to hide, Nero had Britannicus' body cremated *posthaste*, and predictably, his funeral was without pomp or ceremony.

But Nero was not done with exerting his authority. In another move against his mother, Agrippina was banished—once again—this time from the palace. She was moved to a family estate and her *lictors*, German guard, and all the trappings associated with regency were taken away. For a woman who had not only spent most of her adult life in the public eye but had ruled the empire amidst great fanfare, Agrippina had become reduced to the secluded life of a private citizen.

Yet, despite the banishment, things appear to have stabilized between mother and son, until another love interest entered the scene.

Eight years older than Nero, Poppaea Sabina was a married woman when she first took up with the young Nero. Naturally, Agrippina opposed the union; she still nourished unrealized hopes for a reconciliation between Nero and Octavia. But that was not in the cards. The sources contend that Agrippina became so desperate for Nero to give up Poppaea that she tried seducing him herself![39] And according to the ancients, she succeeded in her efforts. There are many stories—some quite graphic—about the pair being caught *in flagrante delicto*. The mere implication of incest tarnished reputations in ancient Rome thus accusations of incest against people of note were not uncommon.

Around this time, Nero would divorce Octavia on the grounds that she was barren. Divorcing her, however, was not enough. According

---

39   Tacitus, *Annals*, Book 14, 2; Suetonius, Nero, Chapter 34. Cassius Dio, Book 62, 11.

to Tacitus he resented that the people loved Octavia so he had her exiled then mercilessly killed.[40] After marrying Poppaea Sabina he resolved to kill his mother. What prompted the decision? It remains a mystery though Poppaea—another strong-willed hence evil woman—is blamed for putting the odious idea into Nero's head.[41] But it may be more complicated than that.

Even in her relative isolation, Agrippina was supported by the fiercely loyal Praetorian Guard and could raise an armed insurrection against her son, if she chose. The truth is Nero was frightened of her, which is why his attempts at killing her sound like a dark comedy. [42]

Because he could not enlist the help of the Praetorian Guard, Nero had to make her death look accidental. The first attempt at this was the specialty of the Julio-Claudian clan: poison. But that failed. Agrippina was well-stocked with enough antidotes to last until the first millennium.

Next was an ill-conceived plan of having a ceiling fall on her while she was sleeping. This came to naught when her workers saw the flaw in the design and promptly fixed it. Lastly, one of Nero's men devised a collapsible boat that would "accidentally" break down upon transporting her. Alas, the boat did break down but only killed her hired hands, whereas Agrippina swam to safety. Like Rasputin, Agrippina survived multiple assassination attempts!

By this time, Nero was in a frenzy. Because of the collapsible boat, his mother now knew he was trying to kill her, so he was afraid of her more than ever. Never known for his bravery, Nero turned the tables on her and reported that it was she who was trying to kill him. Soon after, he hired henchmen to go to her house and finish the deed. When she realized the men were there to kill her, she is rumored to

---

40   Ibid, Book 14, Ch. 64.
41   Suetonius, The Lives of the Twelve Caesars, Otho, 3.
42   Emma Southon, *Agrippina: Empress*, 237-245,

have shouted "Strike here!" pointing to her womb, which bore the monster her son had become.

Nero wrote to the Senate that his mother had hired a freedman to try to kill him but when that failed she killed herself. No one truly believed him but the Praetorian Guard let him live. At 43 years of age, Agrippina was cremated the day she was murdered and accorded no public funeral. In their obsequity, the servile Senate thanked the gods for keeping their matricidal emperor safe.

While they were groveling thusly, there was a partial eclipse of the sun which was always ill-portent. In fact, his mother's death marked the turning point in Nero's reign. When she was alive, either running the government or advising him, Rome was a strong, stable and prosperous state. But after her passing, ruled by fear and paranoia, Nero's reign became increasingly erratic and Rome descended into chaos. After fourteen years and much bloodshed, Nero was declared enemy of the state and ignominiously fled Rome in disguise. Too cowardly to kill himself, he hired a freedman to do the job.

They called her vile when she was strong. They called her defiant when she was tenacious. She was a leader but they called her a schemer. She was a diplomat but they called her a whore. The truth is something we will never really know about Agrippina. What we do know is that the men who wrote about her could not be unbiased toward strong women; a fact which challenges every accusation against her.

In a world where women were irrelevant, Agrippina was in charge and the empire ran more smoothly on account of it. If there were gender equality in ancient Rome, not only would she have been deified but there would have been a month named in her honor.

Selected Reading for Agrippina the Younger

Barrett, Antony A. *Agrippina: Sex, Power and Politics*. New Haven: Yale University Press, 1996.

De La Bedoyere. *Domina: The Women Who Made Imperial Rome*. New Haven: Yale University Press, 2018.

Dio, Cassius. *Roman History: The Reign of Augustus*. New York: Penguin Classics: 1987.

Flower, Harriet I. *The Art of Forgetting: Disgrace & Oblivion in Roman Political Culture*, Chapel Hill: University of North Carolina Press, 2006.

Freisenbruch, Anneliese. *Caesar's Wives: Sex, Power, and Politics in the Roman Empire*. London: Free Press, 2010.

Ginsburg, Judith. *Representing Agrippina: Constructions of Female Power in the Early Roman Empire*. Oxford: Oxford University Press, 2006.

Holland, Tom. *Dynasty: The Rise and Fall of the House of Caesar*. New York: Anchor Books, 2015.

Richlin, Amy. *Arguments with Silence: Writing the History of Roman Women*. Ann Arbor: University of Michigan Press, 2017.

Suetonius. *The Lives of the Twelve Caesars*. Translated by H. M. Bird. London: Wordsworth Classics, 1997.

Southon, Emma. *Agrippina: Empress, Exile, Hustler, Whore*. London: Unbound, 2018.

Tacitus. The *Annals*. Translated by: J. C. Yardley. Oxford: University Press, 2008.

Wood, Susan E. *Imperial Women: A Study in Public Images, 40 BC-AD 68*. Leiden, NV: Brill, 1998.

CHAPTER SEVEN

Hypatia:
The Last Academic

They came to her by land. They came to her by sea. They came to her from the farthest reaches of the Greco-Roman Empire and they came to her from close by. Amongst the literati, acclaimed philosopher and leading mathematician Hypatia (355-415 CE) was a rock star. She was bold, she was beautiful, but most of all—she was brilliant.

Her students, many of them adherents to the then burgeoning new religion Christianity, hung on her every word. They followed her not just in the classroom but also in the public square and even at her home, eager just to hear her speak. Hers was the school all serious students throughout the Roman Empire wished to attend. But students weren't the only ones who were captivated by her. Academics near and far also sought her council.

How did a woman in a deeply misogynist society earn such high acclaim? By the age of 30, Hypatia had become famous in academic circles for fusing the two apparently disparate disciplines, mathematics and philosophy. While well-versed in both areas, academics tended to study either philosophy or mathematics and had schools in one discipline or the other, but not in both. Hypatia's school was novel in this regard. Trained by her mathematician father Theon (335 CE-405 CE), the foremost mathematician in Alexandria,

Hypatia would become his star pupil, assisting him in seminal writings of Euclid and Ptolemy. In fact, Hypatia was so gifted that her father ceded his school to her—retiring at only 55 years of age after it became apparent that her skills surpassed his. For all her mathematical acumen, Hypatia had a strong affinity for philosophy, which she believed led to the highest truth. Her robust background in mathematics and philosophy made her school the perfect venue for students with an interest in interdisciplinary studies.

It's important to have an understanding of what was meant by mathematics and philosophy in ancient times. Today, what two disciplines are more at odds than mathematics and philosophy? While mathematics are considered practical and useful in our highly technical world, philosophy is considered metaphysical and in some circles, relatively pointless. But both were thought sacrosanct by the ancients thus a debate ensued between scholars over which of the two disciplines led to the highest truth. Mathematics, which encompassed arithmetic, geometry, algebra and astronomy, was considered a sacred path to a higher being, or what the ancients termed "the One." Meanwhile, philosophy, a less demonstrable field, was used to develop honor, wisdom, and integrity within an individual. The philosophical goal was to impart a moral code that could bring oneness with the divine. Thus, the goal of both mathematics and philosophy was a transcendent affinity with the sacred, making them both more akin to our notion of religion.

Hypatia taught a type of speculative philosophy called Neoplatonism, which espoused a renunciation of the material world in favor of spirituality. Neoplatonists believed the materiality of the body and the world in general were things to be overcome. Hypatia herself was an exemplar of this creed, choosing to remain celibate so she could focus her energies on scholarship. One famous vignette has her thwarting the unwelcome advances of a student by showing him one of her menstruation rags, quipping "Is this what you love, young man?" Unsurprisingly, his desire for her was quelled. Hypatia's rejection of his advances illustrates how fundamental repudiation of the material world was to Neoplatonism. In this way, it was a philosophy not inconsistent with the essential tenets of Christianity. On account of this compatibility, many of Hypatia's students were both Neoplatonists and Christians. Although a pagan, Hypatia was nonpartisan and encouraged all her students to honor and respect one another and others in the world, regardless of religious affiliation.[43]

While peaceful coexistence was the order of the day in Hypatia's school, Alexandria was a tinderbox of competing factions pitting Christian against pagan and Jew, orthodox against heterodox, sectarian against non-sectarian and finally, religious authority against civil authority. Then under Christian rule, the city of Alexandria—once the center of learning throughout the empire— was fast becoming anti-intellectual and inhospitable to Hypatia and her academic circle. In fact, Christian authorities were oftentimes suspicious of learning, equating it to the work of the devil. Faith in Christ replaced scholarship in this brave new world. An example of this hatred for scholarship was demonstrated in 392 when the Bishop of Alexandria, Theophilus (384 CE-412 CE) led a braying mob of Christian zealots who destroyed the Serapeum, the city's premier temple and library complex.

Elevated by 100 steps on the acropolis of Alexandria, the Serepeum was made of luminous marble and rose above all other structures commanding the city skyscape. Equally impressive, the library within the Serapeum was considered the daughter to the defunct Library of Alexandria, housing hundreds of thousands of scrolls. After the extremists razed the Serapeum complex and set fire to the scrolls, the swarm went on a holy mission. When all was said and done, they destroyed over 2,500 structures and countless artifacts.

---

43   Catherine Nixey, *The Darkening Age* (London: Macmillan, 2017), 131."Hypatia remained determinedly non-partisan in her behavior, treating non-Christian and Christian with meticulous equality."

In 414 CE, Theophilus died and was succeeded by his nephew, Cyril (378 CE- 444 CE) who made his uncle look conciliatory by contrast. Ruling with an iron fist from the get-go, he made his wrath known against another enemy of the Christians—the Jews. When some Christians were killed in a skirmish that broke out between Christians and Jews, Cyril organized an army of thousands called the *parabalani*. Typically from the lower rungs of society and oftentimes illiterate, the *parabalani* gangs were at his beck and call. Some were Nitrian monks who traveled to Alexandria from the desert all fired up against non-Christians. Both groups had a flagrant reputation for violence.

At Cyril's behest, they seized the synagogues, converting them into churches. But defacing their places of worship was not enough for the iron-fisted bishop, he also exiled the Jews from Alexandria and encouraged his Christian disciples to occupy their now abandoned homes and to seize their possessions.

It is emblematic of the staggering influence wielded by religious authority that Orestes—the governor of Alexandria—could do little but stand by the sidelines in horror and despair at this gross injustice. Though a Christian himself, Orestes was a nonsectarian and, like his good friend Hypatia, was appalled by Cyril's barbaric actions against the Jews.

Though it did no good, Orestes reported the atrocious events to the emperor in Constantinople, which put him squarely in the crosshairs of Cyril's band of thugs. One night, while out in his chariot, Orestes was confronted by an angry mob of *parabalani* and Nitrian monks. The monks gashed Orestes' head open with a stone. If not for the help of nonsectarian bystanders, Orestes would have died.

When the stone-hurling monk was apprehended, Orestes had him publicly tortured and the monk ultimately died. In true form, Cyril used the monk's death in a propaganda campaign against the governor, further fueling the fire between the two factions.

Attempts at reconciliation between the two leaders ended in failure. Through it all, the governor sought counsel from the wisest person in the land—Hypatia—who stood resolutely by his side. However, Cyril's supporters saw Hypatia's advocacy on Orestes' behalf not as uniting but as dividing. Alexandria's most acclaimed pagan was an easy target who they blamed for the continuing rift between the two men.

Thus, the rumors began. She has an undue influence on Orestes. She's bewitched him with her sorcery. She is teaching idolatry. Calling her a witch, they even used her famed astrolabe against her saying it was an instrument of Satan. The cacophony of outcries against her became deafening.

Then it happened.

On her daily ride through the city in March of 415, Hypatia had set off for school in her chariot. As a consummate academic, her mind was likely a million miles away. Perhaps she was thinking about her next seminar; about some philosophical dictate or mathematical law she would discuss in class. Being an exemplary teacher, her fortunate students were never far from her mind.

Suddenly, she found herself confronted by a howling mob under the leadership of a church magistrate called Peter. Because she was not a civil authority, she lacked the security detail that Orestes enjoyed. Until then, no academic had needed such protection in Alexandria.

From the beginning, it was violent. They ordered her off her chariot, then dragged her through the streets and into a church. She must have tried to reason with them, but her reasoning fell on the deafened ears of the righteous. After all, theirs was the will of god. They tore the clothes off of the "luminous child of reason"[44] and in God's house, they flayed her with the jagged edges of roofing tiles.

---

44 Synesius of Cyrene, *Dion*, 9, Quoted in *Hypatia of Alexandria* by Maria Dzielska (1995), 48.

As if that were not enough, while still alive and breathing, they gouged out her eyes. Once dead, they further violated her by cutting her body into pieces parading them throughout the streets of Alexandria. At long last, what was left of her ended up in a funeral pyre.

From the farthest reaches of the empire, Christians and non-Christians alike were outraged over the abhorrent slaying of the greatest mathematician of the day. Academics were considered inviolable in the ancient world due to the scholarship and wisdom they contributed to the community. Hypatia was not only an academic, however—she was also an elite woman, which should have been enough protection in and of itself. How could something so horrible happen to someone so beloved? The reality was, Hypatia was part of a dying breed. She was the last champion of a 700-year academic tradition vanishing under a tidal wave of anti-intellectual religious dogma. After Hypatia's death, many pagan academics fled Alexandria in search of more tolerant cities. Eventually, throughout the empire, religion replaced philosophy and clergy replaced academics.

Devastated, Orestes soon left public life. Cyril's star, meanwhile, was still rising. While never formally charged in Hypatia's death, if not for the anti-pagan fervor he stirred up, it is likely the attack would never have happened. Following Hypatia's death, Cyril was given the honorary moniker of "the new Theophilus" for quashing the "last remnants of idolatry." Under his continued leadership, Alexandria became an important Christian hub and Cyril was eventually canonized as a saint. To this day, he is venerated in the Roman Catholic and Eastern Orthodox Churches.

Selected Reading for Hypatia

Deakin, Michael A. B. *Hypatia of Alexandria: Mathematician and Martyr.* New York: Prometheus Books, 2007.

Dzielska, Maria. *Hypatia of Alexandria.* Cambridge: Harvard University Press, 1996.

Nixey, Catherine. *The Darkening Age: The Christian Destruction of the Classical World.* London: Macmillan Press, 2017.

Richeson, A. W. "Hypatia of Alexandria." *National Mathematics Magazine* 15, no. 2 (1940): 74–82. https://doi.org/10.2307/3028426.

Watts, Edward J. *Hypatia: The Life and Legend of an Ancient Philosopher,* New York: Oxford University Press, 2017.

CHAPTER VIII

Empress Theodora: Sinner or Saint?

The hooded gaze of an inscrutable Theodora (c.490-548 CE) (see Figure 11) greets hundreds of thousands of visitors each year as they pay their respects to her mosaic at the Basilica of Saint Vitale in Ravenna, Italy. Encircled in glittering gold and bedecked in crown jewels, her visage befits the powerful Byzantine Roman empress she once was. Theodora is considered to have been one of the most effective and influential of all empresses. While her image on the mosaic is still discernible, the image she presents to history is somewhat less so.

The daughter of a bearkeeper, Theodora rose to the highest office in the land and never lost touch with her humble beginnings. She often advocated for the disenfranchised, particularly women. More than just a titular head, Theodora was an equal partner in Justinian's administration and would become the most powerful woman in Byzantine history.

Alas, much of what we know about her comes from the poisonous pen of Procopius (497-565 CE) of Caesarea, a leading Justinian historian. Prior to *Anecdota* (*Secret History*), Procopius had nothing but praise for the Justinian administration. Thus, it came as something of a surprise to the academic community when his book was discovered centuries after it was written in 550 CE. Brimming with hyperbole and invective against the royal couple, whom Procopius characterizes as "demons," *Secret History* can read like tabloid press.

No character is more impugned than that of the empress. Like many ancient chroniclers of powerful women, Procopius focused on her sexuality. He repeatedly referred to the time when, as a child and young adult, she performed on stage and engaged in the oldest of professions. Licentiousness was not her only sin, according to him. She was also cruel, spiteful, vindictive, and tyrannical. Regrettably, Procopius's fiery invective against Theodora influenced subsequent historians' views on the complicated empress. Notwithstanding, who was Empress Theodora? While her work in the sex trade is unconfirmed, her humble origins are not. In an era not known for social mobility, how did the daughter of a bearkeeper rise to the highest office in the land? And why was her reign in many ways more remarkable than that of her husband Justinian?

The death of Theodora's father when she was five years old left her family in desperate need. Although her mother quickly remarried, when the bearkeeper post vacated by her late husband was denied to her new husband, the family remained financially destitute. Employment options being few and far between for females of any age in sixth-century Constantinople, Theodora's mother had to be resourceful—a trait Theodora must have inherited. She encouraged her three daughters to perform on stage as mime actresses.

But there was a stigma attached to acting in Byzantine society. Employees of the theater were at the very bottom of the social hierarchy. They were denounced by religious leaders and even denied sacraments unless they were on their deathbed. It was assumed—either accurately or not—that actresses were loose with their favors. In the minds of the judgemental public, there was little difference between actresses and prostitutes and as a result both were outcasts from society. Believed to focus on the "sins of the flesh," theater was considered the quintessence of depravity. But forasmuch as entertainers were reviled, people still came out in droves to watch them perform. So important was entertainment in sixth century Constantinople.

When she reached "maturity," likely at the age of 12, Theodora officially began her acting career. When at last she "was ripe for it, she joined the women on stage and promptly became a prostitute," wrote Procopius. He could only have known about her work as a prostitute by hearsay, since he himself was five years old at the time. Be that as it may, with her quick wit, good looks, and precocity, she soon achieved notoriety as a comic actress, capturing the attention of men of means.

Eventually, she moved out of Constantinople to become the live-in mistress of a wealthy governor in Libya. According to some reports, Theodora may have even had one or two children by then, though there is scant mention of them. Sometime after the relationship with the governor soured, Theodora stopped in Alexandria on her way back to Constantinople. Many scholars believe it was while she was in Alexandria that she underwent a full religious conversion that not only changed the course of her life but arguably changed the course of religious belief in the entire region. Her new religion was a branch of early Christianity called Monophysitism, which argued that Christ had *only* a divine nature. This belief was at odds with most of the West and the Byzantine state itself, which believed that Christ had two natures, human and divine.

In a move that may seem contrary to religious belief, it has been suggested that while living abroad in the East—with easy access to circles of influence—the future empress may have been a Byzantine spy. After all, state governments had long been known to use actresses or prostitutes in intelligence-gathering operations.[45] While

---

45   James Allan Evans, *The Empress Theodora: Partner of Justinian*. (Austin, Texas: University of Texas Press, 2004), 17-18.

we have no information as to how she met the heir to the throne, Procopius reckons that they must have met once she returned to Constantinople in the year 520 CE or so.

It would appear that Justinian soon fell under the spell of the brilliant and beautiful Theodora. Unable to marry on account of a law prohibiting nobility from marrying actresses, Justinian entreated his uncle, then Emperor Justin (c.450-527 CE) to intervene. While Justin was amenable to assisting his nephew, his wife Empress Euphemia was not. She resolutely opposed Justinian's intended marriage to the actress. After her death, however, Justin conferred nobility on Theodora, thereby paving the way for Justinian and Theodora to marry. Of this marriage Procopius sneered: "From that moment he lived with Theodora as his legal spouse, thereby enabling everyone else to get engaged to a harlot." Their marriage sent shockwaves throughout the Byzantine aristocracy. In 527 CE, Justin, who was in ill health, crowned both Justinian Augustus as co-emperor and Theodora as Augusta. After Justin's death some four months later, this humble daughter of a bearkeeper and former actress would become empress of the Eastern Roman Empire.

Perhaps it was because of her humble origins that Justinian's court became notable for the groveling it required from visitors. All royal guests—regardless of their lineage—were expected to prostrate themselves face down with their lips touching the imperial feet. However, it was not just Justinian's feet that were thus honored— Theodora's were as well. Reveling in the pomp and circumstance of being royal, Theodora demanded every sign of deference awarded to the emperor. Who could blame her? From the start, she involved herself in all aspects of governance, participating not only in political strategies and planning but in state councils as well. While never officially co-regent, Justinian considered Theodora his equal, calling her *"partner in my deliberations."* He openly acknowledged that he consulted with her on many issues.

From the beginning, one of Theodora's chief goals was to help the unfortunate—particularly women in need who engaged in prostitution. She helped rid Constantinople and cities throughout the empire of brothel keepers for whom prostitutes were virtual slaves. Moreover, Theodora supervised the building of the Convent of Repentance, which housed and supported former prostitutes. She also contributed financial aid to women to buy necessities such as clothing and supplies. Since marriage and security were out of reach for most former sex workers, Theodora aimed to provide women with relative comfort so they would not be tempted into a life of prostitution once again. Justinian would come to rely on Theodora's keen intellect and political acuity, but it was not until the winter of 532 CE that her steely will and strength of character were fully put to the test.

Could the raging riots that burned down more than half of Constantinople have stemmed from something as innocuous as a chariot race? Fan loyalty devolved into street fighting in an event known as the Nika (victory or conquer) Revolt when two sparring factions—the Greens and the Blues—united against Justinian for refusing to pardon convicted felons from each of their camps. Another narrative suggests that the riots were a public outcry against the sovereignty of Theodora.

Regardless of motive, the leaders of the riots are believed to have been the nephews of Justin's predecessor Anastasius I (431-518 CE). Ultimately, they burned down more than half the city, focusing on religious and imperial buildings such as the *Hagia Sophia* (Holy Wisdom), the principal church of Byzantium.[46] Because there was no police force, the emperor turned to his militia, who were soon overcome. The crisis was spiraling out of control. Instead of debating how best to remove the rioters, the senate was debating how best to remove the royals. Meanwhile, Justinian and his retinue

---

46 The *Hagia Sophia* would be rebuilt between the years of 532 and 537 CE and become the crowning architectural achievement of Justinian's reign.

were holed up in the imperial palace, where they began planning their exit strategy to flee Constantinople in a boat under cover of darkness. Theodora, however, had other plans.

Changing the course of history, the empress—ever the actress—took center stage with a stirring speech that roused both the emperor and his attendants.

> While it is the condition of our birth to die, it is unendurable to descend from imperial power to the state of a fugitive. God forgive that I should ever be without this purple robe: may I not outlive the day when I cease to be greeted as empress! If safety is what you want, my emperor, it's easily had. We have plenty of money; there's the sea; there are our ships. But look out that when you are safe you don't discover that death would have been preferable. For my part, I like the maxim, 'Kingship makes a good burial shroud.'

The most esteemed Augusta clearly had no desire to return to the life of a commoner. A sovereign through and through, it would take more than a riot—even one that would burn to a crisp more than half of Constantinople —to drag her from the throne.

Compelled to action by Theodora's moving speech, Justinian and his generals concocted a last-ditch effort to lure the rioters into the Hippodrome by spreading a story that Justinian would be there. Tens of thousands of people—most (but not all) of them rebels—came out for the big event. Alas, once the soldiers sealed off the exits at the Hippodrome, they killed everyone in their path. It is believed that up to 40,000 people were massacred to save Justinian and Theodora's reign. Though stories vary on how the nephews of Anastasius I were brought to justice, most historians concur that while Justinian favored leniency, Theodora—notorious for her 'take no prisoners' approach—insisted on their executions.

While Theodora's authority was significant before the *Nika* revolt, her influence afterward was even greater. This was reflected in many of the reforms Justinian put forward promoting the rights of women. In 534 CE, Justinian passed legislation prohibiting anyone from coercing a woman—slave or free—from working in theater if she was unwilling, or to impede her if she chose to leave it. In another law with enormous implications for women of all social classes, Justinian vindicated the rights of women to own property, to inherit and to retain their dowries. Prior to Justinian's law, husbands had complete authority over the dowry of their wives. Dowry rights refer to how married women could retain possession of their dowries, separate from their husband's property. Moreover, anti-rape legislation was passed, as were laws supporting young girls who had been sold into sexual slavery. Theodora's power was so considerable that she is mentioned in nearly all the laws passed pertaining to the rights of women.

Women were not the only oppressed group whose rights she championed. Theodora was a tireless advocate of her adopted and oftentimes beleaguered faith, Monophysitism. Some background on the split in the Christian church is important here. In 451 CE, the Council of Chalcedon ruled that Christ had two natures—human and divine. Supporters of this edict became known as "Chalcedonians." The ruling, however, was in direct opposition to Monophysitism, which held that Christ had only one divine nature. The schism was, in fact, as much regional and cultural as it was religious. Encompassing the Greco-Roman world, much of the Western part of the Byzantine Empire agreed with the Roman Pope and considered itself Chalcedonian. In the East, however—especially in ancient strongholds like Egypt and Syria—Christians were predominantly Monophysites, represented by various Patriarchs.

Because the Monophysites were often persecuted within the Orthodox Byzantine Empire, Theodora became their vehement advocate. She even provided shelter for covert clergy within the *Boukoleon* palace complex. It is believed that over several hundred of the persecuted clergy at one time or another lived under Theodora's protection. While Theodora was committed to her faction, a dream of Justinian's—himself a Chalcedonian—was to unite the two disparate faiths.

Nevertheless, despite his desire to unify the church—or perhaps because of it—Justinian chose to look the other way when it came to his wife's Monophysite activism. On this issue, they appeared to be at cross-purposes. While Justinian wanted to mend the rift between the Chalcedonians and the Monophysites, Theodora's intervention further deepened the divide.

Over the years, historians have speculated that Theodora's support of the Monophysites kept the schism alive, ultimately crippling the Christian message, especially in the East where the Monophysite presence was most strongly felt. They argue that Monophysitism might have died an early death if not for Theodora. Did Theodora unwittingly weaken Christianity's message in the East, perhaps opening the way for the spread of a new religion in the region? Indeed, a span of just 50 years separates the death of Theodora and the birth of Mohammed. Many believe that Christianity's lack of cohesion—in which Theodora played a role—may have contributed to the expansion of Islam in the region.

Religion and women's rights, however, were not the only areas in which she made her presence felt. In fact, Theodora exerted considerable influence in all facets of governance—and she had the enemies to show for it. Though his jabbering may be questionable at times, Procopius was not the only one reporting how she dispatched some of her foes. She is hardly alone among sovereigns to do so, which may be why they are so seldom canonized—Theodora being, as ever, an exception.

In February of 2000, fifteen hundred years after her birth, Theodora was beatified by the Patriarch of Antioch, the head of the Universal

Syrian Orthodox Church[47]—the church the empress helped found. She is celebrated as Saint Theodora in the Greek Orthodox Church as well.

Canonization aside, overall, history has been unkind to Theodora. She was fearless, she was fierce, and she was female: a combination that does not sit well with many historians—ancient or otherwise. Theodora was a champion of the powerless, which often put her at odds with the powerful. The truth is she did more for women, the disadvantaged, and the religiously persecuted in her short life than most monarchs did in their lifetimes. One of the most triumphant of all female rulers, no empress before or after could boast of having achieved greatness from a background like hers.

Of course, she did not lead alone. It is ironic that the superlative power couple credited with ushering in one of the most productive periods of the Eastern Roman Empire would produce no children. However, when she could not reproduce a dynasty of her own this strong-willed empress tried to manufacture one. Envisioning a Monophysite dynasty, she attempted to marry her nephew to the daughter of Belisarius. If she had lived longer, she might have even pulled it off. Even though she was 15 years his junior, Theodora predeceased Justinian by 17 years when she died—likely from breast cancer[48]— at less than 50 years of age. Aware that the Monophysite religion would suffer with her passing, on her deathbed Theodora begged Justinian to continue to house the besieged Monophysite refugees. She was hardly cold in her grave before the Chalcedonians sought to expel the vulnerable Monophysite clergy from their sanctuary. But Justinian held fast to his promise, and would continue to house the Monophysite refugees for the next 17 years. Her body was laid to rest in the Church of the Holy Apostles in Constantinople.

---

47   The Universal Syrian Orthodox Church traces its origins back to the early Christian community of Monophysites in Antioch (modern day Syria).

48   Evans, 103-104.

Selected Readings for Theodora the Great

Bradshaw, Gillian. *The Bearkeeper's Daughter*. London: Penguin
  Books, 1987.

Evans, James Allan. The Empress Theodora: Partner of Justinian.
  Austin: University of Texas Press, 2004.

Foss, C. "The Empress Theodora" *Byzantion* 72, no. 1 (2002):
  141–76. http://www.jstor.org/stable/44172751.

Mallet, C. E. "The Empress Theodora." *The English Historical
  Review* 2, no. 5 (1887): 1–20. http://www.jstor.org/
  stable/546828.

Pazdernik, Charles. "'Our Most Pious Consort Given Us by God':
  Dissident Reactions to the Partnership of Justinian and
  Theodora, A.D. 525-548." *Classical Antiquity* 13, no. 2
  (1994): 256–81. https://doi.org/10.2307/25011016.

Procopius. *The Secret History*. Translated by G. A. Williamson, New
  York: Penguin Classics, 2007.

Ancient Women
In Mythology

CHAPTER NINE

The Adaptations of Ariadne: Minoan Great Mother Goddess

In the myth of the Minotaur, if not for the humble ministrations of Princess Ariadne, Theseus would not have had a prayer. Although often portrayed as a mere maiden, truth be told, providing backup for a leading man was the very least of her qualities. Springing from the heavens, Ariadne's origins beckon from the primordial mist of Bronze Age Minoan Crete (ca 3000 BCE-1400 BCE). At that time, she was the overarching mother goddess in the Minoan pantheon: an all-important fertility goddess believed to have answered to such titles as goddess-on-earth, weaver of life, and mistress of the labyrinth.

With the destiny of mortals in her hands, Ariadne was considered a bright or fertility goddess. Ariadne is, in fact, analogous to both Demeter, the goddess of the harvest—whose celestial origins are from Crete as well— and her daughter Persephone, queen of the underworld. Predating patriarchy, the great goddess's role was paramount; in agricultural societies religion was centered on fertility and everything was centered on religion. Because Minoan Crete was a matrilineal society with women presumably leading lives of independence, like all goddesses in the Minoan pantheon, Ariadne ruled alone without a male consort. Toward the end of the Minoan civilization—with the Mycenaeans' influence keenly felt—

Ariadne started appearing with a young male consort. Her insignia, the labyrinth—a square or circular structure with multiple circuits spiraling to the center and back again—figures prominently in her mythology. Labyrinths were believed to be places of initiation where mortals moved from one realm to another with the bull god—the Minotaur (Hades-like)—occupying its deepest, darkest center.

The decline of the Minoan Civilization was accompanied by the expansion of the Mycenaeans.[49] As is often the case when one culture contains another, the Mycenaeans rewrote the Minoan myths when they took control around 1400 BCE. The invader gods married or raped the indigenous goddesses, replacing matricentric elements with patriarchal ones. By rewriting mythology, the Mycenaean Greeks provoked the systemic suppression of goddess worship and, by extension, women themselves. This was hardly unique to the Mycenaeans, it continued apace into the Greek culture of the Aegean and much beyond. In reviewing the myths surrounding Ariadne, my purpose is to expose the patriarchal tropes that have dogged her many guises for thousands of years.

Ariadne is best known from a Mycenaean-era myth in which she is reduced to an unassuming princess offering comfort to the legendary hero-king of Athens, Theseus. The tale begins when Poseidon, god of the earth and sea, gifts a rare white bull to King Minos of Crete, expecting it to be sacrificed in his honor. Eager to have the prized bull play stud in his herd, Minos tries to pull a fast one by sacrificing a lesser bull in Poseidon's honor instead. But it is unwise to fool a god. Infuriated, the all-seeing, all-knowing Poseidon casts a spell on Minos' Queen Pasiphae causing her to fall hopelessly in love with the striking snow-white bull.

---

49   In the 18th century BCE, the Mycenaeans invaded the Aegean region conquering the indigenous pre-Hellenic mainland. Representing the first characteristically Greek civilization, Mycenaean Greece dominated the last phase of the Bronze Age from approximately from 18th to 11th century BCE.

Her desire for the bull is so strong that she enlists the help of the famed artificer, Daedalus, to craft a wooden cow with a cowhide covering so that she can copulate with the beast. The product of their coupling is the Minotaur, a monster who is a cross between a human and a bull. Uncared for and unloved, the Minotaur is confined to a labyrinth. First, some context. The Minotaur's hostility toward Athenians is illustrative of the high tension between Minoan Crete and Athens. At this time, Crete is the powerhouse of the Aegean, and Athens a mere fledgling state. King Minos' son, Androgeus, was unjustly killed by Athenians for winning all the prizes in their Panathenaic Games. In retribution, each year Athens had to send seven young men and seven young women as tribute to Crete. Once there the youth were put in the labyrinth where they would either lose their way in the endless passages or be devoured by the man-eating Minotaur who lived in the deepest darkest recesses of it.

This onerous tribute went on for years until Theseus, son of Aegeus, King of Athens volunteered to be one of the seven male victims. Finally, Ariadne enters the myth. The daughter of Minos and Pasiphae, she is instantly besotted with the Athenian hero. Promptly forsaking her family, Ariadne arms Theseus with a sword to kill her half-brother, the Minotaur. In order to escape from the complex labyrinth, she gives him a ball of thread, ingeniously advising him to tie one end of the thread at the entrance and let the thread unspool as he tunnels deeper into the labyrinth's undulating paths. Ever the headliner, Theseus succeeds in his quest to destroy the Minotaur and follows the thread back to the entrance where the love-struck Ariadne awaits. From there they sail off together to Athens with a slight detour to the island of Naxos (Dia), where Theseus promptly abandons Ariadne.

Many ancient writers have come up with theories to explain Theseus' actions. Both Hesiod (c. 750 BCE-650 BCE) and Plutarch (50 CE- 120 CE) say Theseus left Ariadne because he was in love with Aigle, the goddess of good health. In Euripides' (480 BCE-406

BCE) lost play *Theseus* Athena convinces Theseus to leave Ariadne for reasons similar to Aeneas' desertion of Dido in the *Aeneid*— i.e., Theseus had a heroic career ahead of him and Ariadne could prove a distraction. Along these same lines, Latin author and scholar Hyginus (64 BCE-17 CE) suggests that Theseus thought Ariadne would bring disgrace on him in Athens—presumably because she was a foreigner.

Ariadne's story greatly resembles another Mycenaean-era myth concerning another goddess cum princess from a foreign land (Colchis—present-day Georgia), who also acts against her better interests by abandoning her royal family for a Greek hero who ultimately deserts her. Medea helps Jason every step of the way, even at the expense of her father and the murder of her brother. Although their stories differ in substance, both women are cast aside when no longer useful to the hegemonic Greek heroes. Demonstrating the lack of parity between the Greeks and their conquests, the women—often considered part of the spoils of war— represent the subjugated from vanquished lands while Theseus and Jason, play the roles of heedless invaders plundering the resources of the defeated while fleeing with its most valuable possessions. Being vanquished, however, is not the only similarity of the two women.

As granddaughters of the Sun god, Helios, both Ariadne and Medea possess supernatural powers, and as such represent vanquished deities. Some suggest Medea may have been a pre-patriarchal goddess herself. Unlike Medea, Ariadne is not known for vengeance but in a surviving passage attributed to her from Euripides' *Theseus* is the line: *"and yet I will tell a tale worthy of blame..."* Hellenistic poet Catullus (84 BCE-54 BCE) expands on this theme in his epic *Poem 64*, where, taking a page from Medea, Ariadne calls for vengeance against Theseus.

Before he had left for Crete, Theseus had promised his father that if his mission were a success, he would hoist a white sail in place of the black sail upon his return. Ariadne's vengeance takes the form of a curse on Theseus that makes him forget to hoist the white sail. Upon sight of the black sail, Aegeus—believing his son dead—jumps to his death into the sea, which henceforth would be named in his honor: the Aegean. Just as the gods side with Medea, so Catullus says Jupiter comes to Ariadne's defense. Yet she is not good at vengeance. While Medea destroys Jason's bride, progeny, and ancestral line, Ariadne's vengeance ends up making Theseus king of Athens.

As for the recasting of the myth, the Minotaur is a Cretan monster who is more bull-like than human and devours Athenian young. However, bulls in Minoan Crete were not only objects of veneration but quite possibly used in their sanctified rituals as well. In this way, the Mycenaeans took something sacred and turned it into a monster. In his seminal, *Occidental Mythology*, Joseph Campbell asserts: "....terming the gods of other people demons, enlarging one's own counterparts to hegemony over the universe, and then inventing all sorts of great and little secondary myths...validates not only a new social order but also a new psychology." Time and again, the Mycenaean Greeks incorporate their gods and their heroes into the rewritten indigenous myths to reflect not only their patriarchal culture but their predominance.

More powerful still was their marginalization of Ariadne, transforming the great Minoan mother goddess into a lovesick maiden subservient to the Greek hero. The truth is if not for the help of Ariadne, Theseus would be a mere postscript—neither king nor hero. Yet Theseus is the star of this story, and Ariadne is only a bit player. After renouncing her family and homeland, Theseus abandons her—while she is sleeping—leaving her for dead on an alien and desolate island. In some traditions, a heartbroken Ariadne commits suicide.

At this point, the reveler and *bon vivant*, Dionysus, god of the grape harvest, enters the stage. According to one tradition, Dionysus compels Theseus to leave Ariadne to him. Left with little in the way of choice, Ariadne acquiesces. Put another way, a sleeping Ariadne resembles a heedless Persephone picking flowers before being whisked away by another god, in this case, her own Uncle Hades, lord of the underworld. Seen this way, marriage is a violation, which is precisely how the historian Pausanias (115 CE-180 CE) expresses the marriage of Dionysus and Ariadne: "Ariadne asleep, Theseus putting to sea and Dionysus arriving to rape Ariadne."

Here Ariadne is like all Greek girls, whose marriages—arranged by their fathers to total strangers typically twice or three times their age—must have felt like a sort of rape. Dionysus is a foreign deity believed to have been amongst one of the older chthonic (subterranean) gods known for their roles in fertility originating from Thrace or Asia Minor. Ariadne is once again a fertility goddess whose sleeping—suggestive of the period where the earth lies dormant—is analogous to Persephone going underground for a few months each year.

Unlike the love story between the Greek hero and his love-struck aid, the union between Ariadne and Dionysus is cyclical and revolves around the changing seasons. According to Pausanias, when the fertility god's seed lies dormant, the fertility couple separates, and the goddess goes away—perhaps harkening back to an era before marriage when women had more agency in their reproductive lives. Ariadne either sleeps or dies during the dormant season. After all, for a fertility goddess, sleeping and dying are much the same thing. Dionysus also bestows Ariadne with a gift from the gods— a gold crown, formerly Aphrodite's and forged by Hephaestus, with red gems shaped like roses. This crown is eventually placed among the stars, becoming *Corona Borealis* (Crown of Lights) in the night sky.

A remarkable aspect of mythology is the opportunity for multiple endings, and Ariadne's story is no exception. In Homer's *Odyssey*, Artemis—the virgin goddess of the hunt and of chastity known for brutally punishing wayward women—slays Ariadne (then mortal) for her infidelity to Dionysus (her husband all along in this version). According to the *Odyssey*, this was done "on the denunciation of Dionysus." Apparently, the god was upset because Ariadne defiled his grotto simply with her unrequited love for Theseus. Never mind that Dionysus himself was a notorious seducer.

Make no mistake, unlike her previous manifestation in the Minoan pantheon, Ariadne is now merely the wife of a fertility god. Dionysus' exploits and adventures without Ariadne abound, yet Ariadne is mentioned in these myths only in connection with Dionysus. When he returns to her, their marriage is made sacred each year amidst orgiastic celebrations—Ariadne is reborn, and the planet is made fruitful again. According to Walter Burkert's iconic book *Greek Religion*, the celebration of the sacred marriage between Dionysus and Ariadne was called the *Anthesteria* and it commemorated the king, Theseus, giving his wife, Ariadne, to the god. Moreover, there were two Ariadne festivals on the island of Naxos, one joyful, the other mournful. "The marriage with Dionysus stands in the shadow of death," Burkert affirms. As with all fertility festivals, death—an aspect of life's regeneration, is implicated in the revelry.

Death calls again for Ariadne when Dionysus finds himself at war with his nemesis—Perseus, King of Argo—and the Argives. According to the epic poet Nonnus (circa 400 CE -500 CE) in his *Dionysiaca*, a "frail," and evidently mortal Ariadne is turned to stone when "raging Perseus" mistakenly strikes her in battle with a spear.

Perseus, remember, famously beheaded Medusa while she slept. One of the three Gorgon sisters, Medusa's gaze would turn men to stone. She may have once been a pre-patriarchal goddess herself, which could be reason enough for her beheading. There are, however, inconsistencies in the myths. Time and again throughout these later myths, Ariadne is referred to as mortal even though in another tradition, Dionysus descended into the underworld to retrieve her and take her back with him to Olympus as his immortal wife. She proves, however, to be more mortal than immortal when according to Pausanias the goddess is laid to rest in an "earthenware coffin."

Reduced to a woman whose only source of happiness is through a man, the shadow of Ariadne is poles apart from the independent great mother goddess she was over 2,000 years prior. Honored in a religion of the soil that encouraged not only reverence for nature but respect for women, Ariadne became subjugated under a patriarchal society that relegated the female while exalting the male. She was not the only great mother goddess thus subdued. Some believe that under the archetypal guises of the carnal Aphrodite, the jealous Hera and even the patriarchal Athena are vestiges of the great mother goddess tradition from whence they sprang. Much scholarship has been done suggesting that beneath the greater Olympic pantheon—as envisioned by Hesiod and Homer—lay the bedrock of the older great goddess religions.

Selected Reading for Ariadne

Brindel, June Rachuy. *Ariadne: A Novel of Ancient Crete.* New York: St. Martin's Press, 1980

Burkert, Wallter. *Greek Religion.* Cambridge: Harvard University Press,1985.

Campbell, Joseph. *The Masks of God: Occidental Mythology.* New York: Penguin Books, 1991.

Eisner, Robert. "Some Anomalies in the Myth of Ariadne." *The Classical World.* 71, no. 3, (1977): 175-177. https://www.jstor.org/stable/4348823.

Herberger, Charles F. *The Thread of Ariadne.* New York: Philosophical Library, 1972.

Perry, Laura. *Ariadne's Thread.* Winchester, UK: Moon Books, 2013.

Rigoglioso, Marguerite. *Virgin Goddesses of Antiquity.* London: Palgrave Macmillan, 2010.

Webster, T. B. L. "The Myth of Ariadne from Homer to Catullus." *Greece & Rome* 13, no. 1 (1966): 22–31. http://www.jstor.org/stable/642350.

CHAPTER TEN

Hera: Suppression of the Native Queen

Of all the unhappy couples in Greek literature perhaps the unhappiest is that of the Olympian first couple themselves. As the goddess of marriage, a neglected Hera plays the quintessential role of the jealous wife for the ever-unfaithful Zeus—the lord of the gods at Mount Olympus. Often working on the sidelines against her husband's interests, Hera displays a proclivity for instigating strife and mayhem— particularly against Zeus's vast collection of paramours and their offspring. Never mind that his paramours more closely resemble victims than lovers—by no means does she let justice stand in the way of divine retribution.

Hera's facetious depiction in Greek literature as a jealous and vengeful wife is in marked contrast to the piety that her cult engendered. Throughout the Greek world, Hera was bestowed the greatest accolades of all the goddesses in the Greek pantheon; she is regarded as the patron goddess of marriage and the goddess of women and childbirth too. As the only wedded of the original Olympian goddesses, her presence loomed large at weddings where she presided over lawful unions and helped protect women from harm during childbirth. Moreover, Hera holds an exalted place in the Olympian pantheon; not only is she the wife of Zeus but she is also his sister. In Hesiodic genealogy, Hera was the eldest daughter of the king and queen of the Titans: Kronos and Rhea.

In consideration of the multiple honors bestowed on her— oftentimes to the exclusion of more benevolent deities— it is difficult to reconcile the vicious Hera as she is portrayed in Greek literature to the benevolent Hera who is worthy of celebration. So why was Greek literature unkind to Hera? Could the stormy relationship between Zeus and Hera be reflective of a culture clash? What can we learn from her earliest temples and how can we ascertain the historical origins — the pre-Greek roots— of Hera and her cult?

Greek Literature's Hera

Though the stories of Hera's savageness are too numerous to mention in the confines of this article, the following is a sampling of some of her more notorious. First there is the woeful tale of Io, Hera's first priestess. Although Io spurns Zeus's unwelcome advances, ultimately she is powerless to resist the will of this mightiest of all gods. In competing narratives, either Zeus transforms Io into a heifer—ostensibly to hide her from the wrath of Hera—or Hera does the deed herself. Yet Hera goes one step further by fastening Io to an olive tree and employing the hundred-eyed Argus to keep his various eyes on Io to make sure that she has no further assignations with Zeus. Hera's malevolent nature still not quelled, she then sets a gadfly to pester and mercilessly pursue the unfortunate Io to the ends of the earth.

Another of her targets is Sermele, mother of Dionysis by Zeus. In Hera's disguise as a nurse, she encourages Semele to ask Zeus to reveal himself in all his divine grandeur knowing full well that the sight of his unshielded divinity would instantly destroy her —which it does. Zeus does manage to save the baby Dionysis by sewing him into his leg. The next to fall prey to Zeus's unbounded desire—

and Hera's endless wrath—is the lovely nymph Callisto. Once Hera discovers that Callisto is pregnant with Zeus's child, she transforms her into a bear. Finally, there is the tale of princess Alcmene, described as the tallest and the most beautiful of mortal women. Once pregnant with Zeus's child, Hera tries to prevent the birth by tying Alcmene's legs in knots. Her efforts, however, are thwarted and her arch-nemesis, the Greek hero Heracles, is born.

As if that were not enough to rankle Hera, in one tradition Zeus tricks her into nursing the half mortal/half divine creature. Because he was being suckled by a goddess, the infant would grow strong and fierce. After Hera discovers the infant's identity she throws the baby off her breast and her breast milk splatters across the sky forming the Milky Way galaxy. But the fall was not enough to foil the infant hero, so Hera sent two snakes to strangle him while he lay sleeping in his cot. The snakes would lose the contest when baby Heracles strangles them instead using their dead carcasses as toys. The enmity between Hera and Heracles is legendary and continues into his adulthood when she finally drives him into madness causing him to kill his wife and children.

The Pre-Greek History

Before delving into why Greek literature treated Hera poorly, it is important to have an understanding of pre-Greek (or pre-Hellenic[50]) history. In the 18th century BCE, the Mycenaeans invaded the Aegean region[51] conquering the indigenous pre-Hellenic mainland. Representing the first characteristically Greek civilization, Mycenaean Greece dominated the last phase of the Bronze Age from approximately 18th to 11th century BCE. They are

---

50 The Greeks referred to themselves as Hellenes and the ancient Greek world was termed Hellas. The word "Greek" comes from the Latin "Graeci."

51 Likely the Mycenaeans invaded from the north though there is not full consensus on this within the academic community,

called the "first Greeks" because they were the first to use the Indo-European Greek language. To be sure, subsequent DNA testing has revealed a common genetic heritage between today's Greeks and their Mycenaean ancestors. As an advanced warrior society, the Mycenaeans were renowned for their palatial states, urban centers, and seafaring skills. For a time they were under Minoan political hegemony but by 1400 BCE they added the legendary Minoan island of Crete and nearby islands to their long list of conquests, thus becoming the dominant power in the entire region.

While their building achievements are unmistakable, when it comes to extolling their other triumphs, the Mycenaeans are silent. In their heavily bureaucratic society, their writing system—syllabic Linear B— was used chiefly for record keeping and inventories. Though they were without writing, they were not without stories. The oldest legends of humankind were hymns or songs that preceded the written word by hundreds, if not thousands, of years. Narrative writing in the Greek world does not come into being until the eighth century BCE—relatively late in the hourglass of the ages.[52] The poet (or poets) known as Homer was the beneficiary of a rich tradition of mythological and historical stories—an intermelding of traditions by both the conquerors and the conquered—that had been passed down from countless generations of oral poets who had preceded him.[53]

---

[52] Between the Mycenaean era and the Archaic age of ancient Greece lies a four-hundred year period known as the Greek Dark Age or the sub-Mycenaean period characterized by the absence of writing and most forms of culture and the destruction and or abandonment of the great Mycenaean cities and palaces.

[53] "For literature Homer is the beginning, though every scholar is aware that he is nowise primitive.....Homer presents, not a starting point, but a culmination...beneath this splendid surface lies a stratum...at once more primitive and more permanent." Jane Ellen Harrison, *Prolegomena to the Study of the Greek Religion.*

When the Mycenaeans subsumed the pre-Greeks, they recast the indigenous myths and adopted some elements of the local culture as their own. Thus the pre-Hellenic myths of the vanquished people became appropriated by the conquerors; the invader sky gods married or raped the indigenous earth goddesses and replaced matricentric elements with patriarchal ones. Deeply buried beneath the greater Olympian pantheon, lay an underpinning of the old great goddess religions. By reframing the mythology, the great goddesses were absorbed into the reformulated myths and recast as wives, sisters, or daughters; Hera, Demeter, Athena, Aphrodite, and Artemis were all great mother goddesses in the pre-Greek world.

Hera Before Zeus

Based on archeological evidence, such as artifacts and temples (which will be discussed later), it is evident that Hera originated in the pre-Greek Aegean. Thus the mythological marriage of Hera and Zeus symbolized the union of the pre-Hellenic Hera with the Olympian pantheon. In part, derived from iconography, legends, and the numerous plants and animals with which she was associated, Hera was once an earth mother goddess, mistress of animals, the queen of heaven, and the female origin of all things[54] who ruled over the earth and sky— notably without a male consort. She was the goddess of women, fecundity, and connected to the three stages in a woman's life. Her dominion also included vegetation and had underworld or chthonic associations. Indicative of her great goddess status was her link to parthenogenesis or virgin birth. Her parthenogenetic ability is referred to several times in Homer; she gave birth to both Hephaestus and Hebe in this fashion. The prehistoric notion that women could bear children without the help

---

54   One of her many titles in the pre-Greek world. Rigoglioso, *Virgin Mother Goddesses of Antiquity*, 65.

of males is emblematic of an archaic matrifocal era—before the Mycenaean invasions.

Herodotus reports that Hera was an indigenous deity associated with agriculture. Often referred to as "cow-eyed" in the *Iliad*, Hera is associated with cows who symbolized motherhood, abundance, and fertility in general. Because the pre-Greeks far surpassed the Mycenaeans in farming, the Mycenaeans quickly adopted Hera from the Pelasgians[55]—the name used by the ancient Greeks for the indigenous pre-Greeks.

Not just a foil...

Over the course of several hundred years Hera's status was brought down; this greatest of goddesses from the pre-Greek world was disempowered and ultimately transformed into a quarrelsome wife— used as a foil for the all-mighty sky god, Zeus.[56]

The quarrelsomeness that Hera generates is indicative of the clash or the forced merging of the indigenous and invading cultures. Noted Hellenic scholar Carl Kerenyi argues: "the tension between Zeus and Hera..... is not merely a poetic fiction."[57] Time and again, Hera, the formidable native queen, refuses to subordinate herself to the invading sky god. While other gods are deferential to Zeus, Hera gives Zeus as good as she gets. Unafraid of his wrath, she steadfastly asserts herself. Even though she is married to the mightiest of gods, who threatens her beyond measure, Hera perseveres as an independent agent.

---

55   Herodotus. *Histories*, 2.50

56   "Compulsory marriage of Hera and Zeus reflected the subjugation of a 'primitive race' to Achaean (Greek) invaders." H. D Muller, footnoted in *Prolegomena to the Study of Greek Religion*, Harrison, 316.

57   Kerenyi. C, *Zeus and Hera: Archetypal Image of Father, Husband, and Wife*, (Princeton: Princeton University Press, 1975, 57.

In Homer's the *Iliad*—one of the oldest extant written stories of humankind— Hera's strength and sovereignty are demonstrated by her continual clashes with Zeus when she tries to thwart his attempts to favor the Trojan army. The antecedent action leading up to the events in the *Iliad* helps explain her animosity toward the citadel of Troy. In a narrative referred to as the "Judgment of Paris," Paris—prince of Troy— selects Aphrodite (goddess of love) as the most beautiful of the three Olympian goddesses, which also include Athena and Hera. It is Paris's insult which fuels her intense hatred of the Trojans. Hera defies Zeus's orders and collaborates with Athena to provide the Greeks with every advantage.

In Chapter One the clash between Zeus and Hera is laid out. On account of a slight to her son Achilles, the sea-nymph Thetis, beseeches Zeus to grant the Trojans "victory after victory til the Achaean (Greek) armies pay my dear son back." In this scene, even the almighty Zeus is fearful of a clash with Hera. First he replies: "Disaster. You will drive me to war with Hera." Then a panicked Zeus asserts: "Away with you now, Hera might catch us here." Nevertheless, he agrees to Thetis' request. Afterward, in the hall of the gods, while the other gods obsequiously genuflect to the authority of Zeus, Hera confronts him as an equal and instead berates him: "So, who of the gods this time, my treacherous one, was hatching plans with you? ....Dread majesty, son of Cronus.....I suspect you bowed your head in assent to her (Thetis)..." In reply Zeus becomes angry and threatens to harm Hera if she disobeys him. "Maddening one ...be quiet now. Obey my orders, for fear the gods are powerless to protect you when I come to throttle you with my irresistible hands." His threats to harm Hera are continual throughout the epic, but although Hera knows his punishments only too well, she never acquiesces. No other god had the courage to give the lord of gods his due.

Hera is both covertly and overtly defiant of her husband's interests in Chapter Fourteen titled "Hera Outflanks Zeus." "What could she do? Queen Hera wondered, her eyes glowing wide....how could she outmaneuver Zeus, the mastermind, this Zeus with his battle-shield of storm and thunder?" She decides that her best strategy is to seduce him then lull him to sleep with the help of the goddess Sleep. Her plan works and she helps the Greeks gain the upper hand. When Zeus discovers her perfidy, he screams "Uncontrollable Hera—you and your treachery...I'll whip you stroke on stroke. Don't you recall the time I strung you in mid-air and slung those two massive anvils down from your feet and lashed both hands with a golden chain you could not break?" Zeus is referring to the punishment he thrust upon Hera after discovering one of her attempts to sabotage his beloved son, Heracles.

Despite Hera's immortality she is capable of being destroyed or severely injured by the mightiest of gods. Consider the sad fate of the Titan god, Prometheus, who had the temerity to go against the will of Zeus by giving humans fire—hence progress. As a result of his transgressions, his liver is devoured each day by an eagle—one of Zeus's sacred animals —and regenerates itself each night to be devoured the following day in a never ending cycle. Yet for all Zeus's threats, Hera never backs down. Many scholars contend that her overt willfulness against Zeus is an expression of how powerful a deity Hera was in the pre-Hellenic world.

Cultural Integration: The Union

While Hera was the supreme pre-Hellenic goddess of the Aegean, Zeus held the position of supreme deity among the Mycenaeans. Based on archaeological evidence, there is a clear difference in origins between Zeus and Hera. Acclaimed German scholar of archaeology, Erika Simon posits: "Zeus was brought along into the Aegean by Greek tribes migrating from the north. Originally, he was worshiped in the open sky...it is no accident that his wife there (in Dodona —northwestern Greece) was not Hera but Dione, who like him, was worshiped under the oak trees."[58] As two supreme deities who each ruled autonomously, Hera and Zeus were imperfectly matched as husband and wife. If their tumultuous relationship indicates a clash between the two disparate cultures, could their courtship give us a glimpse into how the two cultures began to integrate?

In yet another seduction scenario, after attempting unsuccessfully to court a reluctant Hera, Zeus resorts to trickery to win her affections. The traveler and geographer Pausanias reports that after becoming separated from other gods and goddesses, Hera gets caught in a thunderstorm—put in action by the thunder god Zeus himself. During the storm, one of her sacred animals, the cuckoo, lands on her lap half frozen and shivering. After covering the creature with her robe, she cradles the cuckoo against her breast whereupon the bird transforms himself into Zeus— her steadfast suitor—and proceeds to rape her. In true patriarchal fashion, *she* was shamed by the rape he committed so she agrees to marry him. In another version of the myth, due to the prohibition of brother and sister unions, she appeals to her mother for permission to marry Zeus.

Hungarian scholar in classical philology, Carl Kerenyi, tells how the tale demonstrates Zeus as an intruder to the matriarchal domain in which Hera was enthroned as ruler. The union of siblings, however, was allowed only for the gods, thus Hera could become Zeus's wife.[59] The sacred marriage between Hera and Zeus is termed *hieros gamos* and is used as the prototype for human wedlock in order to ensure abundance, prosperity, and fertility. In the Greek world, all lawful marriages were sacred to Hera and Zeus and the union of the

---

58 Simon, Erika. *The Gods and Goddesses of Ancient Greece*. Madison: University of Wisconsin Press, 39.

59 In matriarchal traditions incest between brother and sister was forbidden. C. Kerenyi. *Zeus and Hera*, 123. Although not in the Greek world, sibling marriage (between royals) was sanctified in many ancient cultures most notably, Egypt.

first Olympian couple—symbolized by the lunar cow with the solar bull —was celebrated amid much fanfare each year.

According to the ancient Greek poet, Callimachus (305 BCE-240 BCE), Hera and Zeus' wedding feast— or in some translations "their desire" —lasted for three hundred years. Some believe that three hundred years may indicate a period of theological flux when Hera's place in the Olympian pantheon was not yet fixed.[60] In fact, the Olympian pantheon as we know it today was not determined until the sixth century BCE when in 522 the Athenian tyrant, Pisistratus established the Altar of the Twelve Gods.[61]

Hera's House: Ancient Temples

In an example of mythology mirroring history, three hundred years comes up again. Evidence was unearthed of Hera worship in the form of a prehistoric wooden structure dating back to the ninth century BCE[62]—nearly three hundred years before the Olympian pantheon was etched in stone. Greek temples, renowned for their massive stone columns, were originally wooden structures; oval prehistoric-style dwellings resembling wooden houses. Though some scholars believe that Hera may have been worshiped in such dwellings long before the first millennium BCE, Hera's cult—more than any other—greatly influenced the development of Greek temple architecture.[63] Famed Hellenic scholar, Walter Burkert contends: "Hera has a unique connection with the temple: the earliest and most important temples are dedicated to her."[64]

The following are some noteworthy examples of her earliest temples. The Heraion of Samos in Hera's birthplace on the island

---

60   M. Rigoglioso. *Virgin Mother Goddesses of Antiquity*, 67.
61   Thucydides. *History of the Peloponnesian War.*
62   Simon, 40.
63   Simon, 39. Burkert, 131.
64   Burkert, *Greek Religion*, 131.

of Samos and her temple at Perachora near Corinth both date to the ninth century BCE; other than the Temple of Apollo in Thermon, no other temple has been unearthed in post-Mycenaean Greece earlier than this. Dedicated exclusively to Hera, they predated the Greek Doric order of architecture—the oldest of the three orders— by two hundred years.

The Heraion of Samos was considered the greatest engineering feat of its day superseding all other sanctuaries.[65] It was also the first roofed temple sanctuary. In fact, the first indications of Hera worship in the area date back to the latter half of the second millennium, illustrating that the Hera cult was already active when the Mycenaeans invaded.

Called "Argive Hera" in the *Iliad*, Argos was another of her major cult centers with an extensive sanctuary—which served several communities —reaching back into the eighth century BCE. A pre-Hellenic aniconic depiction of Hera in a pillar (no longer extant) suggests that she may have been worshiped there long before this time.

The Temple of Hera at Olympia, also called the Heraion of Olympia, is a site where evidence of cult activity reaches back to the tenth century BCE. Originally built from wood in the seventh century BCE then replaced with stone, the temple was still extant when Pausanias in the second century CE commented that Hera was seated on a throne, while as an afterthought a bearded and helmeted Zeus stands by her side.[66] Simon notes that Hera's temple was in existence a century and a half before the Temple of Zeus at Olympia was built and goes on to say that wherever temples to both

---

65   The Heraion was rebuilt in the sixth century BCE over its Mycenaean foundation four times larger than the majestic Parthenon in Athens. Hera became visible as Zeus's wife in the Samian cult as late as the seventh century BCE but even then evidence indicates that Zeus's influence on her cult was minimal. Rigoglioso. *Virgin Mother Goddesses of Antiquity*, 69.

66   Pausanias. *Description of Greece*, 5.17.1

Hera and Zeus exist, excavation has revealed that Hera's temple is always the oldest.[67]

The ninth and eighth centuries BCE saw the construction of two temples dedicated to Hera in Perachora. In a testament to how aligned her cult was to temple architecture, clay or limestone houses are among the votive offerings for Hera in Perachora, Argos, and Samos. According to Simon, the votive homes from Perachora depict the structure in a transitional phase between prehistoric and Doric building styles.[68]

An article about Hera's association with temples would be remiss without mentioning her ruins at Paestum. Located south of Naples on the coast of the Tyrrhenian Sea, posterity owes a debt of gratitude to its swampy marshlands for helping preserve some of the earliest examples of Doric architecture in the Greek world. From the fall of the ancient world in the fourth century CE through the Middle Ages, malaria would emerge, making Paestum uninhabitable. During a time when Greek temples were systematically dismantled and quarried for their stone, the Doric temples of Paestum were largely forgotten and left alone. Two of the three Doric order (sixth and fifth century BCE) temples (see Figure12) were dedicated to Hera.

More than any other Greek deity, Hera served as the inspiration for the creation of the Greek temple—an iconic symbol that for many has come to characterize ancient Greece itself.[69] Though we may never know how Hera was worshiped by the pre-Greeks, in the early Greek world, the development of temple architecture on her behalf is witness to the reverence the population must have had for her. It is ironic that evidence of her early worship is permanently fixed in a time period as overlooked and undervalued as she is. The Greek

---

67 Simon, 39.

68 Ibid, 40.

69 Because most are accustomed to classical architecture appearing in whiter shades of pale, it is hard to fathom that Greek temples were once adorned in a kaleidoscope of colors.

Dark Age—or more appropriately termed the Sub-Mycenaean age (ca 1100 BCE-800 BCE) —is an era distinguished by a decline in wealth and advancement when, ostensibly, no discernible progress was made. Perhaps it is a testament to Hera's greatness that in an era characterized by poverty and an overall lack of engineering, the early Greeks found the resources to build colossal monuments in her honor, some still standing to this day.

Crumbling Status: Hera's fall from Grace

While the passage of time may have been kind to her temples, Hera has not always fared as well. In the beginning, she reigned supreme as the great mother goddess in a religion of the soil that honored nature and celebrated women's extraordinary reproductive powers. After the Mycenaeans invaded her sovereignty was suppressed and she had to share the spotlight with an oftentimes cruel and warlike male who would eventually take center stage. With the advent of writing, she was further reduced to a woman whose only identity is through her husband and degraded to the pettiest of characters; a caricature of unlikeability. In a nod to the power of cultural memory, despite her many diminutions, Hera remained the paragon of goddesses that the population, particularly its women, continued to celebrate in artwork, shrines, temples and annual festivals, from the dawn of the Archaic Age to the twilight of the Hellenistic Era.

Selected Reading on Hera:
Suppression of the Native Queen

Burkert, Walter. *Greek Religion*. Cambridge: Harvard University Press, 1985.

Harrison, Jane Ellen. *Prolegomena to the Study of Greek Religion*. New York: Forgotten Books, 2012.

Haynes, Natalie. *Divine Might: Goddesses in Greek Myth*. New York: Harper Perennial, 2024.

Herodotus. *The Histories*. Translated by Tom Holland. New York: Penguin Books, 2015.

Homer. The *Iliad*. Translated by Robert Fagles. New York: Penguin Books, 1991.

Kerenyi, C. *Zeus and Hera: Archetypal Image of Father, Husband, and Wife*. Princeton: Princeton University Press, 1975.

Rigoglioso, Marguerite. *Virgin Mother Goddesses of Antiquity*. New York: Pelgrave MacMillian, 2010.

Simon, Erika. *The Gods of the Greeks*. Madison: University of Wisconsin Press, 2021.

Spretnak, Charlene. *Lost Goddesses of Early Greece*. Boston: Beacon Press, 1992.

Thucydides. *The History of the Peloponnesian War*. Translated by Richard Crawley. https://www.gutenberg.org/files/7142/7142-h/7142-h.htm

CHAPTER ELEVEN

The Bronze Age Queen: Helen of Sparta

Celebrated as the most beautiful woman in the world, Helen of Troy née Sparta was the yardstick for which all women were measured—and found inadequate. Her scandalous abduction by Paris triggered a 10-year siege on Troy that killed countless Trojans and Greeks alike. Mired in carnage, Helen nonetheless escaped Troy without a hair out of place. In one tradition, Helen wound up in Egypt after the war, but if Herodotus is to be believed, she spent the entire war there. Doubtless, the Greeks were obsessed with a heroine they loved to hate, and they certainly have the stories to show for it.

Unsurprisingly, most of the myths surrounding this fairest of all women involve rape. Helen herself was the product of the rape between Zeus almighty, king of the gods, and the lovely Leda, queen of Sparta. While Leda was sunbathing on the banks of the River Eurotas, an enamored Zeus turned himself into a magisterial swan and had his way with her. Leda then gave birth to the radiant Helen, whose beauty caused her problems even at a young age.

By some accounts, long before her abduction by Paris, at the tender age of seven Helen was kidnapped or raped by Theseus, the mythological king of Athens. Theseus, like Zeus before him, was accustomed to defiling the gentler sex but a romantic interest in another daughter of Zeus—Persephone herself, queen of the underworld—would soon lead him astray. Ultimately, Helen's twin brothers—Castor and Pollux— restored her to their Spartan home.

All the same, in the *Iliad,* Helen the "richly tressed" Spartan queen is best known for fleeing with Paris to Troy after his so-called diplomatic visit to Sparta. A question that has plagued many throughout the ages is whether or not Helen eloped with the flamboyantly handsome Prince Paris of her own volition? Did the goddess of love, Aphrodite, play a role in her kidnapping? Finally, could the kidnapping of a queen—even one as dazzling as Helen— really have been the *sole* reason behind a 10-year war between East and West?

Recognized throughout the ages as Helen of Troy, she was always Helen of Sparta to the Greeks. In fact, it must have come as no surprise to them that the face, which launched a thousand ships, was of Spartan origin. Renowned for their beauty, Spartan women were notorious for being loose with their virtue as well. In a city-state that encouraged its citizen-wives to engage in marital infidelity, it is no wonder that they should be considered wanton by other Greeks. Doubtless, Helen as an unchaste foremother was an unequivocal role model who was even worshiped as a deity in her native home.

Although Helen was writ-large in the collective imagination of the ancient Greeks, it might be surprising to learn that, technically, she was not from 'ancient Greece.' Instead, Helen hailed from the late Bronze age kingdom of Sparta. A gold-glittering powerhouse, the Mycenaean civilization preceded ancient Greece by several hundred years when these fierce seafaring warriors—known as the first Greeks— conquered the Aegean peninsula from its earlier native inhabitants in the eighteenth-seventeenth century BCE. Considered an advanced civilization, the Mycenaeans had a writing system called syllabic Linear B that was used chiefly for record-keeping in their heavily bureaucratic culture. Unfortunately, when it comes to lauding their cultural achievements for posterity, the Mycenaeans are silent; no narrative literature exists from them.

After the collapse of the Mycenaean civilization in the eleventh century BCE,[70] ancient Greece entered a period known as the Greek Dark Age (or the Sub-Mycenaean period). During this time Bronze Age settlements and palatial states were abandoned, there was little or no cultural output, and there is no evidence of any form of writing. Nevertheless, though they were without writing, they were not without stories. The story of Helen and the siege of Troy is believed to be amongst the oldest of humankind and would have been widely known to most Greeks. The so-called Greek Dark Age lasted until ancient Greece became ascendent in the eighth century BCE beginning the Archaic Age. Within a few generations, the poet (or poets) known as Homer would transcribe his two epic poems— the *Iliad* and the *Odyssey*— finally giving voice to the voiceless and chronicling a time over 500 years prior, when the Mycenaean civilization was still dominant.

Many now believe that the Trojan War pitting Mycenaean Greece against Troy was an actual event, and may have contributed to the collapse of the Mycenaean civilization. Troy was a vassal state of the Hittite Empire in northwestern Anatolia (present-day Turkey). The most robust ancient 'historical' account of the Trojan War comes to us from the *Iliad*. Yet for all its endurance, the *Iliad* recounts a mere 52 days in the 10-year siege. It ends not with the Trojan citadel's fiery finale, but with the somber funeral of the Trojan hero, Hector. While the story of the Trojan War is incomplete in the *Iliad*, Helen's character is most decidedly not. Homer leaves us in no doubt about whose behalf the war is being waged.

In Book Three of the *Iliad*, Helen's first utterance to King Priam of Troy is a gloomy one: "if only death had pleased me then, grim death

---

70   In addition to external invasions and internal unrest, natural disasters are among the theories as to why the Mycenaean civilization collapsed.

that day I followed your son to Troy, forsaking my marriage bed, my kinsmen and my child...." [71] Helen constantly mourns the deadly consequences of her abduction, but she is no fool. In order to appeal to the sympathy of others, Helen continually berates herself. The general response to this by others—primarily males who are dazzled by her splendor— is to hold her blameless. Even King Priam himself contends: "I don't blame you, I hold the gods to blame."[72]

Conversely, a feckless Paris is quick to cast blame on the gods for the Trojans' predicament. For his trouble, he is treated unsympathetically throughout the epic. The prince "with the skin of a leopard slung across his shoulders" [73] flauntingly parades himself on the rampart in front of the Greeks. As soon as he sees his counterpart, Helen's deceived husband—the "war-like" Menelaus—a cowardly Paris, slinks away, "cringing with death." Paris's own brother, Hector, berates him for his spinelessness: "You...curse to your father, your city and all your people, a joy to our enemies, rank disgrace yourself."[74] Reluctantly, Paris finally agrees to a contest between himself and Menelaus. Throughout the epic, Helen and Paris are contrasted as opposites in accountability. While Helen takes too much responsibility for her role in the abduction—or elopement— Paris puts the blame solely on Aphrodite. Does he have cause to do so?

The antecedent action preceding Helen's removal from Sparta comes from a myth referred to as the "Judgment of Paris." Upon discovering she was not invited to a lavish Olympian wedding party, a furious Eris, goddess of strife, tosses a golden apple at the banquet table with the inscription *"calliste"* or "for the fairest." Naturally, the three Olympian goddesses in attendance each believe the golden

---

71   Homer, the *Iliad*, tr. Robert Fagles, (London: Penguin Books, 1990),3.209-211.

72   Ibid. 3.199.

73   Ibid. 3.18.

74   Ibid. 3. 57-59

apple is for her, so a scuffle between them ensues. To restore order, Zeus is asked to judge the fairest. Unwilling to make enemies among two of the goddesses— especially since one of them was his wife— Zeus enlists the help of Paris.

Athena, the stalwart warrior goddess, promises Paris wisdom and great luck in battle if he chooses her as the fairest. Hera, the goddess of marriage, childbirth, and wife to Zeus, promises Paris power and throneships if he chooses her. Aphrodite, goddess of love and beauty, promises Paris the most beautiful woman in the world—Helen of Sparta—and the contest is over before it even begins. It is of no consequence to the callow Paris or the goddess of love herself that Helen is already married to Menelaus—king of Sparta.

Geopolitically, long before Paris kidnapped Helen, the Greeks had set the stage. In an agreement called the "Oath of Tyndareus" at Helen's wedding to Menelaus, the Greeks agreed to unite and provide military assistance if Helen was ever stolen. Thus, the military might of the Mycenaean Greeks soon descended on the solitary citadel of Troy.

If Trojan Prince Hector had his way, the fighting would have ended before all was lost. In order to quell the bloodshed, Hector pleads with the Greeks to "hear the challenge of Paris, the man who caused our long hard campaign"[75] urging Trojans and Greeks to lay down their arms while Paris and Menelaus "fight it out for Helen and all her wealth in a single combat."[76] The contest between a strong-armed Menelaus and a flashy featherweight should have been over in short order, and it nearly was. "Lunging at Paris, he grabbed his horsehair crest, swung him round....was gouging his soft throat— Paris was choking, strangling...."[77]

---

75 Homer, The *Iliad*, tr Robert Fagles, Book 3, 105-106.
76 Ibid, 86.
77 Ibid, 428.

Witnessing the battle in horror, Aphrodite straightaway saves her favorite from certain death on the battlefield. After all, Paris was a lover, not a fighter. Imagine Menelaus's dismay, finding an empty helmet in his raised fist instead of the lifeless head of Paris.

Without delay, Aphrodite installed Paris in his bedroom and invites Helen to join him. "Quickly—Paris is calling for you, come back home...he's glistening in all his beauty and his robes!"[78] Not merely the goddess of love, Aphrodite's very nature induces desire in others, regardless of the consequences. Helen, however, has been through this once before, and does not want to live through it again. It is at this stage that Helen gives as good as she gets. Of all the mortal characters in the epic, she was the only one brave enough to defy a deity. Although Helen is the daughter of Zeus, her mother is mortal thus she is considered semi-divine and is not immortal "Maddening one, my Goddess, oh what now? Lusting to lure me to my ruin yet again? Where will you drive me next?" [79] These were strong words for a mere mortal to utter to a goddess, and Aphrodite does not like it. "Don't provoke me—wretched, headstrong girl!..... I might make you the butt of hard, withering hate from both sides at once, Trojans and Achaeans (Greeks),....." [80] Because the goddess could indeed make life even more unpleasant for her, Helen begrudgingly accepts her role, but later rebukes Paris. "So, home from the wars! Oh would to god you'd died there, brought down by that great soldier, my husband long ago."[81]

Alas, life was wearisome for the world's most beautiful woman. Her strings constantly pulled by Aphrodite, this most-desired woman was incapable of fulfilling her own desires. While Helen is the most contrite of the three characters who had a part in the kidnapping,

---

78   Ibid, 450.
79   Homer, The *Iliad,* tr. Robert Fagles, Book 3, 460.
80   Ibid, 481-484.
81   Ibid, 499-501.

she is the least culpable of them. After all, even Paris had some agency in determining which goddess's gifts he most desired.[82]

Helen is a paradoxical figure: the Greeks love to blame her for starting the war, but they just as quickly come to her defense.

Did they come together solely to recover Helen? The answer to that question is likely no. As desirable as she was, in point of fact Helen was not the only Spartan booty Paris pilfered. In addition to stealing away with the Spartan queen, Paris nicked the Spartan treasure as well. To the Mycenaean Greeks, Helen was much more than meets the eye: it was through her that Menelaus became king. Thus, the Spartan treasure was the queen's, not the king's. Women from royal families were kingmakers in the Mycenaean era, even a plain-looking Helen from a powerful state would have been highly desirable to a foreign power.

Eight of the seventeen times Helen's name is used in the *Iliad*, the word *"ktema"* (treasure) is mentioned alongside it. In the duel when Paris squares off against Menelaus, we hear— time and again— how it is "Helen's treasure,"[83] not Menelaus's, for which the battle is fought. Is the war waged to restore the treasure, or to restore the queen? That question has plagued scholars throughout the ages. One must remember that Menelaus, without a heritable queen— and her significant treasure—would have been vulnerable to internal strife and foreign invasion. What choice did Menelaus have but to fight to get her back?

As literary and archaeological artifacts of the Mycenaean era surface, a portrait has emerged of prominent royal women who had access to great wealth and power. Even as goods were traded rigorously between foreign powers, in order to secure state

---

82 In the "Judgement of Paris" which precedes the *Iliad*, it is Paris who decides that Aphrodite is the fairest of the goddesses so that he can win the prize of Helen.

83 Homer, The *Iliad*, tr. Robert Fagles, Book 3, 339.

relations, royal women could have been traded as well. Thus, it is not improbable that the kidnapping of a royal woman could have severed ties between nations.

After the downfall of Troy, what became of the Spartan royal couple on whose behalf so many died? In one tradition, an enraged Menelaus storms through the scorched Trojan citadel intent on slaying his errant wife but instead was literally starstruck, famously dropping his sword upon first sight of the ever-resplendent Helen. In the end, once all had been fought and won Menelaus quietly reunites with Helen (see Figure 13) and the two return to Sparta living happily ever after— or so they say.

Selected Reading for Helen

Blondell, Ruby. "'Bitch That I Am': Self-Blame and Self-Assertion in the *Iliad*." *Transactions of the American Philological Association (1974-)* 140, no. 1 (2010): 1–32. http://www.jstor. org/stable/40652048.

_____. "Refractions of Homer's Helen in Archaic Lyric." *The American Journal of Philology* 131, no. 3 (2010): 349-91. http://www.jstor.org/stable/40983352.

Farron, S. "The Portrayal of Women in the Iliad." *Acta Classica* 22 (1979): 15–31. http://www.jstor.org/stable/24591564.

Foley, Helene. *Female Acts: In Greek Tragedy*. Princeton, NJ: Princeton University Press, 2001.

Homer. The *Iliad*. Translated by: Robert Fagles. New York: Penguin Books, 1996.

Hughes, Bettany. *Helen of Troy: Goddess, Princess, Whore*. New York: Knopf, 2005.

Maguire, Laurie. *Helen of Troy: From Homer to Hollywood*. New York: Wiley Blackwell, 2009.

Roisman, Hanna M. "Helen and the Power of Erotic Love: From Homeric Contemplation to Hollywood Fantasy." *College Literature* 35, no. 4 (2008): 127–50. http://www.jstor.org/ stable/25114378.

_____. "Helen in the *Iliad* "Causa Belli" and Victim of War: From Silent Weaver to Public Speaker." *The American Journal of Philology* 127, no. 1 (2006): 1-36. https://www.jstor.org/ stable/3804922.

Rozokoki, Alexandra. "The Significance of the Ancestry and Eastern Origins of Helen of Sparta." *Quaderni Urbinati Di Cultura Classica* 98, no. 2 (2011): 35–69. http://www.jstor.org/stable/23048961.

CHAPTER TWELVE

Clytemnestra: The Twilight of the Matriarch

As any self-respecting Greek hero knows, sacking a city and raping its female inhabitants is hard work. So it is no wonder that after Agamemnon (see Figure 14) returned from the decade-long Trojan war—where he slew their males, captured their prize princess, and ultimately set their kingdom ablaze—he was expecting a hero's warm welcome home. His wife Clytemnestra, however, had other plans. After drawing a bath for the weary warrior, Clytemnestra wrapped Agamemnon in robes and then hacked him to death. Murder, however, was not her only crime.

Known for her intelligence, duplicity, and ambition, this archetypal matriarch is one of the most reviled of all female characters in Greek literature. More to the point, she struck fear in the hearts of Greek men by turning the dominant paradigm on its head. In Agamemnon's absence, not only did she take command and replace her husband on the throne, she replaced him—with his estranged cousin Aegisthus—in her bed as well.

Unaccountable to anyone, Clytemnestra displayed the reckless, swaggering nerve of a fearless Greek hero. Clearly, she was a woman who did not know her place. For her trouble, she has long been reviled— but was it ambition alone that induced her to kill

Agamemnon? Moreover, how did her role as matriarch precipitate her downward trajectory?

Is it no wonder that she was of Spartan origin. Indeed, she was the mortal half-twin of the semi-divine Helen.[84] Known for their fierce independence, Spartan women were an anomaly in the Greek world. In Sparta, women ruled while their men were off on one military campaign after another. Thus Clytemnestra, her husband occupied with the Trojan war, took the power that was hers and went one better.

In light of this, perhaps unsurprisingly, Clytemnestra is ushered into Greek literature by way of an insult. With characteristic disregard for his wife, Agamemnon announces to all and sundry in the *Iliad* that he prefers the company of his concubine over that of Clytemnestra. Alas, his predilection toward concubines would become legendary and almost lead to the Greeks' defeat: "I love her better even than my own wife, Clytemnestra," he says of one concubine.

The next time Clytemnestra emerges is in the *Odyssey*, when Agamemnon recounts his cruel homecoming to Odysseus from the underworld. This time, the chief perpetrator of the crime was his estranged cousin Aegisthus, who slays Agamemnon while at the dinner table. According to Homer, Clytemnestra merely plays the supporting role of willing accomplice to her lover, Aegisthus. Clytemnestra acts as a foil to Odysseus's devoted wife Penelope, who faithfully stitches away the years as her husband embarks on one adventure—often erotic—after another. Agamemnon, however, gets the last word when he says: "A song of loathing will be Clytemnestra's among men, to make evil the reputation of all womankind, even for those whose acts are virtuous." Never a friend

---

84 Clytemnestra was the mortal twin of Helen's. Her father was King Tyndareus of Sparta, whereas Helen's father was the lord of the Olympian gods, Zeus almighty himself.

to women, Agamemnon's departing words censure them all, even those, like Penelope, who are seemingly irreproachable.[85]

While she plays a bit part in the *Odyssey*, Clytemnestra takes center stage in Aeschylus' The *Oresteia* Trilogy. Considered one of the greatest achievements of Greek literature, it was penned in 458 BCE and is the only surviving example of a Greek tragic trilogy. Epic in scale, the three plays chronicle the curse on the house of Atreus, a family notorious for kin-murder, with an unfortunate proclivity toward filicide. While Clytemnestra's presence is felt in all three plays, it is most formidable in the first play, *Agamemnon*.

Leadership qualities considered virtuous in a man are viewed as monstrous in Clytemnestra. Playing the role of matriarch, she is often rebuked by the chorus for "thinking like a man." Yet it may have been something else entirely that led her to kill her husband. Some speculate that it was when he brought his unwilling concubine, the Trojan princess-cum-slave Cassandra, into their home that sent Clytemnestra over the edge. Poor Cassandra! To be caught in a tug-of-wills between Agamemnon and Clytemnestra—a worse fate cannot be imagined. Once Clytemnestra slaughtered her husband, the hapless prophetess was unceremoniously dispatched—an end she had in truth foreseen.

With calumny heaped upon Clytemnestra throughout the ages, it's easy to forget that she was once a victim herself.

In fact, if not for Agamemnon, their daughter Iphigenia might well have lived to see old age. The grievous tale begins with Agamemnon's calculated promise of a betrothal for Iphigenia to the most eligible bachelor of the Greek world— the semi-divine war hero Achilles. It was standard practice in ancient Greece for the

---

85 Agamemnon's disrespect for females is notorious, even insofar as insulting Artemis, Olympian goddess of the hunt.

father to bargain with his future son-in-law without the knowledge or consent of either mother or daughter.

The betrothal lures Iphigenia and her mother to Aulis, where Agamemnon and the Argive fleet are stuck at port. Unbeknownst to the women, the marriage was a ruse. Agamemnon was in big trouble with the goddess Artemis. Enraged by his swaggering boast that he was a better hunter than she—goddess of the hunt—Artemis quelled the winds so that the Greeks were stranded at the bay of Aulis, stymied from launching their offensive on Troy. Artemis would only release the winds if Agamemnon sacrificed his eldest daughter—the virginal Iphigenia—in her honor.

Faced with the choice of certain defeat at Troy or filicide, the ever-vainglorious Agamemnon chose to sacrifice his daughter: her life the price for victory.

Dressed in the flowing saffron vestment robes of a Greek bride, Iphigenia walks down the aisle eagerly anticipating her betrothed at the altar. Imagine her horror when, at the altar, instead of handsome Achilles she saw a wild-eyed, ax-wielding Agamemnon. "'My father, father!'" she cried, while he bellows to his henchmen: "'Hoist her over the altar like a yearling, give it all your strength, she's fainting— lift her, sweep her robes around her....here, gag her hard, a sound will curse the house'...the bridle chokes her voice.....her saffron robes pouring out over the sand.'"

Treating her with no more regard than he would a goat, alas, Iphigenia is even prohibited from screaming lest another curse fall on the house of Atreus.

Barbarous and cruel, Agamemnon took more care in safeguarding his name than in protecting his child. What follows next is unspoken. The sheer brutality of the act renders the chorus speechless. Eager to put the gruesome episode to rest, Agamemnon removes all traces of Iphigenia, affording her no funeral rites as she quietly slips away from the story—unlike her mother's wrath.

The savage slaying of her daughter unhinges Clytemnestra, who vows revenge against her husband. Representing the matriarch— domineering and unyielding—she is Demeter-like, harking back to a Neolithic, pre-marriage era when the mother-daughter dyad was the primary bond. Like Demeter, Clytemnestra is a fierce champion of her daughter. As old as the Earth, before joining the Olympian pantheon, Demeter—goddess of the harvest— was once a chthonic earth goddess and pre-dated Zeus by hundreds, perhaps thousands, of years. Although initially inconsolable at the loss of their daughters, both Demeter and Clytemnestra become enraged, finally taking matters into their own hands. As Earth-mother, in an effort to bring Persephone back from the land of the dead, Demeter stops the seasons.

Likewise, Clytemnestra, ultimately, made Agamemnon pay for his horrific crime. Not that she needed another reason to kill him, but in a version of the myth recalled by Euripides, Clytemnestra's first husband and young son are both slain by Agamemnon. Slaughtering her family, however, was not enough for the hero. Agamemnon would go on to rape Clytemnestra forcing her to be his wife. When it came to his characteristic cruelty, even his own daughter was not immune.

The legends of powerful matriarchs from which these myths sprang are emblematic of another era long before patriarchy became the law of the land. The Late Bronze Age or Mycenaean Era (1600 BCE-1100 BCE) was marked by the upheaval of the Mycenaean/ Indo-European invasions. While there is still much debate about the period, literary and archeological evidence suggests that antecedent to the Mycenaean civilization women led lives of relative autonomy. While the historical veracity of matriarchal rule is still debated, early societies were likely matrilineal, meaning kinship was traced from the maternal line. This makes instinctive sense, as lineage is more easily and reliably traced through mothers and the birthing process. In the era before the Mycenaean invasions, the notion of patriarchal marriage did not exist, and there is evidence[86] that the mother-daughter relationship was primal. Recalling a time before marriage, the matriarch viewed her child as a possession while the father figure was largely a nonentity.

Bringing an end to life with her mother on earth was a common enough event for women of ancient Greece whose marriages were patrilocal, meaning that the bride had to live with her new husband's family sometimes miles away from her natal home. Because of this, mothers and daughters could be separated sometimes forever hence marriage could be a sort of death. Never to see her mother or the light of her mother's earthly domain, the newlywed Persephone is as dead as any goddess can be. Likewise, with her bridal vestments doubling as her winding sheet, Iphigenia's sacrifice is itself a parody of marriage. For the Greek maiden, marriage and death went hand in hand. It is useful to note that most brides were between twelve and fourteen years of age, while the grooms were at least twice or thrice that age. Because of their tender ages, it was not uncommon for adolescent wives to die in childbirth.

So perhaps it is no coincidence that the marriage rites for women in the Greek world were eerily reminiscent of their funeral rites. Common for both were garlands, ritual absolutions, the shearing of hair, the dedicating of songs, a feast, and the focus on the transition from home to grave or from natal home to husband's home. Moreover, the thinking by some is that the marriage-death parallels evoke the feminine opposition to marriage; mourning women's loss of autonomy hallmark in the era before the Mycenaean invasions.[87] After the invasions, Greek culture became stridently patriarchal, as

---

86   Gimbutas, Marija. *The Living Goddess* (Berkeley, CA: University of California Press, 2001), 112.

87   Rigoglioso, *Virgin Mother Goddesses of Antiquity,* 12.

illustrated by the Homeric epics. This paternalism would eventually become deeply layered into all of Greek literature and ultimately passed onto Western civilization at large.

Androcentrism is keenly felt in *Oresteia*. Although the focus is on one family, the trilogy is culturally expansive. Tracing the path of justice from the primordial code of blood vengeance believed characteristic of early matriarchal societies who revered the Earth mother, the story takes us to a court of law under the patriarchal rule of the Olympian pantheon. Blood-vengeance defines the first two plays of the trilogy. In the first play, *Agamemnon*, the sacrifice of Iphigenia spurs Clytemnestra to murder her husband—-the crime of mariticide. In the second play, *Libation Bearers*, the death of his father pushes Orestes into killing his mother in retaliation—the crime of matricide.

In the final play of the trilogy, *Eumenides*, the main characters are chthonic[88] female deities known as the Furies. They punish men for crimes against the natural order and more closely resemble *Macbeth*'s witches than our modern notion of divinities. The Furies harass Orestes for committing matricide by driving him out of the palace and relentlessly pursuing him to the Temple of Apollo at Delphi. There he is offered sanctuary by Apollo—the god of reason and harmony—who had originally commanded Orestes to avenge his father's death.

While the Furies and Apollo square off one against the other over the fate of Orestes, steely-eyed Athena materializes in full regalia to arbitrate, creating a tribunal where citizen jurors hold forth in cases of homicide. Even as Agamemnon is memorialized by Apollo as "a noble man to die" the justice behind Agamemnon's murder—Iphigenia's cruel sacrifice— is long forgotten as over and over again Clytemnestra is deemed monstrous and depraved for killing

---

88 Deities representing the earth or the soil and as such are related to the underworld.

her "noble" husband for seemingly no other reason than a lust for power. As they harangue and harass Orestes over matricide, the Furies pointedly ignore Clytemnestra's own maternal revenge. As for Iphigenia, we hardly hear of her again.

Maternity itself is put on trial when Apollo makes his case. The god of reason damns motherhood for all time and proclaims: "The man is the source of life—the one who mounts. She (the mother), like a stranger for a stranger keeps the shoot alive unless god hurts the roots. I give you proof that all I say is true. The father can father forth without a mother. Here she stands our living witness look"....indicating Athena. "Child sprung full-blown from Olympian Zeus, never bred in the darkness of the womb but such a stock no goddess could conceive!!"

In Apollo's counterfactual screed, not only do fathers have parthenogenetic abilities, but mothers are incidental to reproduction, a mere incubator to the all-important seed the father provides. By marginalizing maternity, what crime is matricide?

When the all-male jury comes back deadlocked, motherless Athena casts her lot with paternity, saying: "I am entirely my father's child. And this is why the killing of a woman who killed her husband, guardian of the house, can have no overriding claim on me. Orestes wins, even if the votes be equal." Time and again, the audience is reminded of how far greater a crime it is for a wife to kill her husband than for a son to kill his mother. Like Athena, Orestes is considered his father's child, after all. In this patriarchal world order, the mother now plays a supporting role to the all-important father.

From matriarch to nursemaid, Aeschylus used Clytemnestra to paint a portrait of the "fortunate fall" of the matriarch. He uses her story to question the importance of motherhood itself. There can be no fierce matriarch if the essential maternal is removed.

In order to retain cultural dominance, men rewrote the older myths. After all, where would patriarchy be if the subjugated half became empowered? Clytemnestra, for her part, is often referred to as the female Odysseus. Resolute, fierce, and vengeful, Clytemnestra shares all the attributes of Greek heroes—while enjoying none of their accolades. The reason for her outrage is often forgotten. Even with the odds stacked squarely against her, the indomitable Clytemnestra may best be remembered for having no regrets and making no apologies.

Selected Reading for Clytemnestra

Aeschylus. *The Oresteia.* Translated by Robert Fagles. New York: Penguin Books, 1975.

Anderson, Florence Mary Bennett. "The Character of Clytemnestra in the Agamemnon of Aeschylus." *Transactions and Proceedings of the American Philological Association* 60 (1929): 136–54. https://doi.org/10.2307/282814.

Foley, Helene P. *Female Acts in Greek Tragedy.* Princeton: Princeton University Press 2001.

Gimbutas, Marija. *The Living Goddess.* Berkeley: University of CA Press, 2001.

Hall, Edith. *Greek Tragedy: Suffering Under the Sun.* Oxford: Oxford University Press, 2010.

Jacobs, Amber. *On Matricide: Myth, Psychoanalysis and the Law of Mother.* New York: Columbia University Press, 2007.

Moss, Leonard. "The Critique of the Female Stereotype in Greek Tragedy." *Soundings: An Interdisciplinary Journal* 71, no. 4 (1988): 515–32. http://www.jstor.org/stable/41178448.

Rigoglioso, Marguerite. *Virgin Mother Goddesses of Antiquity.* New York: Pelgrave, 2012.

Zeitlin, Froma I. "The Dynamics of Misogyny: Myth and Mythmaking in *Oresteia.*" *Arethusa* 11, no. 1/2 (1978): 149–84. http://www.jstor.org/stable/26308158.

_____. *Playing the Other: Gender and Society in Classical Greek Literature.* Chicago: University of Chicago Press, 1996.

CHAPTER THIRTEEN
The Curse of Cassandra

With a name that defines incredulity itself, it is no wonder that Cassandra—the cursed Trojan prophetess—has a hard time being taken seriously. Scorned throughout the ages, Cassandra was infamously disregarded and frequently reviled by her countrymen—even her own mother ridiculed her. Today she has a psychiatric syndrome named in her honor for those suffering from undue hysterical negativity. In short, she gets no respect. But why such indignation toward her?

If her compatriots had only heeded her guidance, the Trojan War might have ended differently—or it may not have begun at all. It was Cassandra, after all, who foretold the demise of Troy on account of a trip to Sparta made by her errant brother, Paris. In one tradition, she even suggests that her parents kill him as an infant—which in hindsight may have been sage advice. What is more, she predicts Troy's destruction if they accept the gifted horse. "But by god's will," she said, predicting their response, "Troy would never listen." Ever disbelieved, her dire predictions were spot on. Even so, there is no point in being an incredulous prophetess. Why was Cassandra always disbelieved and how was her form of soothsaying different from those of her historical contemporaries, specifically the highly-revered Oracle of Delphi?

Born a princess to King Priam and Queen Hecuba of Troy, Cassandra's early life was one of privilege. Known for being a virgin priestess to Apollo, virginity had more than one meaning in the ancient world. Besides signifying chastity, it also served to draw attention to the fact that a woman was not married. Markedly, Cassandra never married—and so perhaps this was reason enough to distrust her. After all, as a free agent, no man had authority over her.

She is also reputed to be the most beautiful of Priam's nineteen daughters; Homer describes her as the "peer of Aphrodite." Because of her great beauty, dashing Apollo, god of just about everything including poetry, truth, and oracles, promises her the gift of prophecy in return for sexual favors. Yet for all his good looks, Apollo is unlucky with the ladies. Cassandra accepts Apollo's gift of prophecy and then clings to her virginity like a badge of honor, refusing to own up to her end of the bargain. Being a soothsayer, she should have known that spurning the advances of a god is ill-advised. Unable to revoke a divinely decreed power, Apollo retaliates by ordaining that all Cassandra's prophecies are never to be believed.

Surprisingly, of the four times Cassandra is mentioned in the *Iliad*, Homer does not refer to her soothsaying skills. It is not until Aeschylus's *Agamemnon* (458 BCE) that Cassandra shows up as the famous seer she has since become.

In the play, being a disbelieved prophetess was only half of Cassandra's troubles. This virgin priestess, who prizes her chastity amongst her dearest possessions, is twice violated by Greek "heroes" after the sack of Troy. During the pillage, Cassandra had taken refuge in the Temple of Athena, where the appropriately named Ajax "the Lesser" drags her from the temple and savagely rapes her. For this sacrilege, Athena—acting in concert with the god of the sea, Poseidon—-dispatches a storm that would sink most of the Greek fleet on its long journey home. But that was not the end of Cassandra's troubles. A blight to women everywhere, Agamemnon, king of Mycenae and commander of the Greek fleet, takes Cassandra as *pallake* (concubine). After 10 long years of raping and pillaging his way through Troy, the play begins when Agamemnon returns to Mycenae with the hapless Cassandra in tow.

In her only scene of the play — at over two-hundred-fifty lines— Cassandra's part is larger than that of the eponymous hero, Agamemnon himself. Soon after the play begins, although Agamemnon is given a warm welcome home by his wife, Clytemnestra, she is eager for him to meet his maker and quickly dispatches him.

Although Cassandra does not advance the play's action, her words give fresh insight into her prophetic nature. Her first utterance is a scream, Cassandra's mad ramblings do nothing to inspire the chorus's confidence in her prophetic abilities. Regardless, she goes on to accurately describe not only her own slaying but that of her captor Agamemnon, howling, "she gores him through and now he buckles, look, the bath swirls red".

On account of Apollo's curse, the chorus is unable to comprehend her. "We'd heard your fame as a seer," they said, "but no one looks for seers in Argos." Unlike *manteis* (soothsayers—predominantly male) in the historical record, the indifference of the chorus toward Cassandra's prophecies stands in marked contrast to how soothsayers were valued in the Greek world.

Although seers may have been misunderstood from time to time, they were never wholly disregarded. From gods' lips to the prophets' ears, soothsayers acted as intermediaries between the mortal and immortal realms. Vulnerable to life's thousand natural shocks, divination helped the ancients feel the gods were either for or against some of their actions. Commoners clung to soothsayers' every word, frequently recording and analyzing them for content.

While incredulity is part and parcel of Cassandra's story, there are other divergences between Cassandra and historical seers in ancient Greece. Gifted with "second sight," Cassandra is able to see not only the future, but also the past. It is perhaps an irony that soothsayers in the Greek world did little in the way of actually forecasting the future as Cassandra is wont to do. Instead, their work involved either approving or disapproving certain courses of action based on the seer's interpretation of omens and signs. Oftentimes the seer would read the entrails of sacrificed animals, analyze cosmological phenomena, or in the case of bird-divining, take omens from the flights and cries of birds.

How piously the Greeks followed the guidance of seers is evident in the following historical examples. In *Histories*, Herodotus reports how in 479 BCE the city-state of Plataea chose not to go into battle when their seer repeatedly received bad omens over several days in the pre-battle sacrifice. But that was not the end of it. In a demonstration of incontrovertible faith, when the Persians finally invaded, the Plataeans refused a counter-attack because their seer continued to receive bad omens for battle—which in hindsight, had then become a self-fulfilling prophecy.

Even in the hyper-martial city-state of Sparta, complete faith in divination was demonstrated when the king and his commanders ordered soldiers to turn back if the seer decreed inauspicious battle omens. Often, such retreats came at a high cost militarily.

More such examples abound, in the cold, hard face of reality, Greeks remained steadfastly pious to the sacred sight of their soothsayers. This faith is notably exhibited in Greek literature when in time-honored tales disbelieved prophets are ultimately redeemed when their predictions come to pass and the skeptics find their untimely ends. Half out of her mind for always being disbelieved, Cassandra is vindicated when everything she predicts comes to pass.

Another priestess of Apollo with whom Cassandra has frequently been compared was the Oracle of Delphi (the *Pythia*). Unlike Cassandra, the Pythia was widely believed. Inhabiting the most important sanctuary in the Greek world, the Delphi's (see Figure 15) origins may reach back to the Great Goddess (Gaia) tradition which preceded the invading Mycenaeans (1700 BCE-1050 BCE) by hundreds if not thousands of years. Considered the center of the Greek world, the sanctuary was once named *Pytho* after Gaia's she-serpent who guarded it. Under the Greeks, Apollo replaced Gaia by slaying the Great Earth Goddess dragon.[89] The Python's rotting corpse was called the *pythein*—from which the word *Pythia* is derived— in reference to the stench "which arose from the fissure that Apollo had thrown the slain serpent".

In fact, the Pythia refers not to one seer but to a "sisterhood of mystics," whose term was for life (though they only worked one day a month and only nine months out of the year). Because chastity was of great importance given their holy union with Apollo, originally the Pythias were young maidens or virgins. That changed in the third century BCE, when Echecrates the Thessalian kidnapped and raped a Pythia priestess, according to Diodorus. After that, only older, married women of fifty and above could be Pythias. Although married, they had to remain chaste during their service to Apollo.

Unlike traditional soothsayers who made their prophecies by reading external signs, the cave at the shrine of Delphi was a gateway from which the god Apollo issued forth his sacred prophecies. In this way, the priestesses were conduits for him. The Pythia would sit on a stool or tripod punctured with holes and placed at the opening of the cave so that the gasses from the cavern could enter her

---

89   Snakes, serpents, and dragons have long been associated with the Great Mother Goddess religions of the pre-Greeks and other indigenous populations. The mythic slaying of these animals symbolizes the destruction of the Great Goddess religion in favor of the patriarchs such as in this case, Apollo.

womb. In fact, the word "Delphi" is believed to come from the Greek *delphus* meaning hollow or womb.

Although the Oracle of Delphi was famed for being female, the Pythia priestesses were not free agents. They worked under the supervision of a male priesthood that enforced what the Pythias should wear, how old they should be, and how often they should have sex. Looming larger in life than Apollo himself, these male overseers controlled when and with whom the priestesses should prophesy. Nothing was left to chance in this male-supervised religious order. Questions from the public were evaluated by the priests beforehand and, in fact, even when the Pythia was prophesizing, male personnel were always present. With every move directed by their male overseers, is it possible that the Pythia priestesses were merely actors playing the roles of seers?

Skepticism aside, perhaps it was their tight scripting that led the Oracle of Delphi to be the most respected and authoritative seer in the Greek world. Advising the likes of Sophocles, Aristotle, and Alexander the Great—even areligious Thucydides believed the Delphic oracle's predictions. Unlike the incredulity that Cassandra inspired, people from all over the world would come to consult with the Pythia, even though she was known for her cryptic and enigmatic predictions which were not always understood.

Croesus of Lydia is perhaps the most famed for misinterpreting the oracle's prophecy. He had consulted with her on whether or not he should invade a neighboring country and was told "If you go to war you will destroy a great empire." Thinking it would lead to the destruction of the enemy nation, he went to war. Not only was Croessus defeated, he was captured. Later, he wanted to know why the oracle had misled him. He was not misled, the Pythia replied. He had been told that war would lead to the destruction of a great empire and it had led to an empire's destruction—his own. Croesus—

like so many others—had simply misinterpreted the Delphic oracle's somewhat ambiguous prophecy.

Over the years, many believed that the Pythia's divinations were delivered in a frenzied fashion, much like Cassandra's delivery in the play *Agamemnon*. The fumes rising from a chasm in the rock beneath the temple were believed to have induced her manic ravings. But most of these reports came from later Roman historians and early Christians who may have had an inherent bias against the Greek female mystics. Many scholars today base their accounts on earlier Greek historians where it was said that the Pythia dispensed her prophecies in a non-manic, staid fashion. It was the manner in which the Pythia delivered her predictions that helped inspire confidence in them. This was in stark contrast to the frenzied nature of Cassandra's prophecies, which provoked fear and doubt. Yet, given her true gift of prophecy, can you blame Cassandra for raving when she foresaw the doom of those around her?

Although she was cursed by the god, Apollo, it was no accident that Cassandra was female and thus easily disbelieved in a hyper-patriarchal society. The story of her incredulity would have been far less credible if she were a male soothsayer, who—even at his most dubious—was consistently given the benefit of the doubt.[90] The same held true for the famed Oracle of Delphi and her male overseers. For a woman to be credible in ancient Greece, she had to be associated with the male order. As a single woman not yoked to marriage and representing no one but herself, Cassandra was ridiculed by everyone she met.

An allegory for all time, Cassandra was the voice in the wilderness who persistently told people what they did not want to hear. Though she predicted the future with ruthless accuracy, her guidance was neither sought nor respected. Brandishing the courage of her

---

90   There was inherent ambiguity present in the predictions of soothsayers leading their words to be open to interpretation.

convictions, a nation's scorn did not stop her from prophesying. In *Agamemnon,* she cried: "I loved and they hated me, they were so blind to their own demise."

Alas, hers was not a happy ending. Try as she might, she saved no lives. In the end, she could not even save her own. As always, she looked ahead, preparing to die as she had always lived "Oh men, your destiny. When all is well a shadow can overturn it. When trouble comes a stroke of the wet sponge, and the picture's blotted out. And that, I think, breaks the heart." These are her last words.

Selected Reading for The Curse of Cassandra

Aeschylus. The *Oresteia*. Translated by Robert Fagles. London: Penguins Books, 1975.

Broad, William J. *The Oracle: The Lost Secrets and Hidden Message of Ancient Delphi*. New York: Penguin Press, 2006.

Debnar, Paula. "The Sexual Status of Aeschylus' Cassandra." *Classical Philology* 105, no. 2 (2010): 129–45. https://doi. org/10.1086/651713.

Dillon, Matthew. "Kassandra: Mantic, Maenadic or Manic? Gender and the Nature of Prophetic Experience in Ancient Grece." *Sydney Open Journals* (2023): https://openjournals.library. sydney.edu.au/AASR/article/view/2341/2763

Doyle, Andrea. "Cassandra: Feminine Corrective in Aeschylus' *Agamemnon*." *Acta Classica* 51 (2008): 57–75. http://www. jstor.org/stable/24592655.

Foley, Helene P. *Female Acts in Greek Tragedy*. Princeton: Princeton University Press 2001.

Flower, Michael A. *The Seer in Ancient Greece*. Berkeley: University of California Press 2008.

Mason, P. G. "Kassandra." *The Journal of Hellenic Studies* 79 (1959): 80–93. https://doi.org/10.2307/627924.

Pickle, Linda Schelbitzki, and Christa Wolf. "'Scratching Away the Male Tradition': Christa Wolf's 'Kassandra.'" *Contemporary Literature* 27, no. 1 (1986): 32–47. https://doi. org/10.2307/1208596.

Schein, Seth L. "The Cassandra Scene in Aeschylus'
'*Agamemnon*.'" *Greece & Rome* 29, no. 1 (1982): 11–16.
http://www.jstor.org/stable/642925.

Scott, Michael. *Delphi: A History of the Center of the Ancient World.*
Princeton, NJ: Princeton University Press, 2014.

Figure 1: Ptolemaic Queen, likely Cleopatra 51 BCE-30 BCE.

Figure 2: Granite head attributed to Caesarion. 1st century BCE.

Figure 3: Statuette of Isis Nursing Horus. c. 664 BCE-332 BCE.

Figure 4: Egyptian limestone statue identified as Cleopatra and Marc Antony's twins Cleopatra Selene and Alexander Helios. c. 50-30 BCE.

Figure 5: Kleopatra Selene, Queen, Wife of Juba II 25 BCE-24 CE.

Figure 6.: Julia Caesaris Filia. c. 9 BCE.

Figure 7: Augustus of Prima Porta. c. 20 BCE.

Figure 8: (Vipsania) Agrippina the Elder. Marble
Bust. c 1st half of first century CE.

Figure 9: Etching of Sejanus arrested and condemned to death. 18th century CE. by G. Mochetti.

Figure 10: Nero and Agrippina the Younger depicted upon his ascension as emperor. c 54-59 CE.

Figure 11: The Empress Theodora. 547 CE.
In Basilica San Vitale, Ravenna.

Figure 12: Paestum: Temple of Hera I (in background)
and Temple of Hera Ii (in foreground).

Figure 13: Krater depicting Recovery of Helen by Menelaus. 550 BCE.

Figure 14: Gold death-mask known as "Mask of Agamemnon. " 16th century BCE.

Figure 15: Ruins from the Oracle of Delphi,
Temple of Apollo. Delphi, Greece.

Figure 16: Krater of the Flight of Medea. c. 400 BCE.

Figure 17: Demeter
Knidos. 350 BCE.

Figure 18: Peplos
Kore. 550 BCE.

Figure 19: Zeus. Late First Century CE.

Figure 20: Detail of Pluto (Hades) as Serapis. Mid 2nd century CE.

Figure 21: Figurine of Demeter with Pig. 5th century BCE.

Figure 22: Red Figure lekythos of woman
throwing pig into megaron. 5 century BCE.

Figure 23: Thesmophoriazusae Red Figure Krater. 370 BCE.

Figure 24: Amazon and the Hoplites fight with chariot. Attic black figure krater. 510 BCE.

Figure 25: Bronze statue of Spartan Woman. c. 500 BCE.

Figure 26: Asherah Ivory Box. c. 1300 BCE.

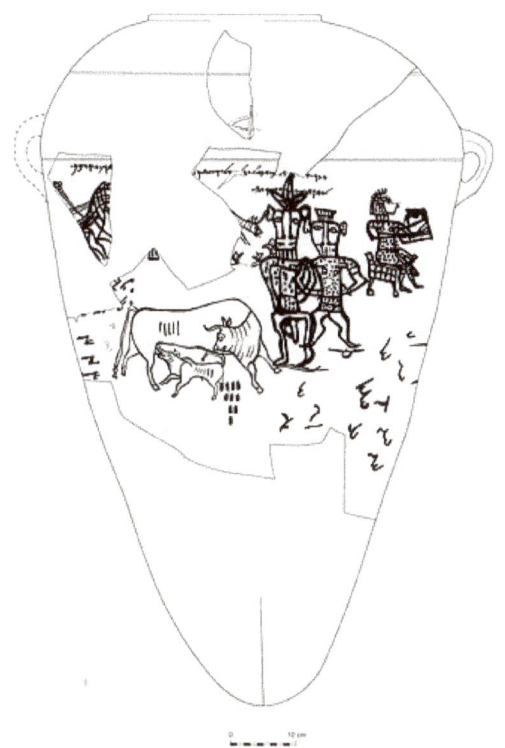

Figure 27. Drawing of Kuntillet Ajrud. 9th century BCE.

Figure 28: Judaean female clay pillar figurines. 9th century to 587 BCE.

CHAPTER FOURTEEN

Analyzing Antigone

The playwright Sophocles (497 BCE-405 BCE) might have been amused to find that nearly twenty-five hundred years after writing about Antigone, his long-suffering heroine is still making her resolute voice heard.

While she cannot compare to her dear old dad-brother Oedipus—whose pathology is nothing short of institutional—the truth is that Antigone has been psychoanalyzed for at least as long as there has been psychoanalysis. Perhaps because she was the progeny of an incestuous union, Antigone's head has been examined by some of the world's finest minds, from psychotherapists to political theorists, poets, and philosophers alike expound on her constancy while exploring her myriad motivations and mindset.

The founder of psychoanalysis himself— Sigmund Freud—believed Antigone was the product of primitive unconscious drives. The modernist author Virginia Woolf praised her as an "exemplar of heroism itself," comparing her to the fearless suffragist, Emmeline Pankhurst. Most recently, American philosopher and gender theorist Judith Butler argued that Antigone portrays a dangerous form of feminism because she is an icon of defiance against patriarchy. While experts may have tried to find common ground, in the end, there are as many theories about Antigone as there are theorists. As a result, she has been burdened with a wide range of labels: from matriarchist to anarchist. Yet for all that has been written about her, who is Antigone, and what makes her so intriguing?

To truly appreciate Antigone, it is important to first understand her past. Because mythology was ubiquitous to the ancient Greeks, they would have been all too familiar with Oedipus's woeful tale and the cursed Laius family. Each play of Sophocles' Theban saga—*Oedipus the King*, *Oedipus at Colonus,* and *Antigone*— is a unit unto itself. Although the events in *Antigone* come last in the saga, in actuality, Sophocles wrote *Antigone* first (in about 442 BCE), preceding *Oedipus the King* by about 12 years. Thus, the Creon in *Antigone* has an altogether different persona than the Creon in *Oedipus the King*.

Cursed Family of Laius: A Summary

On account of a prophecy that an infant son will kill his father— Laius, king of Thebes, and his wife Jocasta— abandon their baby on a desolate mountainside. But just to be certain that the infant perishes, they pin his ankles together. As in most myths about child abandonment, the suckling survives to become a torment to its natural parents. In short order, Corinth's king and queen adopt him and give him the name Oedipus (tender-footed). After finding out he is adopted, Oedipus journeys to Delphi, where the Oracle predicts he will murder his father and marry his mother. Horrified, Oedipus vows never to return to Corinth.

Traveling by foot on the road to Thebes, Oedipus gets into a skirmish with an old man who attacks him, eventually killing the old man in self-defense (his biological father, Laius). Upon entering Thebes he discovers that the town is besieged by a Sphinx, a monster with the body of a lion and the head of a human female. The Sphinx will only release the Thebans if someone successfully answers her riddle. All who have tried have failed, only to be devoured by the monster. But when Oedipus tries to solve the riddle, he succeeds—

forcing the Sphinx to fling herself onto rocks, disappearing forever. In gratitude, the Thebans make Oedipus king, and he marries the widowed Queen Jocasta (his biological mother).

Even though mother and son marry, all is well for many years during which Oedipus and Jocasta beget four children—Eteocles, Polynices, Antigone, and Ismene. Then plague strikes, thrusting Thebes into a tailspin. To ease the suffering, Oedipus consults the Oracle at Delphi—yet again—who proclaims that the plague will cease only when the murderer of Laius is found. In order to rescue Thebes, Oedipus is determined to find the identity of the murderer and in the process discovers his own identity. Upon hearing the truth, Jocasta hangs herself.

When Oedipus finds Jocasta's lifeless body, he is grief-stricken. With tears rolling down his face, he takes the glittering gold pins holding her robe in place and puts out both his eyes with them. Jocasta's brother Creon assumes temporal power in Thebes, ruling alongside Oedipus's two sons. Blind Oedipus, dressed in rags, leaves Thebes to become an itinerant beggar with Antigone at his side. In *Oedipus at Colonus,* when Oedipus discovers that his sons have banished him from Thebes, he curses them, predicting they will kill each other. Although Oedipus is not present in Sophocles' *Antigone*, his prophetic curse is realized before the play begins. Oedipus' son Eteocles refuses to relinquish authority to his brother, so Polynices goes abroad to gather an army in order to attack Thebes. The day before the play begins, brother kills brother in armed conflict, and Polynices is defeated.

Obeying Which God?

The dead lie unburied and the living become buried in this story about a devout and determined young woman who defies a despot's harsh edict forbidding the burial of her deceased brother. In this work, Sophocles "marks the historical bridge between matriarchy and patriarchy," according to French philosopher Luce Irigaray. Antigone, representing the matriarchal tradition—which includes duties toward family and tradition— frequently invokes the chthonic *khthonios* (underworld) deities concerned with mysteries inherent in the cyclical patterns of death and rebirth believed to govern the fertility of the earth. The two most prominent chthonic deities are Hades and Persephone, lord and queen of the underworld, respectively.

Creon, on the other hand, represents the realm of patriarchy overseen by Zeus. Human laws of states and governmental bodies fall under Zeus's eagle eye. As an agent of civic authority, Creon makes the burial of his nephew Polynices a crime punishable by death. His first act as king strikes at the heart of the chthonic tradition, which regards non-burial as blasphemy.

But exposure was only half of it, even mourning Polynices is made a capital offense.

The play begins when Antigone informs her sister Ismene of Creon's edicts in the hope of enlisting her to help bury their brother. Antigone begins by expressing her sisterly devotion to Ismene: "My own flesh and blood–dear sister, dear Ismene." As close as they are biologically, as the scene unfolds it is clear that they could not be farther apart. A study in contrasts, a passionate Antigone charges full-speed ahead, unafraid of the consequences of her actions, while Ismene is wary, contemplative, and helpless to do anything about it, saying "think what a death we'll die...if we violate the laws and override the fixed decree of the throne."

"Remember we are women," she later tells Antigone, "we're not born to contend with men." As a Greek woman, Ismene knows her place— that of the docile, obedient, and modest woman who is never a challenge to male authority. Clearly, Antigone did not read that handbook.

Furious at Ismene's lack of cooperation, Antigone calls her a coward. "I will bury him myself," she says. "And even if I die in the act, that death will be my glory." When it comes to soothing the soul of her brother's shade and appeasing the chthonic gods, Antigone is Achilles-like, preferring to die a youthful heroic death rather than living a long life of mediocrity.

A Woman's Deadly Domain

Although Creon's refusal to bury Polynices is directed against his nephew in retribution for attacking Thebes, it is Polynices' surviving sisters who bear the brunt of it. In a society notorious for keeping women under wraps, it may seem surprising that funereal rites—one of ancient Greece's most sacred of duties—were largely under their dominion. The Greeks, particularly their women, took special care of their dearly departed in rites that were almost akin to ancestor worship.

Wailing and tearing out their hair, women offered a public display of grief. They were also responsible for bathing the deceased, anointing the body with oil, and adorning it with flowers, ribbons, and jewelry. However, of all funeral rites, burial itself was considered the most sacred. Unless properly buried, it was believed the shade would be left in misery and pain, doomed to flit about endlessly for all eternity instead of resting quietly in Hades.

While burial rites were all-important to the ancient Greeks, it was not unusual to deny burial to enemy combatants or traitors. In this way, Creon's edicts were not irregular. To be sure, the abandonment of enemies' corpses outside city walls—where they would not pollute the city—was more or less the convention during times of warfare. Nevertheless, even enemy combatants left outside the city walls were later retrieved by family members for proper burial.

The collection of the deceased during war time is exemplified in one of the most moving scenes from the *Iliad*. Never known for his compassion, even the brutal war-hero Achilles eventually renders the slain body of his arch-enemy, Hector, to his grieving father, Priam, for burial. Creon's refusal of burial goes above and beyond, especially considering that Creon himself was part of the family, being twice uncle to Polynices.

Creon seems to delight in envisioning a decaying Polynices, often alluding to his rotting corpse with such phrases as "carrion for the birds and dogs to tear." In fact, Creon mentions Polynices' decaying remains more than he praises the heroism of Eteocles. Often at cross purposes with Creon, Antigone was fiercely loyal to both her deceased family and the traditions of the *chthonic* gods calling for filial piety and burial for her brother.

The Act of Defiance

Therefore it should come as no surprise that before long, Antigone is caught burying her brother's corpse. The burial is largely symbolic—simply a matter of throwing some dirt on the corpse and saying a prayer—yet it is considered a burial nonetheless. Decisive and assertive, Antigone's burial of Polynices is effectively an act of treason for which she takes full responsibility. When she is brought before Creon on criminal charges, he sets the tone by asking, incredulously, how "she had the gall to break the law?" Antigone is not only unafraid of death, she is also unafraid of Creon. With characteristic defiance, she retorts: "Of course I did. It wasn't Zeus, not in the least who made this proclamation—not to me. Nor did that Justice, dwelling with the gods beneath the earth, ordain such laws for me."

Defending the sacred over the secular with a piety rivaling that of a priestess, Antigone points out that a mere mortal could not override "the great unwritten, unshakable traditions." This is a direct reference to the laws of the chthonic gods governing not only the dead but also family and traditions.

The contempt Creon heaps on his nephew is nothing compared to the profanity he piles on the *chthonic* gods, displaying disdain for them throughout the play. Antigone will learn, he says, "what a waste of breath it is to worship death." A despot, Creon's attitude toward the *chthonic* gods who, unlike Zeus, are not inclined to advance his dynastic ambitions, is on par with the *hubris* he displays toward the powerless masses subject to his rule. "Am I to rule this land for others—or myself?" he asks rhetorically, clearly disregarding the idea of ruling for the common good. "The city is the king's—that's the law!"

Creon's Authority

Surrounding himself with sycophants, it is no wonder that the autocratic Creon is taken aback by Antigone. Moreover, that such impertinence should come from a woman is doubly egregious. After all, women were supposed to be confined to the domicile; forbidden from taking part in the operation of the polis or activities in the public square. Throughout the scene between Antigone and Creon, an emasculated Creon repeatedly refers to her as "manly," trying to link her with a sort of perverse masculinity "I am not the man, not now she is the man if this victory goes to her and she goes free," he says.

The absolutism of his authority is threatened by Antigone's resistance. According to Creon's authoritarian logic, if she wins, he loses. In her seminal book *Antigone's Claim*, Butler affirms that not only does Antigone's defiance unman Creon, but her act of defiance is a law unto itself. "Antigone comes, then, to act in ways that are called manly not only because she acts in defiance of the law but also because she assumes the voice of the law in committing the act against the law." [91]

All the same, while Antigone acts like a Greek hero, the truth is she is not even a Greek heroine; she does not hold power like semi-divine Medea or sovereignty like Queen Clytemnestra. On the contrary, as a young unmarried woman—likely no more than 16 years old— she has no rights and even less authority. In view of the fact that power relations between the two protagonists are greatly unequal, not much time elapses before this battle of wills devolves into a death sentence for Antigone. Creon boasts, "Never! Sister's child or closer in blood than all my family clustered at my altar worshiping Guardian Zeus—she'll never escape, she and her blood sister, the most barbaric death."

As young unmarried women whose father is deceased, both Antigone and her sister Ismene are under the guardianship of none other than Creon himself. The very man who is supposed to be protecting them is actually trying to kill them.

A defiant Antigone takes her death sentence in stride. Willing to die nobly for her cause, she retorts, "If I am to die before my time, I consider that a gain." When Ismene tries to share the blame for the burial, Antigone will have none of it. Wearing her death sentence like a badge of honor she is unwilling to apportion it to someone she considers unworthy of it— like sister Ismene: "You chose to live, I chose to die."

Death's Embrace

Throughout the play, Antigone continually embraces death. When she is initially brought before Creon she says: "Who on earth alive

91   Judith Butler, *Antigone's Claim: Kinship Between Life and Death*. (New York: Columbia University Press, 2000), 11.

in the midst of so much grief as I could fail to find his death a rich reward?" When Creon pronounces his death sentence, a stoic Antigone responds: "I gave myself to death, long ago, so I might serve the dead."

If any in the audience are still doubtful of Creon's tyranny or the virtue of Antigone's act, those doubts are laid to rest when Haemon, Creon's own son and Antigone's betrothed, relates how the commoners feel about the death sentence. "The man on the street, you know, dreads your glance, he'd never say anything displeasing to your face," he tells Creon, adding, "the city mourns the young girl." People don't believe she deserves "such a brutal death for such a glorious action."

Creon is deaf to them. He accuses Haemon of being a "woman's accomplice" and a "woman's slave." Disheartened, Haemon vows to die alongside Antigone, to which his father responds presciently: "Now by heaven, I promise you, you'll pay....she'll die now, here, in front of his eyes, beside her groom."

Only as Antigone is approaching her death vault does the audience catch a glimpse into her deepest feelings: her love for her brother. She would not have done this for anyone but a brother, she says, explaining that if it were a husband "there might have been another" or a child "another too, if I had lost the first." Her brother is something else altogether. With "mother and father are lost in the halls of Death," unable to bear more children, "no brother could ever spring to light again."

This astonishing comment from the child of an incestuous union has led more than one scholar to opine that in addition to fraternal love, Antigone may have harbored an incestuous love for Polynices. In fact, her incestual feelings for Polynices are apparent early on in the play when talking to Ismene about his burial she states: "I will lie with the one I love and be loved by him."

Furthermore, her "loyalty to family" extends only to its deceased family members: her incestuous parents and her insurgent brother—whom she more than a little resembles. While a besotted Haemon and loyal sister Ismene are both prepared to die for Antigone, clearly, she would not have done the same for them. After the first scene, she has nothing but contempt for her "cowardly" sister and never once mentions her betrothed in any of her protracted dialogues about loyalty to the chthonic gods and family.

Alas, poor Haemon; he is more loving than loved. After following Antigone into her crypt, he finds it is already too late—Antigone has hung herself. Meanwhile, at the palace, Creon begins to waver. With the help of the blind seer, Tiresias, Creon recognizes the impiety of his acts and orders the burial of Polynices and the release of Antigone from her underground vault. As Creon approaches Antigone's tomb, he is met with the piercing scream of his son "wailing for his bride," and witnesses in horror as Haemon plunges a sword into his chest.

Defiant to the last, Antigone's death brings an end to Creon's patrilineal ambitions.

It is not, however, the end to Creon's grief. When his wife Eurydice discovers that their only surviving son has killed himself, she follows suit. Alone and desolate, the play leaves Creon, "a wailing wreck of a man" with the chorus affirming "....reverence towards the gods must be safeguarded, the mighty words of the proud are paid in full..." Like all good despots, Creon is right until history proves him wrong.

In the end, the gods do not come out for their devout disciple. There is no *deux ex machina* descending from the heavens to rescue our heroine from her grim fate. Remote and inaccessible, they nonetheless endorse Antigone by orchestrating events that cruelly condemn Creon. Steadfast, heroic, and fiercely defiant, Sophocles could not have known that he was creating a heroine whose voice was as compelling in the ancient world as it is today.

Selected Reading for Antigone

Butler, Judith. *Antigone's Claim*. New York: Columbia University Press, 2002.

Foley, Helene P. *Female Acts in Greek Tragedy*. Princeton: Princeton University Press 2001.

Hame, Kerri J. "Female Control of Funeral Rites in Greek Tragedy: Klytaimestra, Medea, and Antigone." *Classical Philology* 103, no. 1 (2008): 1–15. https://doi.org/10.1086/590091.

Hall, Edith. *Greek Tragedy: Suffering Under the Sun*. Oxford: Oxford University Press, 2010.

Jacobs, Carol. "Dusting Antigone." *MLN* 111, no. 5 (1996): 889–917. http://www.jstor.org/stable/3251251.

Kirkpatrick, Jennet. "The Prudent Dissident: Unheroic Resistance in Sophocles' Antigone." *The Review of Politics* 73, no. 3 (2011): 401:24. http://www.jstor.org/stable/23016517.

Robert, William. "Antigone's Nature" *Hypatia* 25, no. 2 (2010): 412–36. http://www.jstor.org/stable/40602713.

Said, Suzanne. "Aeschylean Tragedy." *In A Companion Guide to Greek Tragedy*. Edited by Justina Gregory. Hoboken, NJ: Wiley-Blackwell, 2008.

Sophocles. *Antigone*. Translated by Robert Fagles. New York: Viking Penguin Group, 1982.

Tutu, Ioana. "The Motivation of Antigone," https://www.mcgill.ca/classics/files/classics/2009-10-07.pdf

Walsh, Keri. "Antigone Now." *Mosaic: An Interdisciplinary Critical Journal* 41, no. 3 (2008): 1–13. http://www.jstor.org/stable/44029635.

CHAPTER FIFTEEN
In Defense of Medea

In Euripides' *Medea* (431 BCE) Medea's wrath against Jason's betrayal was so fierce that the phrase "hell hath no fury like a woman scorned" might have been written with her in mind. In the play the ever-ambitious Jason deserts his foreign-born wife Medea and their two sons for an advantageous marriage with the Princess of Corinth. Using her sorcery *against* Jason—for a change—Medea kills both her rival and her rival's father, King Creon, at whose connivance the ill-fated union between Jason and his daughter had been hatched. These two murders seem rational, even justifiable. Not only is she being replaced by someone younger, blonder, and more socially elevated but to add insult to injury, the king is banishing her from her adopted home in the city-state of Corinth. Can you blame her for being furious?

Yet Medea crosses the line into depravity with the cruel slaying of her two young sons whose only sin was being borne from Jason's seed. In a move that hurt her as well as him, the killings seem extreme. In the dramatic conclusion of the play, Medea is suspended aerially, rising triumphantly above the stage as the *deux ex machina*—god from the machine (see Figure 16). Looming large above her human adversaries, with her two dead children in tow, she is seated majestically in a dragon-drawn golden chariot sent to her by her grandfather, the Titan sun god Helios.

Looking up at her in helpless resignation, a bewildered Jason curses Medea, calling her a "hateful thing....utterly loathed by the gods." Like much of what Jason utters throughout the play, he is wrong. In fact, quite the contrary is true. Instead of cursing Medea and defending Jason, the gods are squarely on her side, ignoring Jason's pleas. Despite killing four people—two of them her own children— Medea is supported by her Titan and Olympian forebears. Displaying her divinity for all the world to see, she rises above the troubles and the carnage—which she herself created—to the safety and asylum that awaits her in Athens.

How could the gods support a monster who killed her own children out of revenge? According to the chorus, who has the last word in the play, "...the gods accomplish many startling things. What we expect does not take place, and the gods make way for what we don't expect." Alas, the indifferent gods are blind to human justice. But before we ourselves dispense justice unfairly, it is important to have some background on the mythology hovering around Medea lo these thousands of years.

The bones of the story come to us in fragments and precede Euripides (484 BCE-406 BCE) by hundreds of years. In fact, Jason and the Argonauts' adventures were "well known to all" in Homer's *Odyssey* (8th century BCE). The first time we hear from Medea is in Hesiod's *Theogony* (8th-7th century BCE) she has been "conquered in love" with a mortal (Jason} " thanks to golden Aphrodite." We then discover "she was subdued by Jason " and they had a son named Medeius, who was raised in the mountains by one of the Centaurs. The next time we hear from Medea, she is made queen of Corinth. In his poem *Corinthiaca,* Eumelus, (ca 8th-6th centuries BCE) reveals that she has been married to Jason, who becomes king of Corinth. From this same source, Pausanias reports that in an effort to immortalize the children she bore Jason, Medea conceals them in Hera's temple and is saddened by the result—the implication being the children died. Jason blames her for the children's passing and leaves Medea. Many believe that this accidental infanticide gave Euripides the idea of making Medea a child-slayer. Although her children may have died in some of the myths, it is interesting to note that Euripides was the very first to burden Medea with filicide.

Then there is a plot twist. From the poet Creophylus, who was—according to Plato—a contemporary of Homer, the Corinthians' are instead blamed for the deaths of Jason and Medea's children. In the myth, as punishment against Medea for killing King Creon, the Corinthians kill her children. Medea often alludes to the possibility that the Corinthians might kill her children in the play, citing that as a reason for killing them more humanely herself.

The most complete pre-Euripidean history of Jason and the Golden Fleece comes to us from Pindar in his *Fourth Pythian* (462 BCE). In it, he narrates the adventures of the Argonauts in detail. When he discusses Medea, he mentions her sorcery and Aphrodite's love magic that helped Jason seduce Medea "so that he might take away her respect for her parents." Her obsession with Jason forces Medea into acting against her better interests in securing the Golden Fleece for him. It is important to note that all the myths about Medea cast her as a victim whose feelings for Jason are preordained by the gods, hence beyond her control. But who is Jason and the Argonauts and what is the Golden Fleece? And just how does Medea get involved?

In a myth that is believed to have predated the Trojan War (ca 1300 BCE), Jason's father, King Aeson, is overthrown by his half-brother Pelias on the Greek mainland in the city-state of Iocolus (modern Volos). In order to win back the kingship, King Pelias challenges Jason to take the Golden Fleece—a fleece from a golden-winged ram that symbolizes the crown—located on the outermost edge of the ancient world in Colchis (modern Georgia) by the Black Sea.

Agreeing to the quest, Jason assembles a band of heroes—prominent among them are Heracles, Orpheus, and by some accounts Theseus—called the Argonauts in honor of their nimble ship, the *Argo*. Embarking on seafaring adventures rivaling those of Odysseus, the crew finally arrives in the wealthy state of Colchis where the precious Golden Fleece is hanging in the sacred grove of the war god, Ares. Jason intends to take the Golden Fleece as his own, but before he can do this, Colchis' King Aeetes—son of Helios, the Titan sun god—gives Jason three seemingly insurmountable tasks.

First, he must yoke himself to fire-breathing oxen and plow a field with them, then he has to sow the teeth of a dragon onto this same field, and finally, he has to overcome the ever-sleepless dragon that guards the Golden Fleece. In other words, Jason does not have a prayer. However, he has a champion in the form of Zeus's wife, Hera.

In an uncharacteristically selfless deed, Jason helps Hera—in the guise of an old lady—cross a treacherous ravine. Like all great goddesses, Hera never forgets the act and comes to Jason's aid in his impossible mission. At Hera's behest, Aphrodite asks her son Eros to pierce Medea's heart with an arrow shot with undying lust for Jason.

Medea, the granddaughter of Helios, priestess of Hekate, sorceress, and semi-divine princess, unknowingly becomes a hapless pawn in Jason's perilous quest. Indeed, Jason would have been a mere legendary postscript if Medea had not come to his aid every step of the way. Although it is against the will of her father—King Aeetes— one by one, she removes the intractable obstacles that stand in the way of Jason's quest.

It is Medea who provides the ointment that protects Jason from the fire-breathing oxen, Medea who helps Jason sow the field with the teeth of a serpent, sorceress Medea who predicts that the serpent's teeth would sprout into an army of warriors, and Medea who proceeds to tell Jason how to defeat them. Finally, it is Medea who crafts a potion that put the ever-vigilant dragon guarding the Golden Fleece into a deep slumber. It is only then that Jason beats the serpent. Or did he? Some myths posit that it was Medea herself who kills the watchful serpent. It must have come as no surprise to the ancient Greeks that the land from which Medea sprung was also home to the Amazons. Fierce and fervent, she greatly resembles the legendary female warriors.

Thus, thanks largely to Medea, the Golden Fleece is now Jason's. Enthralled with lovesickness for Jason, Medea goes against the wishes of her father, her family, and her homeland by providing aid to him.

But the story does not end there. In an effort to convince Medea that the Golden Fleece should remain in Colchis, her brother Absyrtus meets up with the couple. Ever-rapacious, Jason has no intention of returning his precious bounty. Indeed, the couple's unhappy fate is sealed when Medea stands by in resigned horror as Jason slays Absyrtus. Neither ordained by the deities nor killed in self defense, it is simply a murder of convenience—Absyrtus stood in the way of Jason's self-indulgent quest. In his seminal *Argonautica*, Apollonius of Rhodes (3rd century BCE) recounts how Jason hacks Absyrtus' body into pieces and scatters them into the sea so that King Aeetes would be distracted by the task of collecting his son's mutilated body, thus thwarted from pursuing the fleeing couple as they sail away on the Argo.

Hereafter it is clear that nothing good could spring from Medea and Jason's doomed union. From there they set sail to Jason's home of Ioclous to present King Pelias with the Golden Fleece. Tenaciously, Pelias still refuses to give up the crown to Jason. Determined to take it back, Jason persuades Medea to talk Pelias' daughters into using sorcery to make their aged father young again, though in reality making Pelias young again was the very last thing Jason wants. After convincing the daughters to cut their father into pieces in order to make him young again, Medea fails to use her sorcery to bring him back to life again. Deeply distressed at the consequences of their act, the daughters and the son (who upon his father's death is now king) run Jason and Medea out of Iocolus.

Once again, the couple is on the run. Permanent exiles, both are turned away from their homelands. Finally, they land in Corinth and settle down with their two sons until Jason leaves them for the Princess of Corinth—his primary object being the ever-elusive king's crown. This is where Euripides begins the story.

Although his plays deal with the Heroic Age (ca 17th-11th century BCE) in the mythical past, the Greek tragedian Euripides was famous for dramatizing issues relevant to fifth-century BCE Athens. One of the social conventions Euripides took on was the lack of parity between the sexes. As background, in ancient Greece, marriage was transactional between the father of the bride and the bride's prospective groom. Women, including mothers, were wholly excluded from the decision-making process. In order to achieve maximum reproduction, women were wed young; brides were typically between 13 and 15 years old, while their prospective grooms were often twice their age. When a girl married, she left her home and family to reside in her husband's home with his family— sometimes a great distance from her natal home. This was called virilocal or patrilocal marriage. Once married, the wives led lives of confinement and were considered lifelong minors living under their husbands' authority.

As we see in *Medea*, in ancient Greece it was not unusual for a husband to desert his wife for no other reason than growing tired of her. Conversely, a woman could never divorce her husband regardless of how badly she was treated by him.

It is in this milieu that we find an inconsolable Medea. As if in mourning, she is wringing her hands, pulling her hair, and beating her breasts. In a state of deep lamentation, she curses her husband for leaving her and calls on the gods to witness the suffering he is putting her through, "Oh, my father! Oh, my country! In what dishonor I left you, killing my own brother for it," she cries.

Unlucky Medea had been struck by a love spell for an unworthy man who encouraged her to act against not only her family, but also her better interests. Although Euripides ultimately turns Medea into a child slayer, forsaking her family for the love of an undeserving man makes her an extremely sympathetic character with whom the chorus strongly identifies throughout much of the play.

When Medea speaks to the women of Corinth, she speaks for every woman when she delivers these lines:

> Of all the things which are living and can form a judgment, We women are the most unfortunate creatures. Firstly, with an excess of wealth it is required for us to buy a husband and take for our bodies a master; for not to take one is even worse. And now the question is serious whether we take a good or bad one: for there is no easy escape for a woman, nor can she say no to her marriage. [92]

Medea's words reflect how unjust the institution of marriage was for women. Moreover, not only is the chorus sympathetic to Medea's plight, but throughout the play, they quietly endorse her plans for revenge against Jason.

Still, as difficult as it was being a woman living in ancient Greece, Medea was also laden with the role of foreigner, another issue relevant to 5th century BCE Athens. Although the notion of Greek identity slowly began to take form through the colonization of foreign lands beginning in the eighth century BCE, it was not until the war against Persia at the beginning of the fifth century BCE that Greeks began defining themselves as a separate culture. Questions of ethnic identity and foreign assimilation were common topics in fifth-century Athens. To understand how deeply seated Greek

---

92   Euripides, *Medea*, 229-230

ethnicity was becoming, in 451 BCE, twenty years before *Medea* was written, a law was passed in Athens that restricted citizen rights only to children born of both an Athenian mother and an Athenian father thus a child could not be a citizen of Athens if one of his parents was not Athenian. A bias against foreigners was even baked into the word "barbarian" which comes to us from the Greek word *"barbaroi"* which meant babbler and was an onomatopoeic term labeling foreigners as 'bar-bar' speakers.

Derisive and mocking to those who spoke a language other than some dialect of Greek, foreigners were ridiculed as being inferior, savage, and unworthy in every way to their Greek counterparts. Woeful about the struggles of being a refugee in ancient Greece, Medea further laments to the Corinthian women:

> Yet what applies to me does not apply to you. You have a country. Your family home is here. You enjoy life and the company of your friends. But I am deserted, a refugee, thought nothing of by my husband—something he won in a foreign land. I have no mother or brother, nor any relation with whom I can take refuge in this sea of woe.

Brought to a foreign land, with a strange language and customs, Medea represents the precarious existence of all foreigners in ancient Greece. Her ill-fated love of Jason cost her her family, her homeland, and her good name. In his quest for the Golden Fleece, Jason has often been compared to a Greek invader, plundering the resource-rich Colchis and fleeing with its two most valuable possessions: the Golden Fleece and Medea.

Perhaps due to her divine origin, Medea allowed for the expression of a different kind of female archetype—one that went well beyond that of the meek, docile wife. Unlike traditional Greek women, known for their obedience and acquiescence, Medea is strong-willed and fierce, more an avenging Achilles fighting for honor than a Penelope content to stitch away the years while her husband wanders abroad.

Moreover, it was because of her speaking out against the crime Jason and the House of Creon perpetuated on her that the king exiles Medea and her two sons; demonstrating how easy it is for a sovereign to banish a barbarian. But Medea should count her herself lucky, the ever-oblivious Jason blusters: "It's my view that you got much more out of my being saved than I ever did. First of all, you are living in Greece, not some foreign country. Here you find justice and the rule of law."

Tone-deaf words to the freshly banished Medea. But Jason is not just heedless about human relations, the primary reason for his ultimate downfall is his carelessness and hubris in his relations with the gods.

Throughout the play, we hear from both Medea and the chorus about how Jason broke his oaths, among them his union with Medea. In our modern world, oaths do not generally carry the same weight they carried in Medea's time. In fact, oaths were the very foundation of the ancient world. To the pious, oaths were of absolute importance and their breach often unforgivable.

But what oaths are they referring to? Unlike most marriages in the Greek world, Medea was not passed from her father to her husband like her Corinthian counterparts but came into the union on her own sovereignty. The alliance between the star-crossed couple came into being outside the boundaries of societal norms—in part due to Medea's semi-divine status— and resembled something more akin to a treaty between two countries rather than a marriage. Their union took form in a series of sacred oaths sanctioned by the gods. The importance of this is demonstrated in the play— Athens' King Aegeus is stunned when he hears about Jason's deception and Creon's complicity. Sympathetic to Medea's plight, Aegeus agrees to provide her sanction in Athens upon banishment from Corinth. Time and again, the chorus echoes the importance of the oaths made to the gods: "Wronged, she calls on the gods. On the justice of Zeus, the oath sworn, which brought her away to the opposite shore of the Greeks." Although the gods could give a royal fig about the various and diverse infidelities of mortal marriages, they cared profoundly about the oaths sworn to them. Thus, Jason's betrayal of Medea is a betrayal of the gods he swore to when he pledged to be with her.

Jason, of course, is a materialist. Self-centered and vain, he cares more about status and creature comforts than about gods and basic human decency. Taking him to task, Medea says: "Whether you think the gods whose names you swore by then have ceased to rule and that new standards are set up, since you must know you have broken your word to me." Characteristically dismissive of Medea's words, Jason boasts that his marrying the princess was "A clever move....what luckier chance could I have come across than this. An exile to marry the daughter of the king." Just as he used Medea to get the Golden Fleece, he uses the princess to seek the crown. Yet Jason is not alone in his impiety and greed. He has company in the form of King Creon. As a sovereign, Creon knows full well the importance of oaths but ignores them at his own peril when he carelessly orchestrates the match between the Greek hero and his daughter.

As for the princess, her greed is her undoing. Medea reckons that the princess would be enticed by gold that she does not lack, so she weaves poison into the golden-fibered garment and gives it to her sons to present to the princess. Although the princess blanches when she sees her stepsons her countenance brightens upon noticing the glittering frocks they bring her: "She, when she saw the dress, could not restrain herself....She took the gorgeous robe and dressed herself in it and put the golden crown around her curly locks."

All that glitters is not gold, however. As soon as the princess dons her wedding gifts, an exquisitely gilded garment and crown, they burst into flame, burning away her flesh, which then begins to drop off. When her father the king tries to save her by pulling the garment from her body, he himself is ignited. Alas, they both die most ignominiously, flesh falling from their bones, stripped of the identity which in life they too conspicuously revered. As horrific as their deaths are, the chorus still stands resolutely by Medea's side. "Heaven, it seems, on this day has fastened many evils on Jason, and Jason has deserved them." What the chorus will not support is what the gods ultimately sanction—the murder of the innocent children.

Why, then, did Medea kill her beloved children? The reasons are complex and manifold. Time and again throughout the play, Medea ruminates about killing them. "I lost heart, my friends, as soon as I saw their beaming faces. I can't do it. So much for my plans!.... But wait! Can I really bear to be laughed at and let my enemies go unpunished? I have to steel myself. I can't be weak and let those tender thoughts take over." As a mother, she loves them and agonizes over them, but as an avenging deity defending the sanctity of oaths, justice must prevail. When humanity and divinity pit forces within her, divinity wins out.

This process is set in motion with the death of Creon, the King of Corinth, and his daughter. Surely, the Corinthians will take revenge on her by killing the children, so she must beat them to it and kill them herself to save them suffering. Although female, Medea has masculine, duty-bound traits that call to mind Greek heroes like Agamemnon, who sacrificed his daughter for a Greek victory over the Trojans. In a sense, the children's deaths are a sacrifice to the gods who preside over oaths. In the name of all that is holy, Medea must erase all traces of her blasphemous relationship with Jason. She does this by erasing her sons.

About his sons, Jason is blatant at implying they are his alone. Describing his plans to sire more children with the princess, he informs Medea: "You need no children," indicating that Medea was a mere incubator for them. Patriarchal to the core, in ancient Greece, children were born to reproduce the father's line. By killing her children, Medea denies Jason's line continuity. Not only does she remove the two sons from his lineage, but she removes all possible future children by killing his young wife as well. By destroying Jason's progeny, she erases his ancestral line thus she more than kills Jason, she erases him. Yet by killing the children Medea loses something in the process as well—her humanity. In the final scene, looking larger than life in her dragon-drawn golden chariot from on high, Medea is transformed from a passionate, relatable woman into an avenging goddess who cares more about settling scores than basic human decency.

When Jason discovers what she has done, he bellows: "You abomination, most hateful of women to the gods, to me! I was wrong to have brought you with me from Colchis." At long last, is this superficial and haughty man finally learning introspection and humility? In fact, in the end, it is as though Medea and Jason have traded places. Now it is she who exhibits imperial hubris and unfeeling arrogance and he is the victim.

When Jason begs to at least bury the children, Medea will have none of it. To atone for the blood guilt, Medea establishes a holy feast and sacrifice in the children's honor in Corinth. "I will bury them myself, bearing them to Hera's temple on the promontory; so that no enemy may evilly treat them by tearing up their grave." As if the children's death is not punishment enough for Jason, Medea goes on to predict his ignoble death. "As is right, you will die without distinction, struck on the head by a piece of *Argo's* timber." Perhaps a fitting end for the profane and unheroic hero. Though symbolically dead already, Jason laments: "Oh wretch that I am, how I long to kiss the dear lips of my children." Now he longs to kiss them, yet he had no qualms about leaving them for the princess, Medea retorts. Cursing Medea and calling on the gods to bear witness, Jason has the last word.

Even so, his words fall on the deaf ears of the unforgiving gods he disrespected, while Medea flies away to the safety and sanctuary of a tranquil Athens.

Watching this, the largely male Athenian audience—perhaps sympathizing with the wayward Jason—must have been squirming in their seats at Medea's flight to safety. While Medea has Euripides to thank for her depiction as a child slayer, the truth is up until its tragic end, her character—that of the empowered victim—is not only compelling, but brutally pathos-inducing as well.

Perhaps too bitter a reality pill for many in the Hellenic audience to swallow, alas, *Medea* was not well-received in ancient Greece. For his troubles, Euripides earned third prize in a three-way contest at the Dionysia festival of 431 BCE. History, however, is the ultimate judge and *Medea* has stood the test of time. Over its twenty-five-hundred-year history, it has been one of the most popular of all plays from the ancient world, as relevant today as it was in 431 BCE. By taking on universal struggles like ambition, betrayal, and greed along with the ever-omnipresent issues of misogyny and xenophobia, *Medea* is a story for all time.

Selected Reading for Medea

Apollonius of Rhodes, *Jason and the Argonauts*. Translated by Aaron Poochigian, New York: Penguin Books, 2014.

Blundell, Sue. "The Play Explores Social Conflict Between Men and Women," In *Readings on Euripides "Medea."* San Diego: Greenhaven Press, Inc: 2001. 68-75.

Euripides. *Medea*. Translated by David Grene and Lattimore, R. Chicago: University of Chicago Press, 1955.

Euripides, *Medea: A New Translation*. Translated by Diane J. Rayor. Cambridge, UK: Cambridge University Press, 2013.

Foley, Helene P. *Female Acts in Greek Tragedy*. Princeton: Princeton University Press 2001.

Hall, Edith. "Divine and Human in Euripides' Medea," In *Looking at Medea: Essays and a translation of Euripdes' "Medea,"* London: Bloomsbury, 2014: 139-155.

Knox, Bernard, Medea as a Classic Tragic Hero, In *Readings on Euripides "Medea."* San Diego: Greenhaven Press, Inc: 2001, 91-98.

McCullum-Barry, Carmel. "Medea Before and (a little) After Euripides." In *Looking at Medea: Essays and a translation of Euripdes' "Medea,"* London: Bloomsbury, 2014: 23-34.

Stuttard, David. *Looking at Medea: Essays and a translation of Euripdes' "Medea,"* London: Bloomsbury, 2014.

Van Zyl Smith, Betine. "Black Medeas," In In *Looking at Medea: Essays and a translation of Euripdes' "Medea,"* London: Bloomsbury, 2014: 157-166.

Woolf, Christa. *Medea*. New York: Doubleday, 2005.

CHAPTER SIXTEEN
The Passion of Dido

Commissioned by none other than Emperor Gaius Julius Caesar Augustus after his decisive victory at Actium over Antony and Cleopatra, Virgil's *Aeneid* is a patrilineal tale tracing the pedigree of the Italic people from the mythical, stalwart Trojan heroes. Acclaimed for their imperial achievements, both Aeneas and Augustus were victors of empire who were thought to have ushered in a new "golden age," a *pax Romana*; a time of peace, stability, and hegemonic power. Classics professor Michael C. J. Putnam argues: "On the visionary level it (*Aeneid*) suggests an allegorical parallelism between Aeneas and Augustus."[93]

Forasmuch as the mythical Trojan hero, Aeneas was meant to represent Augustus, most scholars agree that his love interest, Dido, Queen of Carthage, was modeled on the jezebel and much admonished Queen of Egypt, Cleopatra.

Who was Dido, and how was her fate implausibly linked to that of the Roman Empire? First, some personal history. Upon discovering that her brother had a hand in the murder of her beloved husband Sychaeus, Dido, the daughter of the King of Tyre (present-day Lebanon), flees her home to the coast of North Africa. When she arrives she asks the locals for a small bit of land, no more than the

---

93 Michael Putnam, "Virgil's Inferno." *The Poetry of Allusion*, Ed. Rachael Jacoff and Jeffrey T. Schnapp, (Stanford: Stanford University Press, 1991), 94-112.

size of an ox-hide. Resourcefully, she cuts the hide into thin strips marking an area around a hillside as her new domain. Thus, Carthage was born. The colony grew quickly and became prosperous. It is at this point that Aeneas enters the scene.

But he does not come alone. There is a divine force running throughout the *Aeneid* imbuing its will on the mortals of the story. Unbeknownst to Dido, the gods are covertly involved both in Aeneas becoming shipwrecked on Carthage and Dido falling head over heels in love with him.

As Aeneas' mother, Venus[94] plays a capricious role in the events. Concerned that Dido would be inhospitable to her son when he washes up on shore, she makes Dido fall in love with him. She does so by using her son, Cupid, to play the role of Aeneas's young son, Ascanius.

Due to a sacred vow she had taken on the ashes of her late husband, Dido initially resists Aeneas' charms but Venus knows that she is vulnerable to the affection of a child. In Book I, Virgil writes: "That her young godling son, Desire, should take the face and figure of Ascanius, then come and use his gift to make the queen infatuated, inflaming her with lust to the marrow of her bones." Each time Dido caresses the godling, she breathes in the contagion, which eventually beguiles her into falling for the Trojan captain. "To her undoing. Mindful of his mother, he began to make Sychaeus fade from Dido's memory bit by bit." Gradually by breathing in the scent of the child, she begins to fall in love with the father.

It is on account of this equivocation that Juno, the goddess of marriage, joins in. Together with Venus, the two orchestrate a thunderstorm from which the lovers must take refuge in a cavern.

---

94   Rome's version of Aphrodite. Because the Romans borrowed heavily from Greek mythology, the Roman gods e.g. Jupiter, Juno, Venus, Mercury etc line up precisely with the Greek pantheon of gods, Zeus, Hera, Aphrodite, Hermes, etc..

Eager to push things along, the goddesses then stage a wedding for the two in the cave. "Primal earth and pronubial Juno give the signal, fires flashed and heaven was witness to the marriage, from summit top the nymphs shouted. That day was first the cause of death of evils." The marriage scene is ambiguous; while Dido considers it legitimate, Aeneas would disavow its authenticity.

Even though the goddesses are culpable for Dido's love of Aeneas, they are hell-bent on keeping Aeneas faithful to his imperial mission. Dido's fate is in direct opposition to Aeneas' when she ultimately becomes abandoned for his patriarchal duty of founding an empire.

Before embarking on his sovereign adventure, Aeneas is Dido's constant companion. He plays an indispensable role in buttressing the fortifications of her beloved Carthage.

It is at this point in the story that Jupiter—king of all gods—expresses impatience with Aeneas for putting off his hegemonic exploits. The lord of the gods dispatches his messenger Mercury to upbraid the Trojan hero. Chastened, Aeneas promptly executes an about-face, subverting the love of Dido for the duty of an empire. And just as coolly as Aeneas takes up with Dido, he coolly tosses her aside. "He burns to flee from Carthage; he would quit these pleasant lands." Duty bound by a strong sense of mission, Aeneas' patriotism trumps his feelings for Dido. She is subverted for his duty of empire at the will of the gods.

In fact, the word *pietas* (pious or a sense of duty) appears frequently in Virgil's *Aeneid* in reference to Aeneas.

To be clear, while he exhibits *pietas* in his love for country, the term does not apply to the women in his life. When Troy was on fire, Aeneas carried his father on his back and grasped his son by the hand but forgot about his wife Creusa, whom he left to die in the burning city. Likewise, Aeneas leaves Dido behind as soon as he is called away on his mission. Classics professor Christine Perkell submits: "The women's deaths are at least partially attributable to the manner of Aeneas' departure although Aeneas does not acknowledge this. To Cruesa Aeneas is fatally inattentive. To Dido he is also irresponsible, even treacherous."[95]

In Aeneas, Virgil created the prototypical Roman male, both in his stoicism and call to duty. For Roman heroes, personal and political choices could not co-exist; one must be renounced for the other. In this way, Virgil's hero was an antithesis of the hedonist Antony, who was perceived as squandering an empire for a woman, i.e. Cleopatra.

Aeneas, meanwhile, plans to set sail for the land which would become known as Italy—all the while keeping his mission hidden from her. Queen through and through, Dido sees through his plans. Upon discovering his treachery, she laments: "So you traitor, you really believed you'd keep this a secret, this great outrage?"

Disgraced, humiliated, and degraded, Dido is cruelly used by the gods and their golden boy Aeneas. Although her love for Aeneas is beyond her control, she takes full responsibility for it and does the only thing a queen could do in her debilitated position: ends her life.

In the last quarter of Book IV, aptly titled "The Passion of the Queen," Dido is frenetic, overcome with a rage she could neither control nor contain. After plunging the Dardan sword—a gift from Aeneas— into her chest, she climbs atop a funeral pyre, cursing the "cold Trojan" to the last. While Virgil's last words pertaining to Dido's state of being are "inflamed and driven mad" he fails to mention during this episode of chaos that Dido is driven to this state of mania at the mercy of a fate which the gods ordained.

After the tragic sequence ends in Book IV, Book V takes us a world away and we see the great divide between Virgil's star-crossed

---

95   Christine Perkell, "On Creusa, Dido and the Quality of Victory in Virgil's Aeneid," *Women's Studies* 8 (1981), 201-223.

lovers. Detached and completely removed from the horror of Dido's passing, Aeneas is fully oblivious of Dido's last act; he is calmly in charge and fully present to his mission. Women's studies professor Paola Bono affirms: "(Dido's) self-destruction is Aeneas' purification from that part of himself which could have hindered his sacred task....Dido is sacrificed for Rome's future glory."[96] Dido's ashes serve as a building block not only for Rome's future splendor but for Aeneas's renown.

Despite writing under the nascent imperial and authoritarian regime of Augustus about a heroine fashioned on the much-reviled Cleopatra, Virgil's treatment of Dido is balanced and to a large degree sympathetic. The author may have been taken aback to learn that for all its swaggering patriarchy love overcomes mission, after all, in the *Aeneid*. Standing the test of time, throughout the years readers' interest in Dido's destiny has far surpassed that of Aeneas' quest to found Rome.

Traveling to the underworld in Book VI, Aeneas encounters the shade of Dido, who is as cold to him as he was to her on his abrupt departure from Carthage. The last glimpse we have of Dido is of her returning to her former husband Sychaeus, the man upon whose death she took a vow of chastity. Finally, there is a genuine feeling of love between two people, with no deities or spells involved. Only in Virgil's underworld does Dido find redemption.

---

96   Paola Bono, "Rewriting the Memory of a Queen: Dido, Cleopatra, Elizabeth I." *European Journal of English Studies* 10 (2006): 117-130.

Selected Readings for The Passion of Dido

Bono, Paola. "Rewriting the Memory of a Queen: Dido, Cleopatra, Elizabeth I."

European Journal of English Studies, 10 (2006): 117-130.

Desmond, Marilyn. *Reading Dido.* Minneapolis: University of Minnesota, 1992.

Hawkins, Peter S. "Dido, Beatrice, and the Signs of Ancient Love." *The Poetry of Allusion.* Ed. Rachel Jacoff and Jeffrey Schnapp. Stanford: Stanford University Press, 1991.

Perkell, Christine. "On Creusa, Dido and the Quality of Victory in Virgil's Aeneid." *Women's Studies* 8 (1981): 21-223.

Putnam, Michael C. J. "Virgil's *Inferno*" *The Poetry of Allusion.* Ed Rachael Jacoff and Jeffrey T. Schnapp. Stanford: Stanford University Press, 1991. 94-112.

Virgil. The *Aeneid.* Translated by Robert Fagles. New York: Penguin Books, 2006.

_____. The *Aeneid.* Translated by: Robert Fitzgerald. New York: Vintage Classics, 1990.

_____. The *Aeneid.* Translated by: Sarah Ruden. New Haven: Yale University Press, 2008.

Ancient Women in Community

CHAPTER SEVENTEEN

The Thesmophoria: Feminine Consciousness in Ancient Greece

In the indigo light of the early morning wearing white robes and carrying torches, the pious women made their way through the cobbled streets in observance of their multiple-day long annual festival honoring Demeter (see Figure 17), goddess of the harvest and her daughter, Persephone (see Figure 18), queen of the Underworld. Numbering in the hundreds, perhaps thousands, the sound of the women's fervent voices singing in praise of Demeter must have reverberated throughout the city walls. Faithfully, the people came out for them—citizens and slaves alike. They packed the city streets to catch a glimpse of the spirited procession as it ascended the hill to Demeter's sanctuary. From the dawn of the Archaic era to the twilight of the Hellenistic era (800 BCE-31 BCE) in the most highly-anticipated religious festival of the year, citizen wives gathered from around their city-states to celebrate the Thesmophoria, the oldest and most widespread of all religious festivals in the Greek world.

With well over 100 city-states participating, the festival spanned from Crete to the south,[97] Asia Minor to the east, Macedonia to the

---

97 The Thesmophoria was even celebrated in ancient Egypt during the Hellenistic era.

north and Sicily to the west. Scholars believe that its wide reach within the Greek world is testament to its prehistoric origins.[98] The Thesmophoria ushered in the sowing season and was one of a series of cults devoted to fertility, both human and agrarian. In Athens, the Thesmophoria was celebrated in the month of *Pyanopsion* (October-November) on a prominent hill where the general assembly of the polis met, known as the Pnyx[99].

Reflecting its societal weight among the male populace, on the second and most-sacred day of the Thesmophoria there was a cessation of certain civic functions. In Athens, the Boule Council—a citizen assembly that made decisions affecting the community—could not meet and law courts were completely suspended. Moreover, as a magical means of promoting fertility, all prisoners were released from jail. Certainly there were other feminine festivals devoted to fertility but none as honored as the Thesmophoria.

Why was a women's fertility festival in hyper-patriarchal ancient Greece accorded such distinction? After all, a woman's place in ancient Greece was on the margins of society, away from the public sphere. Could the strict demarcation of gender roles actually serve to empower women in the Greek world? This essay demonstrates how women's segregation helped contribute to their empowerment. The Thesmophoria formed an identity around the cult, which promoted feminine consciousness, uncommon in the androcentric dominion of ancient Greece. Against the backdrop of extreme misogyny, unlike other feminine fertility festivals, men held the Thesmophoria in high esteem.

Membership in the Thesmophoria was restricted to citizen wives, that is to say, wives of male citizens who were also daughters of

---

98   Kevin Clinton, *Myth and Cult: The Iconography of the Eleusinian Mysteries* (Stockholm: Svenska Institute i Athen, 1990), 28-37. H. W. Park, *Aspects of Greek and Roman Life: Festivals of the Athenians* (London: Thames and Hudson Ltd, 1977), 82.

99   The Pnyx Hill is considered the first site of democracy.

male citizens. Make no mistake, there were no female citizens in ancient Greece. The citizen wife designation was conferred on these women so that they could reproduce the ever-coveted male citizens. Further, no maidens nor female slaves were allowed to participate in the Thesmophoria. And last but not least, while men—that is to say—male citizens were responsible for the expenses related to its celebration, males were strictly prohibited from enjoying any portion of the festival to the point of death. Unlike other feminine fertility festivals such as Skirophoria and Haloa, the women of the Thesmophoria made sacrifices (much as men did in their festivals) and used instruments of death (sacrificial knives etc) in their rituals.

Because of this and other subversive elements in the festival, men who spied on or witnessed the event in any way risked life and limb by doing so. While Greek citizen wives were typically confined to the seclusion of their domiciles, those participating in the Thesmophoria were away from their families for a minimum of three days and three nights. In Syracuse (in Sicily), it was celebrated for ten days and nights. Their time away from home was exceptional in and of itself.

To appreciate the significance of a socially respected, women-only cult festival supported by male citizens, it is important to understand what life was like for women in ancient Greece. To be sure, a woman's place was in the home tending to such things as nursing children, weaving clothing, and preparing food. They could not participate in the public life of the polis in any way unless they were priestesses. Once married, not only were women confined to the home, but they were considered lifelong minors whose every move was directed by their husbands. Even the simple task of going to the marketplace was off-limits to citizen wives ostensibly because they could not be entrusted with financial transactions as complicated as purchasing fruits or vegetables.[100] Needless to say,

---

100 In addition to distrusting the women, citizen males did not want their wives out in public without their husbands or guardians. Thus slaves or metics did the marketing.

if a woman could not be entrusted with the simple act of making change, there was no question of giving them the vote in this newly democratized society. In consideration of the poor opinion men had of women, how did the close female connection to the Earth serve their better interests?

When one envisions ancient Greece, one imagines it as the seat of Western civilization. Yet for all its seemingly urbane sophistication, it was chiefly an agrarian society[101] where most of the residents worked the land. Frequently rocky, craggy, and subject to drought, much of the Greek world tended to be non-arable.[102] So it is unsurprising that they were obsessed with the notion of fertility, holding several fertility festivals throughout the year in the hopes of boosting their crops. These fertility festivals were a means of appeasing the gods to secure crop fertility. However, crops were not their only concern. Due to their ever-expanding empire, they also needed an ample supply of men to fill military posts. Therefore, they needed women— citizen wives in particular— to produce male citizens.

Considered ancient even during the Archaic era (800-480 BCE), the Thesmophoria's primeval rituals and its ubiquity in the Greek world have led many scholars to believe that its origins may date back to the Neolithic era, which in the Mediterranean region was around 7000-3200 BCE. It is important to remember that marriage as we understand it today did not exist during the Neolithic era. While it is unclear if Neolithic society was ruled by women, most scholars agree that the social structure was matrilineal, meaning lineage was traced through the mother's line which is, in fact, more verifiable. This is evident in the mother and daughter images found

---

101 Victor Davis Hanson, *A War Like No Other* "....agriculture was the linchpin of all social, economic, and cultural life."

102 Because it was known for its mountainous terrain, only one fifth of the land mass in ancient Greece was arable. https://www.worldhistory.org/article/113/food--agriculture-in-ancient-greece/ Herodutus wrote "Poverty and Greece are stepsisters." *Histories* 7.102.

throughout the region while the father figure is largely missing. It is possible that paternity may not have been fully understood during the Neolithic era—thus, the mother/daughter relationship was considered primal. In a society that did not mate for life and traced ancestry through maternal lines, knowledge of paternity may not have been fully comprehensible.

How did these prehistoric origins empower the citizen wives of ancient Greece? The Thesmophoria bestowed a link to an era when women had autonomy in their lives— a period before patriarchal precepts ruled the land. Women played key roles during the Neolithic era, a time known for the advent of agriculture and the raising of livestock. While men were hunting, women stayed behind foraging for plants, leading them to the cultivation of seeds and vegetation. This ultimately became humankind's principal food source and allowed them to settle the land. Women acquired expertise in the use of plants, which were not only appropriated for sustenance but also used for medicinal purposes.

In addition to empowering women through the use of medicinal plants, the rituals of the Thesmophoria were another means of promoting women. Such rituals often involved caverns, which represented the womb of Demeter. Two women called 'bailers' descended into caverns to retrieve the decomposed remains of piglets, which had been sacrificed at an earlier time. Fertility cakes made from baked dough were also retrieved, along with pinecones which were used in the rite because they were known to be prolific thus they represented fecundity. These sacred objects were then placed on the altar of the twin goddesses, Demeter and Persephone, and mixed with seed to produce what was known as 'sacred or divine compost.' In an attempt to magically stimulate the fertility of the earth, noted Helenist scholar, A. B. Stallsmith contends:

"Adding some of this 'divine compost' with their seed before sowing guaranteed a good harvest."[103]

Just as women were barred from the political sphere in ancient Greece, so they were barred from certain rites within the religious sphere as well. Unless they were priestesses, women were forbidden from executing sacrifices thus were unfamiliar with altars in general and slaughter in particular. In contrast, in the Thesmophoria, women performed sacrifices[104] themselves thus had access to sacrificial knives and spits in their rituals. The Thesmophoria was conspicuous among feminine fertility festivals because it had the authority over life and death.

How can one know the details of what transpired at the super-secret Thesmophoria? After all, the rituals were considered women's mysteries and as such, were covert and known only to the female participants. The oldest and best sources on the rituals are *scholia*—explanatory comments found on the margins of ancient documents— found in the Lucian's *Dialogues of Courtesans*. There are many theories on who this Lucian scholiast may have been, among them that this person was one of the actors in the festival herself. After all, who else but an adherent to the Thesmophoria would have had knowledge of their super-secret rituals?

The festival gave women authority, enabling them to have agency in a vital aspect of their lives beside the domestic. Although finding empowerment was inherent in the rituals, women also found expression running the Thesmophoria itself. While voting in the *polis* was out of the question for women of ancient Greece, the Thesmophoria was a politico-religious cult complete with elections. Forming an *ad hoc* type of democracy, women made all decisions

---

103 Allaire B. Stallsmith, "Interpreting the Athenian Thesmophoria," *Classical Bulletin* 84.1 (2009), 43.

104 In most city-states, the participants of the Thesmophoria performed rituals without the help of priestesses.

pertaining to the Thesmophoria, including planning, accounting, communications, and most importantly, practicing feminine ritual— all without male counsel.

In the final analysis, religions may reveal more about their adherents than their deities. After all, the characteristics of religions are often determined by the anthropological climate in which they are formed, and the Thesmophoria is no exception. Harkening back to a pre-patriarchal, pre-marriage era when women had more agency in their lives, the Thesmophoria helped ancient Greek women connect with a reality they might not otherwise have imagined in the hyper-patriarchal world in which they lived. By uniting a feminine community beyond the reach of the patriarchy, the Thesmophoria nurtured a strong feminine consciousness connected to the past and allowing greater freedoms in the present. Confined to the margins of society, women had been denied all power except the one—the essential power of childbearing—which differentiated them from men. Ironically it was this strict demarcation of gender roles that gave women the opportunity to exploit their connection to the natural world in order to harness power on their behalf.

Selected Readings for The Thesmophoria

Blundell, Sue, and Margaret Williamson. *The Sacred and the Feminine in Ancient Greece.* New York: Routledge, 1998.

Cantarella, Eva. "Dangling Virgins: Myths, Ritual and the Place of Women in Ancient Greece." *Poetics Today* 6, no. ½ (1985): 91-101.

Clinton, Kevin. "The Sanctuary of Demeter and Kore at Eleusis, In *Greek Sanctuaries: New Approaches*, Edited by Nanno Marinatos and Robin Hagg. (London: Routledge, 1993, 110-124.

Connelly, Joan Breton. Portrait of a Priestess: Women and Ritual in Ancient Greece. Princeton: Princeton University Press, 2007.

Dobson, Marcia W. D-S. "Ritual Death, Patriarchal Violence, and Female Relationships in the Hymn to Demeter and Ianna" In *NWSA Journal*, 4 no. 1 (Spring 1992): 42-58. http://www.jstor.org/stable/4316175.

Hanson, Victor Davis. *A War Like No Other: How the Athenians and Spartans Fought the Peloponnesian War.* New York: Random House, 2005.

_____. *The Other Greeks: The Family Farm and the Agrarian Roots of Western Civilization.* Berkeley: University of California Press, 1999.

Harrison, Jane Ellen. *Prolegomena to the Study of Greek Religion.* New York: Forgotten Books, 1903.

The *Homeric Hymn to Demeter.* Edited by Helene Foley. Princeton: Princeton University Press, 1994.

Lowe, N. J. Thesmophoria and Haloa: Myth, Physics, and Mysteries," In *The Sacred and the Feminine in Ancient Greece*, edited by Sue Blundell and Margaret Williamson, 149-173. London: Routledge, 1998.

Sourvinou-Inwood, Christiane. "Aspects of the Eleusinian Cult." In *Greek Mysteries: The Archaeology and Ritual of Ancient Greek Secret Cults*, edited by Michael B. Cosmopoulos, 25-47. London: Routledge, 2003.

Stehl, Eva. "Thesmophoria and Eleusinian Mysteries: The Fascination of Women's Secret Ritual." In *Finding Persephone*, ed. Maryline Parca and Angeliki Tzanetou, Indiana: Indiana University Press, 2007.

Stallsmith, Allaire B. "Interpreting the Athenian Thesmophoria." Classical Bulletin 84.1 (2009). https://www.academia. edu/2381368.

Thompson, Homer A. "Pnyx and Thesmophorian." *Hesperia: The American School of Classical Studies at Athens.* 5, no.2 (1936):151-200.

Versnel, H.S. "The Festival of Bona Dea and the Thesmophoria.: In Greece & Rome, 39 (April 1992).

Zeitlin, Froma I. "Cultic Models of the Female: Rites of Dionysus and Demeter." *Arethusa* 15, no. ½ (1982): 129-157. http/ www.jstor.org/stable/26308107.

_____ *Playing the Other*. Chicago: University of Chicago Press, 1996.

CHAPTER EIGHTEEN
Rape of a Goddess

Who were Demeter and Persephone, and why did their myth resonate so strongly with women of ancient Greece? The story of Demeter, goddess of the harvest, and her daughter Persephone, queen of the underworld, has inspired many. While there are twenty-two variations of the myth, it is the Homeric *Hymn to Demeter* (hereafter called the *Hymn*), composed between 650 BCE and 550 BCE, that is believed to be the oldest.

Undoubtedly, the episode that leads up to the narrative found in the *Hymn* is as important as the story itself. It starts when Zeus (see Figure 19), lord of the gods, rapes his sister Demeter. The product of that rape is Persephone. They never married. Indeed, Zeus would have been the husband to hundreds if he married everyone he raped.

Being an absentee father did not stop Zeus from arranging the marriage of his daughter, Persephone to his brother, Hades, lord of the underworld (see Figure 20) . The famous *Hymn* then begins with the reciting of an agreement between Zeus and Hades to allow Hades to kidnap, that is to marry Persephone—without the knowledge or consent of either mother or daughter.

As a result, one day while Persephone was out picking flowers with her friends, the earth cleaves open and Hades, on a horse-drawn chariot, charges out violently, snatching Persephone to be his wife for all eternity in the underworld. Persephone shrieks at the violence of the attack, alerting Demeter to her peril.

Inconsolable at the loss of her daughter, Demeter roams the earth in search of Persephone. No one, god nor mortal, has the courage to tell her what became of her daughter. Finally, through information gleaned by the pre-Olympian goddess Hecate, Demeter is informed of Persephone's rape.

Upon discovering that Zeus made the perfidious bargain with Hades, Demeter withdraws from her residence on Mount Olympus and instead makes her home in an agrarian community populated by mortals. After many trials and tribulations there, a grand temple is built in Demeter's honor with attendant rites to conciliate her spirit. But these honors are not enough to appease the grieving goddess.

It is at this point in the story that Demeter realizes her full strength. As a means of regaining her daughter from Hades, she exploits her power of fertility and stops the seasons, turning the earth into a barren wasteland. Reluctant to see the planet he shepherds wither away, Zeus pleads with Demeter to make the earth abundant once again. But Demeter will not relent until Persephone is released.

Finally, Zeus intercedes on Demeter's behalf and orders Hades to return Persephone to her mother's earthly domain. Ever obedient to Zeus, Hades adheres to his instruction but not until he lures Persephone into consuming a pomegranate seed. The mere act of eating in the underworld binds Persephone to Hades as his wife for a few months out of every year.

So how did this parable of the kidnapped bride ring true for women living in ancient Greece? Living under their husbands' patriarchal thumbs, women were accustomed to being kept out of the loop regarding the matrimony of their daughters, and as such, it was not unusual for a father to bargain with his future son-in-law about the fate of his daughter without the knowledge or consent of either his wife or daughter.

As a girl was often torn from her natal home and forced to marry an unknown man who was—on average—twice or three times her senior, abduction can be seen as the equivalent of rape. After all, men were taking young girls to be their wives, that is to say, the begetters of their sons. Indeed, some military campaigns were undertaken for the express purpose of rape; many Ionians were said to have gotten their wives in that manner.

Furthermore, in patriarchal ancient Greece, marriage was virilocal. In other words, the young girls—most of whom were fourteen to sixteen years of age—were forced to reside in their new husband's family home, which could be a great distance from their original home. This meant having contact with their own family members after their marriage was a rare occurrence.

Consequently, Demeter's sense of powerlessness against the abduction, and the suffering that ensued at the loss of her daughter, could resonate for most women of ancient Greece. Additionally, although males are present in the account, it is a woman's story. All the major roles are played by females, and the areas of concern: marriage, agriculture and sacrifice are indubitably in the feminine domain. To be sure, the dark bargain made by the male deities is a misbegotten one, as the union produces no child and nearly brings an end to the life of the planet. Indeed, although their actions drive the events, Zeus and Hades are remote shadows, whose dark force propels the dissonance felt by mother and daughter.

At its most fundamental level, the *Hymn* is a story about a mother's grief at the loss of her beloved daughter. Told from the perspective of the mother; it is more Demeter's story than Persephone's. At once powerless and inconsolable, Demeter appears more mortal than divine. Suffering profoundly due to the actions of males, Demeter is initially impotent to set things right. It is this sense of helplessness that sets off her sorrow at the loss of Persephone, mirroring the anguish that must have been felt by mortal mothers who lost their daughters to marriage each day.

Although both are parents to Persephone, Demeter's bereavement is in marked contrast to that of Zeus, who had initiated her abduction in the first place. Bargaining with the lord of the underworld, who most would view as an agent of death; Zeus is indifferent to his daughter's banishment into the land of the dead. In other words, he is disinterested in his daughter's fate. Though immortal, Persephone is spirited away from the living cosmos and is compelled to live in the realm of the underworld for eternity.

Indeed, is Persephone's marriage not a sort of death? Seen as a transition, the marriage of a maiden was viewed by many as a symbolic form of death.

It is Demeter, however, who does something never seen before in Greek mythology -- she dares to defy the will of Zeus. Moreover, not only does she live to tell the tale but she very nearly wins the battle. After all, for the majority of the year, Persephone lives with her mother in the light of her mother's earthly domain. Though life can never return to the way it was before the abduction, most mortal women could envy Demeter's achievement. In this way, the *Hymn* was liberating for ancient women, an example of a mother's triumph over all else.

Selected Reading for The Rape of Persephone

Arthur, Marylin, and H. D. "Politics and Pomegranates: An Interpretation of the Homeric Hymn to Demeter" *Arethusa* 10, no. 1 (1977): 7–47 http://www.jstor.org/stable/26307824.

Harrison, Jane Ellen. *Prolegomena to the Study of Greek Religion.* New York: Forgotten Books, 1903.

Homeric Hymn to Demeter. Edited by Helene P. Foley. Princeton University Press, 1994.

Kerenyi, Carl. *Eleusis: Archetypal Image of Mother and Daughter.* Princeton: University Press, 1967.

Rigoglioso, Marguerite. *Virgin Mother Goddesses of Antiquity.* New York: Palgrave MacMillan, 2010.

CHAPTER NINETEEN
A Pomegranate for Persephone

It is assumed with some authority that Western women living in the twenty-first century have more options in their reproductive lives than at any time in history.

But is this true?

Is it possible that women living in hyper-patriarchal ancient Greece had as much contraceptive control as Western women do nowadays? Recent scholarship from the era has found that women may in fact have had *more* agency in reproductive matters than previously believed.

As background to this story, it is important to remember that during the Neolithic age (7000-3200 BCE) women were responsible for ushering in the advent of agriculture. While men were off on hunting expeditions, women focused on foraging, leading them to the cultivation of seeds and vegetation which ultimately became humankind's principal foods.

Because of this gender specialization, women acquired expertise in the use of plants, which were not only appropriate for sustenance but also for their medicinal properties. Some of these plants may have been used by women to manage their reproductive lives.

Many scholars have argued that the participants in the Thesmophoria, a feminine fertility festival, used plants for the purposes of reproductive health. Both archaeological findings and literary evidence reveal that through their expert utilization of different vegetation, women could manage many facets of their feminine well-being, including menstruation, conception, abortion, delivery, lactation, and menopause.

The feminine community that formed around the cult of Demeter was tight-knit. Participants could share information they had acquired on both vegetable and human reproduction. It was within this community that they could impart their knowledge on the use of plants to either encourage or discourage various stages of reproduction.

Meanwhile, the citizen men of ancient Greece stood back and paid for the fertility festival. The health of the land was vital for the health of the polis. Moreover, the procreation of male citizens was essential; the androcentric powers needed manpower to maintain their military endeavors.

Therefore, in an effort to encourage fertility and support their interests, ancient Greek males supported the Thesmophoria.

Although citizen males wanted legitimate heirs, ultimately it may have been the women who decided—through their expertise in plants—how fertile they were. For all its patriarchal fervor, controlling the growth of the populace within each city-state may have been left to the caprices of the weaker sex.

There was, after all, considerable motivation for women *not* to be fertile. Woefully, death from childbirth was common in ancient Greece, primarily due to nutritional deficiencies in females,[105] an overall lack of hygiene and the overly young age of first-time mothers. Thus, child birthing was a risky proposition. That being the

---

105 Except for the city-state of Sparta, men got the choicest cuts of beef, the freshest vegetables, etc whereas the women were left with table scraps as a result they often suffered from nutritional deficiencies.

case, it should come as no surprise that many women might have acted at times to dissuade its occurrence.

While women in ancient Greece could not determine who their marriage partners would be, perhaps choosing amongst a variety of reproductive options—unbeknownst to their husbands—was the one way in which women took charge of their lives.

Ironically, women's restricted roles in ancient Greek society may have empowered them in some ways, as most men had very little knowledge of the use of medicinal plants. This ignorance is aptly portrayed in the *Hymn* when Zeus orders Hades to release Persephone, Hades adheres but not before luring Persephone into eating a pomegranate seed. The mere act of eating binds Persephone to Hades for a few months out of each year.

Persephone, however, has the last laugh. Unknown to Hades, the pomegranate seed has contraceptive qualities. Indeed, no child would spring from that unholy union.

To be sure, the *Hymn* and the rites in the Thesmophoria are rife with plant lore, much of it associated with reproductive agency. Plants ranging from Pennyroyal and Pomegranate in the *Hymn* to Pine and Vitex in the rites suggest that any woman familiar with these plants could control her reproductive life as she chose. Although believed to produce hallucinogenic effects, Pennyroyal was also known as an emmenagogue (encourages menses) and an abortifacient (induces abortions). Similarly, Vitex, known for promoting fertility by inducing menses or lactation, was essential and is still used by women today in an effort to control their hormonal imbalances. Pinecones, because of their prolific nature, were believed to enhance fertility and so female participants used pine for a variety of their fertility rites.[106]

---

106 Lucia Nixon, "The Cults of Demeter and Kore" in *Women in Antiquity,* edited by R. Hawley, (London: Routledge), 1995, 76-96.

Oxford Classical Archaeologist, Lucia Nixon, contends: "....women knew ways of controlling their own fertility and in remembering the anger and power of Demeter negotiating on behalf of her daughter, they helped their own daughters manage their married lives by passing on that knowledge."[107]

In an area as vital as fertility, is it possible that women, despite their general oppression in society, had greater jurisdiction than was previously thought? Were they able to wrest control of their reproductive destinies from the very powers that sought to restrict them? Though we cannot say for sure, it is remarkable to contemplate that through their knowledge and use of medicinal plants, ancient Greek women may have had as much, or *more*, reproductive agency than many of their female descendants do today.

---

107 Ibid, 92.

Selected Reading for
A Pomegranate for Persephone

Arthur, Marylin, and H. D. "Politics and Pomegranates: An Interpretation of the Homeric Hymn to Demeter" *Arethusa* 10, no. 1 (1977): 7–47 http://www.jstor.org/stable/26307824.

The Homeric Hymn to Demeter. Edited by Helene Foley. Princeton: Princeton University Press, 1994.

Keller, Mara Lynn. "The Eleusinian Mysteries of Demeter and Persephone: Fertility , Sexuality and Rebirth." *Journal of Feminist Studies in Religion* 4, no. 1 (Spring, 1988). http://www.jstor.org/stable/25002068.

Nixon, Lucia. "The Cults of Demeter and Kore." In *Women in Antiquity: New Assessments*, edited by Richard Hawley and Barbara Levick. 76-93. London Routledge, 1995.

Pomeroy, Sarah B. *Goddesses, Whores, Wives, and Slaves: Women in Antiquity.* New York: Schocken Books, 1975.

Pratt, Louise. "The Old Women of Ancient Greece and The Homeric Hymn to Demeter. *Transactions of the American Philological Association* 130, no.2 (2000). http://www.jstor.org/stable/284305.

Stehle, Eva. "Thesmophoria and Eleusinian Mysteries: The Fascination of Women's Secret Ritual." In *Finding Persephone: Woman's Ritual in the Ancient Mediterranean,* edited by Maryline Parca and Angeliki Tzanetou, 165-185. Bloomington, Indiana: Indiana University Press, 2007.

CHAPTER TWENTY

Demeter and the Danaids: A Subversive Alliance

A murderous band of husband-slaying sisters allegedly founded the Thesmophoria, the Greek world's most venerable feminine fertility festival celebrated by, of all people, upstanding citizen wives. Why would a festival attended by highly respected married women be affiliated with a subversive myth whose women savagely resisted marriage? What was it about the Thesmophoria—the most prominent ritual honoring Demeter, goddess of the harvest, and her daughter Persephone, queen of the underworld—that was correlative to the rebellious, marriage-hating Danaids? To fully answer that question, it is important to understand what the cult meant to its participants and to the community at large.

Throughout ancient Greece, from the beginning of the Archaic to the end of the Hellenistic eras (800 BCE-31 BCE), citizen wives came from far and wide to gather in their cities to celebrate the Thesmophoria. Archaeological and literary sources suggest that the prehistoric cult had its roots in the Neolithic era (7000 BCE-3000 BCE) when agriculture and hog domestication were the domain of women. Archaeologists claim women played critical roles during this time—they were in charge not only of breeding the population but of feeding it as well. Given this, it is of no surprise a women's festival was centered around rites honoring Demeter, an agricultural and fertility goddess.

According to one theory, because it was an act of aggression against a goddess, Persephone's rape indicated an end to matriarchy while ushering in an era of patriarchy where kidnapping-cum-marriage was routine. In her book, *Virgin Mother Goddesses of Antiquity*, Marguerite Rigoglioso espouses: "In the immortal realms as well as the earthly plane, it (the rape) signaled the usurping of the parthenogenetic power of the female in service to the birthing of the 'sons of gods.'"[108] In this way, the long arm of the patriarchs supplanted the indigenous mother goddesses with their thunderous sky gods and carried with them their custom of virilocal marriage, which they had been practicing for some time.[109] Marriage became a form of ownership; both the woman and her offspring were made the property of her husband. In order to protect a patrilineal succession of property, monogamy was required thus the actions of women became tightly controlled by their husbands.

Independent and fierce, the mariticidal Danaid sisters were compelled into marriages with their cousins against their ferocious wills. Violently resisting male interference, it is no accident the Danaid sisters are the Thesmophoria's founding members. The earliest extant literary reference for the Thesmophoria alludes to the forty-nine notorious daughters of Danaus and comes from the historian Herodotus (484 BCE-425 BCE) in the *Histories:* "About the ritual of Demeter that the Greeks call the Thesmophoria, let me keep a pious silence, except for how much of the ritual can be piously told, The daughters of Danaus were the ones who brought the ritual from Egypt and taught the Pelasgian (indigenous pre-Greek) women."

---

108 Marguerite Rigoglioso, *Virgin Mother Goddesses of Antiquity.* (New York: Palgrave MacMillan, 2010), 100.

109 The invasions of the Mycenaeans in the ca. 18th-17th century BCE brought this about.

The sisters fled from Egypt to Greece and established the sacred rites of the Thesmophoria upon their arrival, according to the legend. The most thorough version of the myth comes from Apollodorus (second century BCE) and begins with a quarrel between twin brothers, Egypt's King Aegyptus, and Libya's King Danaus. To heal a previous rift, Aegyptus proposes a mass marriage between his fifty sons and the fifty daughters of Danaus.

Distrustful of his brother's motives, Danaus consults an oracle, who confirms his worst fears: Aegyptus planned to kill Danaus's daughters (the Danaids) so that his sons can take their dowries. Ultimately, Danaus and his daughters seek refuge in their ancestral homeland of Argos, a principal Mycenaean citadel located in the Peloponnese.

Not so easily dissuaded, the fifty sons of Aegyptus follow them to Argos, insisting upon wedded bliss with their reluctant cousins. When they are rebuffed yet again, the obdurate men lay siege on Argos. To lift the siege, Danaus is forced to acquiesce to the wedding between his daughters and Aegyptus's sons but Danaus equips his daughters with daggers to kill the bridegrooms as they lay sleeping. Forty-nine of the fifty blushing brides comply by beheading their husbands on their wedding night. The only one who doesn't is Hypermnestra, who spares Lynceus because he respects her virginity and leaves her intact. Her act of mercy, however, angers her father Danaus, who has her imprisoned. Eventually, Lynceus rescues Hypermnestra by slaying Danaus to become king. With a loyal wife by his side, the legendary couple would go on to become the founding ancestors of a long line of Argive kings and heroes. But, unless parthenogenesis is involved, how they procreated while she retained her virginity is a mystery of the ages.

In another tradition, for their troubles, the Danaids find themselves in Tartarus: the deepest, darkest, and dreariest part of Hades. Hell-like, it was used only for enemies of the gods who are given some futile task to perform in perpetuity. Because he tried tricking the gods, Sisyphus can be found here, endlessly rolling a falling boulder uphill. Although not enemies of the gods, the Danaids were condemned to ceaselessly carry water in sieves for eternity. British scholar and linguist Jane Ellen Harrison posits that the Danaids' punishment was unusually severe not because they murdered their mortal husbands but because they rejected marriage, which constituted a threat to patriarchy. Worth noting, although no more than a fool's errand, according to Harrison, an ancient method of testing a woman's virginity was for her to carry water in a sieve.

Drawing from the myth of the Danaids, the playwright Aeschylus (525 BCE-456 BCE) wrote his last trilogy on the errant band of sisters often referred to as the *Danaid Tetralogy* of which only *The Suppliants* is extant. In the play, the Danaids are suppliants seeking asylum in Argos—from their persecuting cousins, the Egyptians. The play begins when the Danaids throw themselves at the mercy of the King of Argos (Pelasgus) and its citizens to protect them from unwanted marriages with their Egyptian cousins. The intransigence of the Danaids is demonstrated when they threaten to pollute Argos by committing mass suicide if not granted sanctuary. "As soon as we can, from these gods (statues), we'll hang ourselves." Ultimately both Pelasgus and the Argive citizens agree to give asylum to the Danaids. Yet despite the refuge, the Argives ready themselves for war against the Egyptians who have come to their shores expecting the Danaids to board their boats back to Egypt. "Board the swift boat at once, I order you! Let no one delay when we drag you by the hair, we'll have no compunction for those precious curls." As king of a sanctuary city, Pelasgus defends the women from their cousins: "These women, if they were willing, you'd be welcome to take them with you, provided that pious speech persuaded them: but not against their will."

As is demonstrated in the *Hymn*, it was not unusual for brides to be taken against their will in marriage. However, in the case of the

Danaids, the all-important father is as unwilling as his reluctant daughters to proceed with the nuptials. In the play, when asked by Pelasgus why they have come to Argos, the Danaid chorus leader replies: "So as not to be a slave to Egyptus' sons." Pelasgus then asks, "Is this from hatred, or does the law forbid it?" Disavowing that incest is the reason—after all, marrying family members was *de rigueur* for Egyptian royalty—a Danaid replies: "What woman could like a man she buys as her owner?"

Euripides' *Medea* makes a similar lament: "We have to buy husbands with money and accept them as masters to our bodies." In the Greek world, not only does marriage shackle a woman in bondage but she is meant to pay for the privilege. The Danaids' aversion to marriage is matched in magnitude by the perseverance of their cousins who would have them as wives against their wills. "We, the great seed of a Holy mother, ah me! Grant us that we unwed, unsubdued, from marriage of men may flee." Harkening back to an era before marriage, Aeschylus's reference to a "Holy mother" indicates his belief that the myth reaches back into the pre-Greek era of worship in the Great Goddess religion before the Mycenaean invasions of the 18th-17th century BCE.

The subtext of the tale is women's fear of losing autonomy on the one hand, and the threat of violence to them on the other.

Although the ending for the *Danaid* tetralogy is lost, it is believed to have followed the same pattern as Aeschylus' *Oresteia* trilogy: division, violence, then reconciliation in the establishment of a time-honored tradition. In *Oresteia*, the Court of Areopagus is founded to help pass judgment in murder trials. Similarly, in the *Danaid* trilogy, the Thesmophoria festival is founded as a means of reconciliation, a gift from the patriarchs to women for their compliance in patriarchal marriage. "The women were reconciled to their changed status by the foundation of a festival in which they enjoyed exclusive rights," British scholar and classicist George Derwent Thomson contends.

Because it was a festival commemorating the absence of ancient violence in future marriages the Thesmophoria proved reassuring not only for citizen wives but for citizen husbands as well.

The earliest myth about feminine opposition to marriage, the *Hymn,* supplies the narrative of marriage as violent abduction or rape. Revealing a profound feminine hostility to marriage, many scholars see a symmetry between the *Hymn* and the myth of the Danaids. In a blatant display of male hegemony, the cousins— like Hades before them—forcefully inflict marriage or sanctioned rape, on the unwilling brides. The Danaids play the double roles of Persephone as reluctant wife and Demeter as fierce and vengeful matriarch. The dark bargain made by the males in both stories is a misbegotten one: the anger of Demeter nearly brings an end to life on Earth, while the reluctant Danaids resist marriage by savagely slaying their bridegrooms. In light of the similarities between the two myths, Herodotus rightfully apprehended the link between the Danaids and the cult festival of the Thesmophoria, each with its distinct aversion to matrimony.

Selected Reading for Demeter and The Danaids

Aeschylus. *The Suppliant Maidens*. Translated by David Greene and Richard Lattimore. Chicago & London: The University of Chicago Press, 2013.

Bachvarova, Mary R. "Suppliant Danaids and Argive Nymphs" in Aeschylus *The Classical Journal*, 104, no. 4, (2009): 289-310.

Bernal, Martin. *Black Athena: The Afroasiatic Roots of Classical Civilization*. London: Vintage Books, 1987.

Bonner, Campbell. "The Danaid Myth." *Transactions and Proceedings of the American Philological Association*, 31. (1900), 28-36.

Euripides. *Medea*. Translated by David Grene and Lattimore, R. Chicago: University of Chicago Press, 1955.

Harrison, Jane Ellen. *Prolegomena to the Study of Greek Religion*. New York: Forgotten Books, 1903.

Herodotus. *The Histories*. Translated by : Tom Holland. New York: Penguin Group, 2015.

The Homeric Hymn to Demeter. Edited by Helene Foley. Princeton: Princeton University Press, 1994.

MacKinnon, J. K. "The Reason for the Danaids' Flight." *The Classical Quarterly* 28, no. 1 (1978): 74–82. http://www.jstor.org/stable/638710.

Rigoglioso, Marguerite. *Virgin Mother Goddesses of Antiquity*. New York: Palgrave MacMillan, 2010.

Thomson, George. *Aeschylus and Athens: The Classic Study in the Social Origins of Drama.* New York: The Universal Library, 1968.

Zeitlin, Froma I. *Playing the Other.* Chicago: University of Chicago Press, 1996.

CHAPTER TWENTY-ONE
The Savagery of Citizen Wives

Meeting outside the social constructs of marriage, the Thesmophoria evoked a time when women led autonomous lives—without male restrictions. In a society where men set the rules, a community of empowered women that challenged men's authority struck fear in their hearts but nowhere was this male fear more evident than in the stories about the savagery of the Thesmophoria's citizen wives. Because men were forbidden—to the point of death—from attending or witnessing any portion of this all-female festival, the Thesmophoria was notorious for its undercurrent of ferocity towards them. Stories abound about men who were subject to life-threatening and disfiguring acts of violence perpetrated by the citizen wives when they spied on or interrupted their festival in any way.

First there is the tale of the legendary Messenian hero, Aristomenes (ca 720 BCE-648 BCE), celebrated for his triumphs against the fearsome Spartans. Unfortunately for him, he does not fare as well against the well-bred ladies of the Thesmophoria. According to Pausanias (110 CE-180 CE), citizen wives are taken hostage in Demeter's temple by Aristomenes and his fellow warriors while celebrating the Thesmophoria. Hardly shrinking violets, the women—full of the mighty spirit of Demeter—fight the errant warriors furiously with their sacrificial knives and roasting spits. Pausanias recounts the "mortification" of the Messenians. Imagine their humiliation: renowned for their victories against the supreme Spartans, they fell most ignominiously to the second sex. In fact, Aristomenes himself was "knocked senseless" and only escapes with his life because he receives help from his mistress, one of Demeter's priestesses.

Then there is the hapless King Battus of Cyrene (ca 650 BCE-600 BCE), famed for founding the ancient city of Cyrene (Libya). In an account that sounds suspiciously like thwarted rape, an overly curious and perhaps aroused Battus throws himself at the women during their festival. This made him witness to their clandestine rites. At some point, the ceremony stopped and instead the women turned their attention from butchering the sacrificial victims to butchering Battus. "The female slayers brandished their naked swords," recounts Claudius Aelienus (175 CE-235 CE), later adding: "as if in response to an agreed signal, they leaped upon Battus to remove the part of him that made him a male." Cruelly castrated by the furious disciples, the legendary King Battus was a warning to Greek men everywhere: payment is steep for violating Demeter's sacred and secret rites.

Next there is the legend of unlucky Miltiades (555 BCE-489 BCE), an Athenian statesman renowned for his role in the Battle of Marathon. While battling to secure the island of Paros, he leaps over the wall leading to the Thesmophorian shrine, upon which he is so overcome with terror that he jumps back over the wall, spraining his thigh in the process. He develops gangrene from the wound and later dies. The historian Herodotus (484 BCE-425 BCE) recounts the tale as an admonishment, warning that this mournful outcome was due to Miltiades breaching the sacred sanctuary of Demeter Thesmophoros.

Finally, there is Plutarch's (46 CE-120 CE) narrative of Peisistratus (562-527 BCE), the tyrant of Athens, and the Athenian statesman Solon (638 BCE-558 BCE). Together, they pull a trick on the women of the Thesmophoria. The famed statesmen enlist two beardless men to impersonate the women in the sacred rites of the Thesmophoria, which were taking place in Megara, a town ten miles from Eleusis. Ostensibly, it takes no time for the enraged disciples to discover the impersonators and summarily attack them.

Sanctioned Savagery

As violent as these stories may have been, they were deemed justifiable by society at large since it was believed that the women of the Thesmophoria were acting on Demeter's behalf. "[T]he fact is that a celebration of the Thesmophoria at Eleusis was considered unobjectionable," writes eminent classicist Kevin Clinton.

These narratives demonstrate the fear and curiosity of men toward the Thesmophoria. Because the festival was all-important to the health and prosperity of the *polis*, citizen males turned a blind eye to their wives' temporary emancipation during festival events. Apropos to the Thesmophoria, from the seminal *Greek Religion*, the famed Walter Burkett opines: "Men regard this not without suspicion but cannot impede the sacred."

In discussing the violence associated with male interference in the Thesmophoria, in his article "The Festival of Bona Dea and the Thesmophoria," H. S. Versnel asserts: "They [the stories] also most clearly demonstrate that the festival is essentially wrong, disruptive, and consequently in the eyes of one half of society, threatening." Drawing a primordial connection between the Thesmophoria citizen wives and their ferocious Danaid foremothers, these vignettes reveal the apprehension Greek men felt for the Thesmophoria and its citizen wives.

Besides the subversive misandry inherent in the festival, what else about the Thesmophoria encouraged stories of its savagery? To answer this question, we need to understand the limited rights of women in the Greek world.

Women's Disenfranchisement

In point of fact, women were treated as children. Their every move was directed by a male guardian, typically in the form of a husband, father, or brother. Accordingly, they were confined to the relative seclusion of the home and restricted from the public domain. Moreover, they were prohibited to own or inherit property—even voting was forbidden in this arch-patriarchal society. Make no mistake, the designation citizen wife was merely a title conferred on the wife of a male citizen—who was herself the daughter of a male citizen—so that she could bear the much-coveted male citizen.

Therefore, it should come as no surprise that routine ritual sacrifice considered vital to the health and prosperity of the *polis* was the purview of the male citizen. "Just as women are without political rights, reserved for male citizens, they are also kept apart from altars, meats and blood," writes Belgian classical scholar Marcel Detienne in his paper titled "The Violence of Wellborn Ladies: Women of the Thesmophoria." Except for priestesses, women were strictly prohibited from using the instruments of death: sacrificial knives, sharp-pointed roasting spits, and kettles. Even priestesses were forbidden to make sacrifices in some city-states. Not only were women prohibited from offering sacrifices but they were also forbidden from utilizing tools commonly associated with the home, such as kettles, spits, and knives.[110] Perhaps this was because the

---

110 ""Kept away from meat, Greek women are totally unqualified to handle the instruments that we would see….as naturally belonging to the domestic and feminine world. Women had no rights to the kettle, the spit, or the knife." Marcel Detienne "The Violence of Wellborn Ladies: Women of the Thesmophoria, " *The Cuisine of Sacrifice in Ancient Greece* (Chicago: University of Chicago Press, 1989), 133.

notion of women brandishing instruments of death was entirely incongruous with ideal feminine qualities of subservience and tranquility.

Sacrificing Sectarians

Owing to the Thesmophoria ushering in the sowing season, it had long been assumed by scholars that the festival—like all other feminine festivals—dined on vegetarian fare. We now know this was not the case. In fact, it is now accepted as fact that the citizen wives performed animal sacrifices, thus requiring access to these murderous implements. Archaeological evidence has demonstrated that full-grown sows were killed in a sacrificial manner using knives. These were discovered at various Demeter sanctuaries throughout the ancient Greek world. Furthermore, literary artifacts record meat-eating by the women of the Thesmophoria. "Why at Eretria do the women of the Thesmophoria cook meat in the sun instead of roasting it on the fire?" Plutarch asks.

The Lucian scholiast —the source for most of what is known about the rites of the Thesmophoria—also confirms that citizen wives sacrificed animals and ate their meat. Ever the stand out among fertility festivals, the Thesmophoria was the only feminine cult in the Greek world where animal sacrifices were performed without male authority. The confidence with which citizen wives made sacrifices at the Thesmophoria cues prominent classics professor, Matthew Dillon in his book *Girls and Women in Classical Greece* Dillon to opine: "There is nothing in the stories that mitigates against believing that women could slay animals except for the notion that women should not do so."[111] Aside from anecdotal information, in Delos, financial records from the Thesmophoria between the years

---

111 Matthew Dillon. *Girls and Women in Classical Greek Religion.* (London: Routledge, 2002),115.

of 314 BCE-166 BCE indicate the purchase of sacrificial animals such as pigs.

Dating back to Neolithic times, pigs had long been associated with fertility and harvest, and as such were consistently linked to Demeter. This relationship is demonstrated by artwork highlighting Demeter's connection to pigs. Figurines common to Demeter sanctuaries include the figurine of Demeter with a pig by her side (see Figure 21). On the final day of the celebration, the citizen wives enjoyed roasted pig as part of their culminating feast. But sows were not the only swine that were sacrificed.

Sacred Compost

Sometime before the festival, hundreds of piglets were killed and thrown into caverns. This type of sacrifice was depicted in artwork from the era on an Athenian *lekythos* (a long thin krater) showing a disciple crouched over a cavern holding an unfortunate piglet by his tail before flinging him into the dark and deep recesses of the cavern, or *megara* (see Figure 22).

Always part of the Thesmophorion shrine where the Thesmophoria was celebrated, the cavern symbolized Demeter's womb. In his seminal book, *Greek Religion*, the late German classicist Walter Burkert posits:

> The manipulation of the decomposed remains of the piglets to achieve a good harvest is the clearest example in Greek religion of agrarian magic... unquestionably there is a very ancient tradition here; findings from the early Neolithic Age already point to a connection between corn (wheat) and pig.

Pig remains were part of the "sacred compost" to the double goddesses—hence essential to the health and well-being of the polis. The piglets were not in fact killed for alimentary purposes but for the perceived sanctity of their rotted remains that later became the "sacred compost."

German archaeologist, Erika Simon submits that composting is "a great invention of the prehistoric agrarian culture." The magic of composting was discovered soon after the advent of agriculture. When Neolithic people observed that plants flourished when the soil was mixed with the decomposition of plant and animal matter, it did not take long before the practice of composting was put in place.

Thesmophoriazusae

The theme of subversive women who perform sacrifices comes up in Aristophanes' comedic play, *Thesmophoriazusae* (Women at the Thesmophoria) when one of the chief characters known as Mnesilochos (or the In-Law) impersonates a female disciple at the ritual and is found to be an imposter. To keep himself from getting attacked by the armed and dangerous citizen wives, he snatches a baby from one of the celebrants and threatens to sacrifice it at the altar. "You'll never feed this baby another sop, unless you let me go; nay here atop these thigh-bones by this knife stricken, shall its veins run red. Ensanguinate[112] the altar."

Fear of the armed citizen wife celebrants induces Mnesilochos to stab the hapless infant in a fit of terror. But upon doing so—to his great surprise—the "infant" turns out to be nothing more than a wineskin wrapped in swathing (see Figure 23). Like most of the citizen wives in the play, Mica—the infant's mother—is a confirmed lush and deeply distressed about the perforated wineskin. While making every effort to catch the "precious liquid" she cries: "Give me the blood-bowl so at least I can collect my own little one's blood."

---

112 Bloodletting, as during a sacrifice.

In this spoof of piglet sacrifice, Detienne points out that this act would have no comic effect if the spilled wine/blood were inconsistent with the practices of the Thesmophoria itself. Since they were secret and known only to citizen wives, Aristophanes cannot provide details of the rites, but it was no secret that pigs were involved. The infamy surrounding this, however, had less to do with pigs (or piglets) and more to do with the fact that women—an oppressed and largely segregated population—were handling the sacrificial knives and weapons they were otherwise forbidden to touch.

Because women were restricted from attending theater performances—to say nothing of actually being in the plays themselves—the audience watching *Thesmophoriazusae* was overwhelmingly, if not entirely, composed of men. They would have been all too familiar with the stories about the female savagery portrayed in the play. Though they were suspicious of the Thesmophoria, they could not oppose it without risking the fertility of their lands and women. In contrast, citizen wives were empowered by the Thesmophoria's prehistoric roots, which evoked a time before the social construct of marriage, a time when women are believed to have led independent lives. Even though their power was provisional, an oppressed feminine community suddenly freed from the shackles of male authority and armed to the teeth was a genuine threat to the androcentric rule of ancient Greece. The stories of their violence against men—factual or not—indicate the cult was a force with which to be reckoned.

Selected Reading for
The Savagery of Citizen Wives

Aristophanes. *Thesmophoriazusae.* Edited by Alan H. Sommerstein. Warminster, England: Aris & Phillips Ltd, 1994.

Burkert, Walter. *Greek Religion.* Cambridge: Harvard University Press, 1985.

Detienne, Marcel. "The Violence of Wellborn Ladies: Women of the Thesmophoria," *The Cuisine Sacrifice in Ancient Greece, edited by Marcel Detienne and Jean-Pierre Vernant* Chicago: University of Chicago Press, (1989), 129-147.

Dillon, Matthew. *Girls and Women in Classical Greek Religion.* London: Routledge, 2002.

Griffin, R. Drew. "Cannibal Demeter and the Thesmophoria Pigs," *The Classical Journal* 111, n. 1 (December 2015),137.https://www.jstor.org/stable/10.5184/classicalj.111 2.0129.

Lyons, Deborah. "The Scandal of Women's Ritual." In *Finding Persephone.* Eds. Maryline Parca and Angeliki Tzanetou, Indiana: Indiana University Press, 2007.

Osborne, Robin. "Women and Sacrifice in Classical Greece." *The Classical Quarterly* 43, no.2 (1993). 392-405. http://www.jstor.org/stable/639178.

Simon, Erika. *Festivals of Attica: An Archaeological Commentary.* Madison, Wisconsin: University of Wisconsin Press, 1983.

Tzanetou, Angeliki. "Something to do with Demeter: Ritual and Performance in Aristophanes' Women of the Thesmophoria." *The American Journal of Philology* 123, no.3 (Autumn 2002). http://www.jstor.org/stable/1561692.

CHAPTER TWENTY-TWO
Advance of the Amazons

It was love at first sight when Achilles locked eyes with the famed Amazon warrior queen Penthesilea. Romance, however, was the last thing on his mind; he was on the battlefield. Alas, poor Penthesilea— Achilles would realize his love for her only after driving a bronze spearhead into her chest. The *Aethiopis* reports that Achilles suffered pangs of mourning, as intense as those he felt from the loss of his beloved Patroclus, when her helmet was lifted revealing Penthesilea's savage beauty "undimmed by death."[113]

Achilles was not alone among Greek heroes to fight, then fall, for an Amazon. Indeed, combatting the all-female tribe of Amazons was a yardstick with which to measure the bravery of Greek heroes. During a vignette that sounds worryingly like rape, in the ninth of his twelve labors, Heracles was forced to strip the magical *"war-belt"* or girdle off the Amazon warrior-queen Hippolyta. Evidently unaware of his own brutish strength, the mighty Heracles wound up killing Hippolyta while attempting to disrobe her. Finally, according to one tradition, Theseus battled then married another Amazon queen, Antiope, who then became queen of Athens. This sparked a war between the Amazons and the Athenians called the *Amazonomachy* (Amazon battle) in which the Amazons, unsurprisingly, were routed.

---

113 Adrienne Mayor, *The Amazons* (New Jersey: Princeton University Press, 2014), 297.

In each of these tales, although defeated, the Amazon is treated honorably at the hands of a Greek hero, or in the case of Antiope, is treated no less than a Greek woman or about as much as the fairer sex can expect from a Greek man.

Renowned for their courage and bravery against Greek heroes and gods alike, the Amazons were a force to be reckoned with and were so popular they were often featured in artwork and statuary. Such depictions have been found in public, private, and even sacred spaces across the Greek world. Often depicted sporting pants and hurling javelins from the seats of their attendant steeds, the celebrity of Amazon women could be due, in part, to their being antithetical to everything the Greeks held dear in womanhood. After all, for the hyper-patriarchal Greeks, no other culture of which they were aware stood in such stark contrast to their values than the combatant, independent, male-hating Amazons. This could help explain why in vase art, Amazons were second only in popularity to the colossal Heracles himself (see Figure 24). Even children were influenced by them—dolls depicting Amazons' distinctive headgear have been found in the graves of young girls throughout the Greek world.

The Amazons are acknowledged in Homer's *Iliad* as *antianeirai* or "equals of men" and considered a living, breathing race by the ancients. Since then, however, scholars have placed the Amazons in the realm of mythology. Who could blame them? After all, the notion that the weaker sex could be on an equal footing in battle against male counterparts seemed too absurd to be believed. Since the emergence of DNA testing, however, it has been determined once and for all that the Amazons were not, in fact, a figment of the Greek's fertile imagination.

At first glance, there is nothing unusual about the remains of a young warrior approximately 20 to 30 years old from the fourth century BCE. Like many warriors from the area, this one was buried with a collection of spears, bows, quivers, and bronze-topped arrowheads, along with an armed leather belt and various other instruments of war. As it happens, the most renowned amongst the nomadic horse people were often buried along with their steeds. A battle-ax smashed through the skull demonstrates the manner of this warrior's death. When these bones were first excavated in the 1970s, it was determined, with some authority, that these were the remains of a male warrior.

All that has changed since the advent of DNA testing in the late 1980s. It has since been determined that this warrior was, in fact, female. What's more, she was not an outlier. Thousands of burial mounds like hers can be found from Bulgaria to Mongolia. In some areas, fully 37 percent of all warrior skeletons found were warrior women. Could the ancients have been right all along? Were the livid tales of a raucous band of female warriors fact, not fiction—as had long been supposed? After being erased from the annals of history, at long last—are Amazons finally being restored?

Most experts today believe that the Amazon warriors of the ancient Greeks in fact came from a vast nomadic tribal culture in what is now the Eurasian Steppe. This rugged landscape, known to the Greeks as Scythia, extended from Thrace to the west of the Black Sea across the steppe of Central Asia to beyond the mountains of Mongolia, concluding at the Great Wall of China. In total, their land encompassed nearly 5,000 square miles (or eight thousand kilometers) and shared borders with Greece, Assyria, Persia, India, and China.

It is therefore unsurprising that skirmishes were frequent between the roving Scythians and neighboring countries. Ethnicity was a fluid concept for these nomadic tribes who roamed the vast steppe, often interbreeding with each other. It is likely no coincidence that the area pinpointed as home to the Amazons is rife with the remains of ancient nomadic warriors. When archaeologists first began unearthing thousands of *kurgans,* or burial mounds, from the Eurasian region, they discovered that the nomadic culture dated back to at least the tenth century BCE.

Once they began breeding horses around the ninth century BCE, Scythians flourished, becoming famous for their mounted warfare. Clashes between the Greeks and the Scythians started in 800-700 BCE, when the Greeks first began colonizing the area between the Aegean and Black Seas. Not coincidentally, this was the same time that the Amazons began to capture the Greek imagination. In the eighth century BCE, Homer was the first to consider them in the *Iliad,* which is set in the Bronze Age (2800 BCE- 1050 BCE) several hundred years before the epic was composed. Although the Amazons are roundly defeated by the heroes in Homer's epics, in both cases the phrase "a match for men at war" is used to describe them.

But it was not until the fifth century BCE, that the Amazons truly rode into the historical account with Herodotus—the so-called father of history—chronicling their origins. According to him, after the Greeks defeated the Amazons, they captured the survivors and set sail on three ships. It did not take long, however, for the Amazons to stage a mutiny, killing all the Greeks on board. Unable to sail, the Amazonian landlubbers meet friendly winds that deposited them in a Scythian area on the northern coast of the Sea of Azov. After some minor skirmishes with the locals, the Scythians soon became captivated by the female warriors—and mating ensued. One day, the Scythians told the women: "Let us head back to the main body of our people and live as they do. You are wives for us, you and you alone." But the Amazon women want no part of such an arrangement, replying: "We have never learned to do women's work. We shoot arrows, throw javelins, ride horses."

Finally, the women ask the young men to go home and gather their possessions "to set up home together on our own." Unlike in the

Greek tradition, where females are expected to provide the dowry, in this case the dowry is provided by males. The Amazons and the Scythians eventually leave the area, forming a new tribe called the Sauromatians. In addition to dressing like their male counterparts, women are expected to ride, hunt, and go to war, just like men. Herodotus, however, not only demonstrates parity between the sexes—his account depicts a society where women are clearly in charge. In fact, marriage between the Scythians and the Amazons differ radically from the patriarchal notion of matrimony in the Greek world. Not only are the men expected to provide the dowry, but the women set the rules determining how they and their husbands are to live in their new society:

> The women said to them: 'Not only have we torn you away from your fathers, but we have wrecked immense damage on the countryside. Our joint course of action, then, since you have thought fit to have us as your wives, should be to get out of this country, and settle down beyond the River Tenais.' Once again the young men were persuaded.

Herodotus's account of the Amazon myth and the origins of the Sauromatian people were first considered just that—a myth— but that all changed in 2004 with the excavation of the Sauromatians' burial mounds in today's Volga and Ural regions. Like the burial mounds throughout the rest of the Eurasian Steppe, women were found buried alongside implements of war and articles of horsemanship. Evidence suggests that women also held roles of chieftains and priestesses in Sauromatian society. Researchers have unearthed both material honors commensurate with positions of power and religious objects befitting priestesses in female burial mounds. This has led some scholars to argue that their culture was matriarchal—or at a minimum, matrilineal. Based on religious artifacts from the region, many believe the cult of the mother goddess was worshiped there amongst the nomadic tribes within the greater Scythian region.

However, not all claims made by Herodotus and other ancient chroniclers about the Amazons are backed up by archaeological artifacts. According to Herodotus, Scythians referred to the Amazons as "man-killers" or in the Scythian language, *oiorpata*. The reason for this was the belief that no Amazon was allowed to marry until she had slain a man in battle. Following closely on the heels of this was the idea of the Amazons as "man-hating" and "man-less," characterizing them as a savage, all-female race that kill their males upon birth. As to their being an all-female society, while they likely fought as a group, so far no evidence supports Amazon women existing as a society unto themselves. Burial grounds from the region show that both male and female warriors lived together as a populace. Moreover, it is reassuring to note that no evidence to date supports the claim that Amazons killed their male infants.

While the Greeks hurled tall-tales and innuendo against the warrior women, they were not alone in writing about them. Harrowing legends about the bravery and fortitude of nomadic warrior women can be found in most ancient civilizations bordering the Eurasian steppes, including Egypt, Persia, Caucasus, Central Asia, and China. These tales about the Amazons, however, differ from those of their Greek counterparts in one significant way: often, the Amazons win. Not only do the Amazons beat back their non-Greek rivals in these stories, they often become allies, companions, even lovers to their erstwhile foes. Because the Scythians were a pre-literate culture, regrettably, ancient Greek and non-Greek sources are all we have to fill in the blanks about their lives.

Despite their lack of writing, the Scythians were not without stories. These stories, called the *Nart* sagas, were an ancient oral tradition of the Caucasus reckoned to be as old, if not older, than Homer's famous epics. The sagas depict a race of warrior horsewomen who strongly resemble the Amazons. Largely independent and unmarried, these women were courageous in battle and independent in spirit— characteristics the Greeks generally attributed exclusively to the male gender.

Furthermore, the sagas suggest a possible etymological link to the word Amazon itself. One of their stories portrays a famous Circassian queen called, among other things, Forest Mother, Moon Mother and Lady Amezan, phonetically pronounced *a-maz-ah-na* in Circassian. Resembling Botticelli's Venus, the beautiful Lady Amezan has long, undulating fiery red hair and is secretly in love with a handsome man from another tribe. By a twist of fate, she discovers to her horror that the helmeted warrior she cut down in battle is none other than her secret beloved. Straightaway, Lady Amezan rushes to his side, trying to resuscitate him by kissing his cold, lifeless lips. It is too late. "My sun has set forever!" she cries before bringing down the sword on herself: "They lay dead together, Amezan and the man she loved."[114] According to the saga, a spring appeared where the Earth absorbed the star-crossed lovers' blood.

Amezan is an example of its native origin, but the Greeks had their linguistic equivalent of "amazon" as well. Broken down etymologically in Greek "*a*" means without and "*mazos*' ' means breast. This likely refers to a persistent myth that the Amazons had to cut off their right breasts in order to properly shoot an arrow. Most archaeologists now agree that there is no evidence to support Amazons cutting off their right breasts, or any breasts for that matter. Moreover, it would appear they were fully capable of slinging arrows with their breasts intact. Yet the myth of their only having one breast has endured throughout the ages. Why is that? Perhaps the ancient Greeks were trying to make the Scythian women look even more exotic than they were, putting further distance between them and their secluded Greek counterparts.

---

114 *Nart Sagas from the Caucasus*, tr. John Colarusso (New Jersey: Princeton University Press), 2002.

It must have been astonishing for the Greeks to witness the freedom of nomadic women. After all, in the Greek world, girls as young as 14 were often spirited away by their suitors—men who were frequently much older than they—and confined to their husband's home, where a life of subjugation and domesticity awaited them. In direct contrast, matrimony in the nomadic world often involved men and women of approximately the same age. One account by the naturalist Aelian (175 CE -235 CE) claims that if there was an interest in marriage on the part of the male, then he had to wage a battle with his beloved and the winner controlled the reins throughout the marriage. For these ancient wanderers, there was some parity between the sexes—a foreign concept to the ancient Greeks.

In fact, in the nomadic realm there was no set age for marriage. What's more, nomadic women and men were free to mingle with each other before marriage and even take on other lovers after marriage. Given how seasonal patterns influenced the nomadic way of life, they often migrated from pastures in the summer to campsites in the winter. Springtime brought bands of tribes together as a means of forging alliances. In this way, intertribal unions were accepted, and even commonplace.

Before modern testing methods proved otherwise, many experts believed that most tribal women were warriors until they had children, at which point they stayed with their kin. Modern scientific analysis, however, has disavowed that hypothesis. It has since been determined that many of the uncovered burial mounds were of warrior mothers. Often they were buried alongside infants and children, adding credence to the argument that in addition to being young and unmarried, Amazons were mothers too.

Daughters, lovers, wives, and mothers—while their titles were the same as their Greek counterparts, their roles were worlds apart. Why did the Amazons have greater freedom in their lives than the Greeks? One reason may be that in the resource-scarce nomadic society, everyone was expected to pitch in to do his or her part. In a sense, this was a society that didn't have the luxury of segregated roles. In order to bring in as much food as possible, girls were trained right alongside boys in hunting and warfare. After all, females could be just as effective at riding horseback, thrusting spears, and slinging arrows as their male counterparts. Furthermore, if the enemy should come calling, there was no place for the women to hide. Frequently on the go, their makeshift shelters were fragile. Because there were no cities, there were no surrounding walls to protect the nomads from invading forces. The result was that nomadic women—and men—had to be battle-ready on a dime.

What became of this extensive, relatively equitable culture? Scythians faded from historical and archaeological records after about the second century BCE. Some claim the few that were left were ultimately assimilated into Slavic and Gothic tribes in the early centuries of the Common Era.

Brave, fearsome, adventurous, independent, and forceful....all these words readily describe Greek heroes as much as they do the Amazons. In fact, compared to their usual treatment of people from other cultures, the Greeks were fair to the Amazons. This could be due, in part, to their enchantment with the warrior women. After all, DNA testing has shown that the women were tall, athletic, and fair-skinned, not unlike those believed to reside on the "heavenly threshold"[115] of Mount Olympus. Perhaps their resemblance to goddesses further explains their overall popularity within the Greek world.

Difficult to make out in antiquity's primordial haze, these ancient warrior women begin to take shape. They ride high atop majestic steeds flanked in head-to-foot armor and wielding jagged spears— undoubtedly a forbidding sight to any Greek they encountered.

---

115 Homer, the *Iliad,* tr. Samuel Butler (New York: CreateSpace Independent Publishing), 2010, 1.191

Thanks to modern scientific methods and archeological discoveries, the Amazons are coming into ever-sharper focus. They have moved from the margins of mythology to the *terra firma* of historical fact. Even so, examining a preliterate culture dating back over 3,000 years has its limitations. While much has been discovered about their lives, more remains to be learned about these majestic and mysterious women.

Selected Reading on the Amazons

Bernal, Martin. *Black Athena: The Afroasiatic Roots of Classical Civilization*. New Brunswick, NJ: Rutgers University Press, 2006.

Brown, Frieda S., and Wm. Blake Tyrrell. "'Εκτιλώσαντο: A Reading of Herodotus' Amazons." *The Classical Journal* 80, no. 4 (1985): 297–302. http://www.jstor.org/stable/3296811.

Davis, Malcolm. *The Aethiops: Neo Neoanalysis Reanalyzed*. Cambridge, MA: Harvard University Press, 2016.

Dowden, Ken. "The Amazons: Development and Functions." *Rheinisches Museum Für Philologie* 140, no. 2 (1997): 97–128. http://www.jstor.org/stable/41234269.

Guliaev, Valeri I. "Amazons in the Scythia: New Finds at the Middle Don, Southern Russia." *World Archaeology* 35, no. 1 (2003): 112–25. http://www.jstor.org/stable/3560215.

Herodotus. *The Histories*. Translated by : Tom Holland. New York: Penguin Group, 2015.

Homer. The *Iliad,* tr. Samuel Butler, New York: CreateSpace, 2010.

———. The *Iliad,* tr. Emily Wilson. New York: W. W. Norton & Company, 2023.

Mayor, Adrienne. *The Amazons: Lives & Legends of Warrior Women Across the Ancient World*. New Jersey: Princeton University Press, 2014.

Nart Sagas from the Caucasus, tr. John Colarusso, New Jersey: Princeton University Press, 2002.

CHAPTER TWENTY-THREE
Sparta and its Liberated Women

On the face of it, Spartans might have felt right at home living under the iron fist of the Third Reich given that this city-state—more than any other in the Greek world— sacrificed individuality on the altar of authoritarianism.

In addition to the institutionalized abuse it hurled on its prized male citizens, Sparta was notorious for licensed savagery against the much-maligned enslaved Helot class which they were bent on destroying. It may come as something of a surprise, therefore, that the otherwise primitive Spartans were in many ways out-and-out advanced in their treatment of women.

Alas, it is no secret that even in "enlightened" ancient Greece, members of the second sex were relegated to the margins of society. While Sparta—also known as Lacedaemon— joined other Greek city-states in deeming women unworthy of citizenship, women had the right to own property. In fact, by the early fourth century BCE, Spartan women were believed to have owned as much as 40 percent of their own land. For this and many other such freedoms, a grumbling Aristotle attributes the license of Spartan women to the state's eventual downfall, quipping: "But what difference does it make whether women rule, or the rulers are ruled by women? The result is the same."

What could have induced Sparta to break from their Greek counterparts and give women authority over their lives? In order to answer this fundamental question, it is important to understand how and why Sparta differed from other Greek city-states.

First and foremost, Sparta was a warrior state predicated on a ready militia that was second to none. A diarchy, Sparta was ruled by two hereditary kings who shared power equally. Within the executive branch, the kings governed along with five *ephors* (overseers) who were the only elected positions within the state, ruling for a term of one year. With little interaction from the outside world, Sparta was intensely insular and by most accounts a closed society where an individual's rank at birth determined their rank at death. Nevertheless, by some definitions they were democratic; among its male citizens, everyone was equal, referring to themselves as *homoioi* (the equal ones). The *polis* or city-state was divided into three primary social classes: the Spartans (or *Spartiates*) who were its male citizens, the Helots who were its serfs or slaves, and the *Perioeci* "dwellers around" who worked as craftsmen and made their all-important instruments of war. The *Perioeci* were neither as elevated as citizens nor as suppressed as slaves and lived within the Spartan territories.

As one of the two most prominent city-states of the Greek world, Sparta has often been compared unfavorably to Athens. Athens gave the West its genius for democracy, architecture, theatrical arts, and philosophy, while Sparta— to the exclusion of nearly everything else—focused on physical training and martial might. Sparta's chief preoccupation was to subdue rebellion from within its borders and repel invasion from outside.

Why were the Spartans so obsessed with the notion of military supremacy? According to Hellenic scholar, Paul Cartledge, the moment that "transformed [Sparta] from a *polis* into a military police state" was when they conquered the neighboring state of

Messenia in the eighth century BCE. The conquest was hard won as a result of two long decades of conflict. The victory not only gave Sparta a territory rich in agricultural land--they enslaved the entire population of Messenia, becoming the only Greek city-state to base its agricultural output solely on slave labor. Although slavery was widespread throughout the Greek world, Sparta brought it to a new level. In other *poleis*, slaves were owned by individual citizens, whereas in Sparta, the slaves were the property of the *polis* and primarily assigned to work the state-owned farms. Outnumbering the Spartans ten to one, their denigration created a population of permanently enraged and disgruntled captives. The Spartans called the new enslaved class Helots. Musing on the hatred the Helots felt toward the Spartans, historian Xenophon (430-354 BCE) posits that they "would gladly eat the Spartans raw." Indubitably, the Spartans were sitting on a veritable powder keg of their own creation.

Because the Helots would rise in rebellion numerous times over the centuries, the Spartans were justifiably paranoid about an aggrieved population within their borders who outnumbered them. Thus, their top priority was to do everything possible to subdue the Helots. In other Greek city-states, when male citizens were not fighting, they were farming their land, so vital was farming in the ancient world. But in Sparta, since all the farm work was done by the Helots, the male citizens changed their focus from farming part of the time to soldiering all of the time in order to keep the Helots—whose agricultural labor was critical to their very existence—in check. In fact, the Spartan economy is often compared to the antebellum Southern United States. Like the South, the fear that an enraged slave laborer class could take arms against their Spartan overlords encouraged brutality against the Helots and drove the Spartans to be physically fit and battle-ready on a dime.

At this point, it is important to understand how critical physical fitness was to the Spartan regime. No land for the feeble and weak, only the healthiest male infants were allowed to live. Plutarch writes about how the infants were brought before their tribal elders to be inspected for their physique. Infants deemed physically inferior were exposed and tossed off a chasm at the foot of Mount Taygetus. It should be noted that infanticide was practiced by all Greek city-states to one degree or another. However, in other city-states, the decision was up to the child's parents— not the state.

In Sparta, the toughening up began at infancy—Spartan mothers and nurses were known for their severity. If a male infant were fortunate enough to attain the ripe old age of seven, he was conscripted into an intense military regiment that lasted until his twentieth birthday. He was then deemed a professional soldier, ready to spend his days in battle or training for battle. Away from his home and family, the seven-year-old boy would undergo a rigorous training program called the *agoge* which focused on duty, discipline, and endurance. Walking barefoot regardless of weather conditions was one of a multitude of abuses suffered by the boys. While it is beyond the scope of this paper to go into detail about the harsh conditions of their military training, one particular aspect was noteworthy in its barbarism.

Krypteia, or the secret service brigade, was a group of select eighteen-year-olds ordered to live off the land and fend for themselves. The primary purpose of the *krypteia* was to terrorize and kill the much-besieged Helots. Imagine giving license to kill to a testosterone-fueled, half-starved eighteen-year-old boy. But it was not only this special elite who went on Helot-killing sprees. To keep a check on the growing Helot population, Plutarch writes that the *krypteia* practice was repeated each autumn, when the *ephors* called open season on the Helots, allowing the Spartans to kill them without fear of blood guilt. Grim was the life of a Helot, followed by that of a male citizen who would finally be free from the shackles of military bondage if he was among the fortunate few who lived to reach their sixtieth birthdays.

Before the boys were conscripted into their military regiments, the girls trained right alongside them—oftentimes in the nude. The latter was an important element in physical training, Spartans were notorious for their scant clothing (see Figure 25). Although the girls were sent home when the boys went off to military training, their training was far from over. Their mothers continued their education in running, wrestling, horseback riding, discus, and javelin throwing. Throughout ancient Greece, females received no public education, whereas in Sparta not only were the girls educated right alongside boys, but their intellectual formation would often exceed that of the males. In addition to physical fitness, girls were educated in liberal arts where they learned to read, write, compose music, dance, and write poetry. Additionally, according to Plato and Plutarch, Spartan girls were trained in philosophical discourse and encouraged to make their views heard publicly as well as privately. In fact, Spartan women's voices were so brazen that Plutarch compiled a book of their quotes.[116]

Conversely in much of the Greek world, it was deemed improper for respectable women to speak unless it was through their husbands. According to the prominent Athenian statesman, Pericles (495 BCE-429 BCE), the greatest honor a woman could have is to be least spoken of in men's company—clearly, Sparta did not adhere to his notions. While Spartan women far exceeded their Greek counterparts in education and erudition, the education of Spartan males was believed to have been, well—spartan. Male education was focused primarily on two disciplines: maintaining physical fitness and obedience to authority. Many scholars assert that because of their focus on martial arts, male citizens had little time to learn, making their education in rhetoric and liberal arts far weaker than their Greek counterparts elsewhere. This dearth of scholarship

---

116 *Sayings of Spartan Women* or *Lacaenarum Apophthegmata*. The text is in the public domain at: https://penelope.uchicago.edu/Thayer/E/Roman/Texts/Plutarch/Moralia/Sayings_of_Spartan_Women*.html

is aptly demonstrated in the lack of arts, theater, or notable architecture[117] throughout Sparta. Some experts believe that some Spartan male citizens may have been wholly illiterate.[118]

That is because scholarship was never the goal for male citizens. After an extreme and oftentimes brutal military education, men were tasked to become the best soldiers in the world thereby creating a military without compare. Similarly for Spartan women, through a regimen of intense physical training, their goal was to produce the healthiest offspring in the world. Because of their emphasis on health and fitness, Spartan girls married in their late teens, in contrast to their Greek counterparts who often married in pubescence. The thinking was that females gave birth more easily and produced healthier children when they themselves were not children. Unlike in other Greek *poleis* where the groom was typically fifteen or so years older than the bride, the custom in Sparta was that Spartan wives were typically the same age as their husbands.

To be sure, the state of Sparta was before its time in many aspects. For instance, while a meager diet was imposed on the "weaker" sex throughout the Greek world, often leading to such things as malnutrition and anemia—hardly ideal conditions for mothers to be—not so in Sparta. They understood that healthy women produced healthy children. Because of privations endured during intense military training, not only were women's rations on par with men's but Spartan wives often ate better than their husbands.[119]

---

117 Their lack of monumental architecture is a big reason why there are few remaining ruins in Sparta.
118 In Plutarch's *Life of Lycurgus* 16.6: "Of reading and writing, they learned only enough to serve their turn; all the rest of their training was calculated to make them obey commands well, endure hardships, and conquer in battle."
119 "Spartans were the only Greek women who were well-fed and drank wine." Sarah B. Pomeroy, *Spartan Women*, 133. Additionally. Spartan women had better access to food than their male counterparts. https://www.perplexity.ai/search/did-spartan-women-yHw5X5CPSX2yyqrq8QcHfw

To encourage comradery, Spartan men lived in the barracks with each other up until the age of 30, even after getting married. Further, they were required to take their meals not with their wives but with each other—in the messes—until they were 60. To be sure, homosexuality was not only prevalent amongst the Spartans— it was state-endorsed. The reasoning was that men would fight more bravely if they felt affection for each other. Conversely, newlyweds were discouraged from seeing each other. By building up the urge to procreate, it was believed that a husband and wife would produce more robust progeny. Until they reached the age of 30, men were only allowed to visit their wives surreptitiously under cover of darkness on nights when no moon was out so as not to be seen by the authorities who could arrest them. It should therefore come as no surprise that Sparta had problems maintaining its population. In fact, they even had a term for it: *oliganthropia* which literally means "fewness of persons."

Because husbands were often away, wives became accustomed to overseeing the *oikos* or household. While chiefly involved in farming, Helots were also engaged in housework. Even weaving, a common female occupation in ancient Greece, was left to the enslaved class. Utilizing slaves for domestic activities freed up Spartan women to pursue other endeavors, such as managing household farms. To be sure, women's rights in Sparta began in earnest when men ceded farm work for military life, leaving the responsibility of managing agricultural estates to their wives. On account of the greater responsibilities given to women, it was in Sparta's best interest to educate them well. Education was imperative for women who made management decisions on their estates; decisions that male citizens in other city-states routinely made.

The female management of the family farms led to the institution of Spartan's Lycurgan reforms in the seventh century BCE, which allowed women to own land. Sparta was the only city-state in the Greek world to make such a concession to its female populace.

From the sixth century BCE down to the Persian Wars (492 BCE-449 BCE), Sparta was the most powerful of all Greek *poleis*. Women played no small role in this. Eventually, they would become some of the wealthiest of *all* Greeks, owning nearly 40 percent of their land. Of equal importance, perhaps, is the fact that Spartan women could inherit property. Unlike in other Greek *poleis*, where widows would lose their family estate to the closest male relative if they had no sons, in Sparta, a wife could inherit the entirety of her husband's estate.

Thus, Sparta unwittingly advanced the lives and livelihoods of its citizen-wives, who lived longer on average than their battered husbands. In the rest of the Greek world, by contrast, the mortality rate for women was higher than it was for men. As a result, in Sparta, the women outnumbered the men. It was therefore not uncommon for fertile wives to be shared amongst Spartan men. In a process known as "wife sharing" (or "husband doubling"), a married man could allow another man to father his wife's offspring. The children from these new unions would belong to the second man, i.e. the man not married to the mother of these children.

In other Greek city-states, the strength of the *polis* rested on the strength of the household or *oikos*, thus the chastity of the wife was deemed all-important. In Sparta, building up the population was paramount, so chastity took a back seat. Wife sharing was most common in households with healthy children. This was yet another practice that benefited women. Not only did they run their primary *oikos*, but now they had access and authority over the *oikos* of another male citizen with whom they reproduced. It should come as no surprise, then, to hear that in Sparta, adultery was not sufficient cause for divorce, nor did it threaten a woman's right to own property. This was in stark contrast with other *poleis*, where adulterous wives were at best driven out of their *oikos*, at worst sold into slavery.

Yet despite Sparta's best efforts to boost population, *oliganthropia* would rear its ugly head time and again, leading to Sparta's eventual decline. According to Paul Cartledge, by the early fourth century BCE, Sparta's population was one-fifth of what it was 200 years prior. Some scholars argue that a big reason for that was women's emancipation. Because Spartan women were involved in activities beyond mothering, there was an opportunity cost for raising children—potentially diminishing their incentive for bearing them. In her book *Spartan Women*, Professor Sarah Pomeroy reports that ancient historians had long speculated that one of the reasons for the low birth rate in Sparta was because Spartan women engaged in contraceptive practices. Did Spartan women determine how fertile they wanted to be? By using plants, herbs and other such remedies, most experts believe that Spartan women had relative autonomy in all facets of their lives, including their fertility.

While women may have borne some of the responsibility for the low birth rate, Sparta's brutal focus on military might and harsh segregation of the sexes with little or no regard for human sentiment undoubtedly played an equal or greater role. Without the manpower to maintain its military preeminence, Sparta lost its conquered lands in the fourth century BCE during the third Messenian war. At long last, the Messenians (Helots) were freed from their despotic tormentors, but they were not alone in liberation—their tormentors were liberated as well. No longer soldiering to the exclusion of everything else, Spartan men returned to their family farms and engaged in military obligations for only part of the year. They started living as male citizens did elsewhere in the Greek world. This, combined with losing its army of slaves, meant that women no longer held as much power. Eventually, Spartan women lost their ability to own and inherit property, reluctantly trading emancipation for the secluded and silent life of an average Greek citizen-wife.

It may seem contrary to modern sensibilities that Greeks the world over respected Sparta for its virtues such as integrity and honor. Considered by many to be an idealized state, theoretical concepts which define a polis like equality and unity (amongst its male citizens) were magnified in Sparta. Likewise, Spartans were admired for their sense of duty, loyalty, and devotion to their city-state. Famous for their incomparable bravery, their motto "better to die than to be disgraced" was strictly adhered to. In fact, admiration was especially felt for Spartans by the fifth through fourth century philosophers, particularly Plato and Aristotle who not only praised their economic forbearance and adherence to law but modeled their notion of an ideal polis on the city-state of Sparta. Forasmuch as Aristotle praised Sparta, however, he was not alone in casting blame for its downfall on women. Over the years, while many have blamed women for Sparta's decline, their contribution to the city-state's success is often overlooked. If not for the women administering and managing the family estates, their husbands could not have devoted their lives to the military might for which Sparta became known. Indeed, Sparta would never have become the preeminent military power reaching near-mythical heights if not for the intelligence and resourcefulness of its liberated women.

Selected Reading on Sparta's Liberated Women

Cartledge, Paul. *Spartan Reflections*, Berkeley: University of California Press, 2001.

_____ "Spartan Wives: Liberation or License?" *The Classical Quarterly*, 31 no. 1 (1981).

_____ "Literacy in the Spartan Oligarchy." *The Journal of Hellenic Studies*, 98 1978.

Fleck, Robert K. and F. Andrew Hanssen, "Rulers Ruled by Women," *Social Science Research Network:* https://papers.ssrn.com/sol3/papers.cfm?abstract_id=788106

Kennell, Nigel M. *Spartans: A New History*. Oxford: Wiley-Blackwell, 2010.

Plutarch, "Laconic Women." Translated by A. E. Stallings. *Poetry,* 198, no. 4 (2011): 390-396.

Pomeroy, Sarah B. *Spartan Women*. Oxford: Oxford University Press, 2002.

Redfield, James. 1977. "The Women of Sparta." *The Classical Journal,* 73, No. 2. (1978): 144-161.

Scott, Andrew G. "Plural Marriage and the Spartan State." *Historia Zeitschrift*, 60, No. 4. (2011): 413-424.

CHAPTER TWENTY-FOUR

The Last Priestesses

When the executioners came for her on that otherwise bright, sun-baked June[120] day in Rome, Cornelia (50 CE--91 CE) might have been feeling many emotions, but penitence was not likely one of them. Never one to go gently into the night, she raised her hands in supplication, calling for help from the gods and beckoning her patron deity, Vesta—goddess of the home and hearth—to come to her rescue. Alas, as can happen when appealing to the gods, her cries were greeted with silence. Denouncing what she called trumped-up charges of unchastity, Cornelia railed against Domitian (51 CE--96 CE)—emperor at the time. "Caesar thinks I am impure, I who have performed many rites, by which he conquered and triumphed," she cried out.

Occupying his role as *Pontifex Maximus* (chief priest), Domitian convened a session of the sacred college in order to convict Chief Vestal Cornelia of the gravest crime of the Vestal order—*incestum* (unchastity) and he sentenced her to the gravest of punishments: live burial. Unlike most criminal proceedings against Vestals, this particular session was conducted without the presence of the accused, something so notable that Pliny the Younger (61 CE-113 CE) made mention of it in his description of the entombment of Cornelia.

---

120 Cornelia was executed in the month of June during the Vestalia festival honoring the goddess Vesta. https://www.perplexity.ai/search/what-month-did-MvF.WmScTw.qBbeC_TuD_w

"Domitian generally raged most furiously where his evidence failed him most hopelessly," he wrote. "That emperor had determined that Cornelia, chief of the Vestal Virgins, should be buried alive, from an extravagant notion that exemplary severities of this kind conferred lustre upon his reign."[121]

Who were the Vestal Virgins and why was their sacred oath of chastity so fundamental to the cult? Further, why was the merciless live burial the common method of execution for a fallen Vestal? Though today many believe that the cult of Vesta had Etruscan origins, according to Roman historian Livy (59 BCE-17 CE) the College of Vestals was founded by the legendary second king of Rome, Numa Pompilius (753 BCE-673 BCE) in the eighth century BCE. The cult held sway for more than 1100 years until 394 CE, when Theodosius I (347 CE-395 CE) dissolved pagan religions by decree in favor of Christianity.

The cult of Vesta was so integral to the story of Rome that the mother of its twin founders, Romulus and Remus, herself pertained to it. Vestal Rhea Silvia, like many legendary virgins of the day, was forcefully impregnated by a god—in her case, the god of war, Mars. Despite being a victim of rape, however, she was not absolved of the crime of unchastity. Thus the first Vestal Virgin was also the first Vestal to be executed for breaking the sacred vow of celibacy. But before she was executed, Rhea Silva gave birth to twins who were left to die upon the bank of the Tiber River. A kindly servant set the twins afloat and they were eventually reared by a she-wolf. Or so the legend goes. Although the fate of Rhea Silvia sadly mirrored that of some of her unlucky successors, happily many more lived to see the end of their term.

---

121 Pliny the Younger on the unjust conviction of the Vestal Virgin Cornelia by Emperor Domitian https://www.loebclassics.com/view/pliny_younger-letters/1969/pb_LCL055.271.xml?readMode=recto

Recruited between the ages of six to 10, there were only six Vestals at any given time in the whole empire. These girls were often selected from patrician families and served the deity Vesta for a period of 30 years. While Vestals were permitted to marry after serving their 30-year term of service, they seldom did. The Vestals were the only exclusive female priests in the Roman religion. Why was Vesta so all-important to the Romans? A female deity, Vesta's origins may have been as old as fire itself. Long before ancient Rome, early societies made protecting fire's perennial source part of religious ritual. Fire was believed to have magical origins and was indispensable to everyday life. As Vesta's priestesses, the Vestal Virgins were responsible for keeping Rome safe, symbolized by the sacred eternal flame which the Virgins were tasked with safeguarding. As long as the sacred fire burned, Rome was secure.

The Romans believed that if the sacred Vestal fire should die out, Rome's very existence would be threatened. In addition to maintaining the sacred hearth, the Vestal Virgins also performed other rites and religious duties, such as ritual food preparation, gathering water from the sacred spring, and the care and keeping of sacred objects. Moreover, they looked after vital documents, such as wills from prominent people.[122]

Since they bore the responsibility of keeping Rome safe, the Vestals had more rights than the standard Roman women. For example, they could own property and make wills, with their wealth held under their own name—some of the Vestals became quite rich during their tenure. Perhaps most significantly, they could vote, just like every other Roman *male* citizen.

---

122 The will of Marc Antony was left in the care of the Vestal Virgins, but it was confiscated by Octavian in his propaganda war against Antony and Cleopatra in the lead up to the war with the Egyptian queen. Was the will real or a forgery is the question that historians to this day still puzzle over.

Roman women may well have envied their Vestal sisters. The public treated them munificently. Vestals were transported by carriage (*carpentum*) wherever they went, and always had the right of way. Their person was venerated; the penalty for injury to a vestal, through accident or otherwise, was death. They performed rites before important battles in order to assure a Roman victory, and had the ear of the emperor. They also had the authority to pardon condemned prisoners. Emperor Augustus always included them in all major dedications and ceremonies. Considered guileless, they were entrusted with the wills and testaments of major figures like Julius Caesar and Marc Antony. Such was their authority that the Vestals came to the aid of a young Julius Caesar, gaining him a pardon after Sulla put him on a death list. In light of all this, life wasn't so bad for a Vestal—unless she broke her vow of chastity.

The virginity of a Vestal was considered critical to the health of the state, the loss of which threatened national security. Considered the daughters of Rome, any sexual relationship between a Vestal and a citizen was seen as both incestuous and treasonous. It was believed that if a Vestal broke her vows, there would be a dangerous breach in the *pax deorum* (peace of the gods) assuring the continuity and success of the Roman state. To be sure, the security of Rome depended on the purity of their ritual, and its purity depended upon their chastity.

Given that Vestal's bodies were considered inviolable, "punishable by death" was a vexing proposition for the Romans. It wasn't until the fifth king of Rome, Tarquinius Priscus (616 BCE-579 BCE), that a suitable punishment was found—that of being buried alive. Roman law, however, prohibited burial within city walls. In order to get around that, King Priscus had the errant Vestal buried alive in a chamber containing a bed, some blankets, and a lighted lamp, along with food provisions to last a few days. The thinking was that because Vesta was an underworld goddess, she could rescue her buried priestess if the need arose. Romans were very apprehensive about incurring the wrath of one of their supreme deities. There was a great deal of deliberation over the manner of death so that Vesta would not punish them for the bloodshed of one of her priestesses.

While Romans may have lived in fear of the wrath of Vesta, that didn't preclude them from using her priestesses as scapegoats from time to time. Vestal burials often coincided with times of political upheaval, leading some to think they may have been used as fall guys for the state. Who better to blame for the failures of the state than the priestesses tasked with keeping Rome safe? Ultimately, the fate of the vestals rested with the *Pontifex Maximus* (the supreme pontiff or high priest) and his sacred council of three pontiffs or priests.[123] Was this patriarchal convocation always fair and unbiased toward the priestesses? Alas, it is believed that while some of the executed Vestals may indeed have broken their sacred vows, others were likely used as political pawns.

Only two years away from completing her 30-year term of service, Chief Vestal Cornelia was paraded through the streets in a litter that was so tightly secured that no whimper nor wail could escape from it. In the funeral-like procession toward live entombment, the crowd moved away in horror of the proceedings. "No sight could be more shocking, nor was there ever a day at Rome more gloomy and sorrowful," reports Plutarch.

Resigned to her fate, Cornelia descended the steps of the ladder leading to her underground crypt. Pliny the Younger said she stumbled when her robe caught. Ever the priestess, she remained poised and collected throughout, unfastening the robe and steadying herself as she haughtily shunned the executioner's offered hand of assistance. With the sun on her back and a cool breeze on her face,

---

123 Before Augustus (31 BCE -14 CE) it was strictly a religious role, but Augustus politicized it and as emperor made himself chief pontiff where this tradition would remain.

she made her way down into the pitch-black underground chamber that would soon be her sarcophagus.

The Vestal Virgins were irrevocably suppressed and their eternal flame extinguished in 394 CE when emperor Theodosius abolished all forms of paganism in favor of the burgeoning religion of Christianity. Alas, the twilight of the Vestal Virgins mirrored the fall of the Roman Empire, with only 82 years separating them in a history that spanned a millennium. After the fall of the Roman Empire in 476 CE, many ancients felt it was the brutal exodus of the pagan gods and the subsequent advent of Christianity that led to its collapse. For the first time in 800 years, Rome was sacked. Augustine of Hippo (354 CE-430 CE) book *Confessions* was written as a rebuttal to that argument.

Selected Reading for The Last Priestesses

Beard, Mary. "The Sexual Status of Vestal Virgins." *The Journal of Roman Studies* 70 (1980): 12–27. https://doi.org/10.2307/299553.

Galia, Andrew B. "Vestal Virgins and Their Families." *Classical Antiquity* 34, no. 1 (2015): 74–120. https://doi.org/10.1525/ca.2015.34.1.74.

Kroppenberg, Inge. "Law, Religion, and Constitution of the Vestal Virgins." *Law and Literature* 22, no. 3 (2010): 418–39. https://doi.org/10.1525/lal.2010.22.3.418.

Pliny the Younger, *Letters.* https://www.loebclassics.com/view/pliny_younger-letters/ 1969/pb_LCL055.271.xml?readMode=recto

Wildfang, Robin Lorsch. *Rome's Vestal Virgins: A Study of Rome's Vestal Priestesses* London: Routledge, 2006.

CHAPTER TWENTY-FIVE

In Search of Asherah: The Lost Hebrew Goddess

Ugarit, a second-millenium Canaanite port city, situated on the Mediterranean in today's northern Syria, was the site of a major excavation in 1928 that unearthed a veritable treasure trove of cuneiform alphabetic texts. The tablets date back to the fourteenth century BCE and were written in text very similar to ancient Hebrew and Aramaic. For perhaps hundreds of years before Abraham (17th century BCE) migrated to what would become known as Israel, Asherah was revered as Athirat, the Earth Mother and Fertility Goddess. Upon entering the region, the ancient Israelites adopted her and gave her the Hebrew equivalent name of Asherah. "The discovery of the Ugaritic material has established the existence of a goddess Asherah at Ugarit without any doubt. Although in Ugaritic her name appears as Athirat, this is etymologically equivalent to Hebrew Asherah."[124] The Ugarit excavation put Asherah the goddess on the map after having lost her place for thousands of years (see Figure 26).

Who was Asherah to the ancient Israelites, and why is she often paired with Yahweh, their supreme god? Historians and

---

124 Judith M. Hadley, "Yahweh and his Asherah: Archaeological and Textual Evidence." *Ein Gott allein?* Eds. Walter Dietrich and Martin A. Klopfenstein (Gottingen: Vandenhoeck und Ruprecht, 1994), 236.

archaeologists have gradually pieced together her narrative based on artifacts from the region and the sacred scriptures of the Hebrew Bible itself. Evidence suggests that Asherah was honored in ancient Israel and Judah as early as the twelfth century BCE until before the fall of the Southern Kingdom of Judah (ca 587-588 BCE).

Researching the presence of a Hebrew goddess begs the question: how monotheistic were the pre-exilic Israelites and Judeans? Certainly, the very notion of polytheism is inherent in the quest for Asherah. Moreover, the many artifacts representing Asherah and her cult from the region belies the biblical prohibition against the creation of idols. Although discussing the intricacies of the Bible is beyond the scope of this article, we will assess a portion of the research associated with the Bible pertaining to Asherah, the goddess, and asherah, her cult symbol.

For our study it is important to distinguish between popular or folk religion practiced by the majority of the people in the rural areas, and the official or book religion of the high priests and ruling classes in Jerusalem. Popular religion was primarily practiced away from the metropolis out in the country or in rural communities of which most Israelites were a part; it served as a kind of redress for what could not be practiced in the official religion.[125] Since most Israelites and Judeans lived a good distance from the Temple of Jerusalem, they were not as influenced by the book religion and instead had their own religious beliefs and practiced their faith locally. Biblical scholar Meindert Dijkstra maintains: "In all periods of history, religion in ancient Israel has been more pluriform than the biblical writers wanted to indicate."[126] In contrast, Jerusalem produced a definitive text written entirely from the perspective of the upper class.

125 Karel Van Der Toorn, *From Her Cradle to Her Grave* (Wiltshire: Sheffield Academic Press 1994, 112.
126 Meindert Dijkstra, "Women and Religion in the Old Testament," in Only One God? Eds. Bob Becking and Meindert Dijkstra (New York: Sheffield Academic Press, Ltd, 2001), 165.

In rural communities of the ancient world, literacy was all but non-existent. Writing was done by professional scribes paid by the ruling classes. "In the ancient world generally, the populace was almost entirely illiterate. Even priests and kings could not read and depended on a small cadre of professional scribes to communicate and to carry on their affairs."[127] asserts William Dever, Professor Emeritus of Near Eastern Archaeology. Indeed, even rudimentary writing did not become widespread until the eighth century BCE, at which time many were able to write their names, numbers, and trade commodities. It was a long way from being able to read the literary achievement that is the Hebrew Bible.

How, then, can we know how common people worshiped? While artifacts found in the region help piece the puzzle into place, we can also find many of the rituals practiced by the common people in the Bible itself. By and large, biblical writers were unhappy that Asherah or the "Queen of Heaven" shared the platform with their male deity, Yahweh, and repeatedly tried to dissuade their union. Some scholars suggest that one can define folk religion as everything the Bible expressly condemned.[128]

But did women have a role in religious life? Thousands of figurines suggestive of female veneration have been found in the region, suggesting that women played some role in religion. Some of these figurines are thought to be associated with fertility. The Bible also mentions women, such as Queen Maacah. While clearly no commoner, she is chastised for making an "obscene object" for the Asherah in 1 Kings 15:13. Later, in 2 Kings 23:7, we find women being scolded for expressing their devotion to Asherah by weaving veils for her. Lastly, in Jeremiah 7:17, women are admonished for baking cakes for the Queen of Heaven. These are just a few examples

---

127 William G. Dever, Did God Have a Wife? (Grand Rapids, MI: Wm. B. Eerdsmans, 2005), 28.

128 Susan Ackerman, "Digging Up Deborah," Near Eastern Archaeology Vol 66, no 4 (December 2003): 179. http://ehis.ebscohost.com.

of many more in the Bible pertaining to women's role in religion. While these women are found disreputable, the fact that they are mentioned at all speaks to their presence within the religious community.

To be sure, aniconism[129] was, and still is, inherent in the Hebrew Bible. Ample archeological evidence, however, suggests that those who lived outside Jerusalem—and indeed, sometimes right inside it—idolized statuary and cult objects as part of their popular or folk religion. While we have no text or sacred scriptures from their folk religion, we do have much in the way of artifacts from the region. Thirty or so years ago, most biblical archeologists were also biblical scholars and tended to accept without question the stories we find in the Judeo-Christian Bible as historical fact. Today, biblical archeologists tend to be more objective, and their research is more revealing. As such, archaeological sourcing is now a fundamental means of interpreting the ancient Israelite religion.

Iconography tends to be more redolent of the past than mere words. Examined alongside sacred texts, they can provide us with a deeper understanding of the religio-historical evolution. Because most people in ancient Israel and Judah were functionally illiterate, iconography was of primary importance to them. Though nearly one thousand years subsequent to this time, a quote by Pope Gregory I (590 CE-604 CE) is apt for this discussion: "What scripture is to the educated, images are to the ignorant who see through them what they must accept; they read in them what they cannot read in books."[130]From the many tens of thousands of artifacts excavated from the region, Israelites and Judeans expressed devotion through

---

129 Aniconism is opposition to the use of icons or visual images to depict religious figures or deities.

130 Caecilia Davis-Wyer, *Early Medieval Art 300-1100: Sources and Documents* (Englewood Cliffs, NY: Prentice Hall, 1971), 48. Quoted in Leslie Ross *Art and Architecture of the World's Religions, Vol 2 (*Santa Barbara, CA: Greenwood Press, 2009), 231.

statuary and iconography. The idolatry that is often scorned in the Hebrew Bible may be indicative of the prevailing activity of the region.

While Asherah is mentioned in the Hebrew Bible forty separate times, the findings at Kuntillet Ajrud and Khirbet el-Qom have further solidified the role she played in the Yahweh pantheon. An obscure ancient Hebrew inscription and accompanying diagram have sparked a lively debate within the academic community. Excavated in 1975-76 in northeast Sinai near Judah's southern border, Kuntillet Ajrud was a ninth to eighth-century BCE Israelite caravanserai [131] with an attached shrine. The inscriptions under contention were found on shards from two large *pithoi,* or storage jars, that were uncovered within the caravanserai. The ambiguous inscription reads: "I have blessed you by Yahweh of Samaria and his Asherah." The same text is found a number of times with geographical differences, leading one scholar to speculate that perhaps the locations—Samaria, Jerusalem, and Teman—were sites of Yahweh sanctuaries.[132] Thus, the scribe at Kuntillet Ajrud may have had familiarity with the Yahweh sanctuaries in which the presence of "his Asherah" would be felt.

As background, it is interesting to note that the possessive pronoun or the Hebrew pronominal suffix "his Asherah" appears in probably the oldest text we have referencing the goddess in the Hebrew Bible. In Deuteronomy 33:2-3, "at his right had his own Asherah." Because "Yahweh....his Asherah" is quoted in both biblical and extra-biblical texts the phrase may have been widely recognized and perhaps used often in the region indicating a close relationship between the pair within the cult.

---

131 A caravansary was an inn or a central courtyard for travelers to take respite in desert regions.

132 Dijkstra, 117.

What is "his Asherah" supposed to mean? Most scholars agree that both Asherah, the goddess and asherah, the cult object were associated with Yahweh. Nevertheless, regardless if the inscription referred to the goddess herself or her cult object, it reveals the same thing: Yahweh is linked to Asherah.

The associated cultic object for which Asherah was known was a wooden or sacred pole, which is referenced many times in the Bible such as in Deuteronomy 16:21-22, "You shall not plant any wooden thing as an Asherah beside the altar of the Lord your God which you shall make. And you shall not set up a pillar, which the Lord your God hates." That prohibitions need to be set implies observance at some level. Religion and Theology Professor John Day contends: "The presence of the symbol of the goddess Asherah next to Yahweh's altar most naturally suggests that she was regarded in syncretistic circles as Yahweh's consort."[133] Arguably, the worship of Asherah was happening, or forbiddance would have been superfluous. Since the findings of Kuntillet Ajrud, much of the academic community is in agreement that Asherah functioned as Yahweh's consort, if not in the official religion then most assuredly in the popular religion of the average people.

A drawing of three figures was found next to the text of "Yahweh and his Asherah" (see Figure 27). Two figures are in the foreground, and another in the background. Because the sherds contain both the inscription and the drawing, it is assumed by some that the sketch is representative of "Yahweh and his Asherah." Might this drawing be further proof that it was Asherah, the goddess, and not her cult object who was referred to in the inscription? But if that is the case, why are there three figures? That question has stumped many scholars. Some conclude the text and the drawings are unrelated. Ultimately, as with most of the findings on Kuntillet Ajrud,

---

133 John Day, "Asherah in the Hebrew Bible and Northwest Semitic Literature," in *Journal of Biblical Literature* 105, (1986): 392.

the scholarly community is divided on whether the inscriptions are related to the diagrams or not.

One of the ancillary drawings found near the inscription is of the "Asherah Tree." The wooden pole with which Asherah was associated was also symbolic of the "tree of life.[134]" Old Testament Historian Mark Smith writes, "Asherah was a nurturing mother goddess. The religious symbol of the goddess, the asherah was in Israel a wooden pole, or perhaps a tree, representing the 'tree of life.'"[135]

The "'tree of life" was a recurrent theme in the ancient Near East. An arid region, trees were revered as symbols of life and nourishment. They therefore became associated with the goddess and her cult. The "tree of life" also appears in the Garden of Eden allegory.

In her seminal book *When God Was A Woman*, feminist theologian, Merlin Stone discusses the acrimony the patriarchy felt toward the "asherim" (plural of Asherah) which she calls a major symbol of the female religion, she writes:

> It would not be too surprising if the symbolism of the tree of forbidden fruit, said to offer the knowledge of good and evil, was included in the creation story to warn that eating the fruit of this tree had caused the downfall of all humanity.

Because Asherah's name was commonly linked to Yahweh's, biblical writers may have felt the need to propagandize against it. By integrating the story of the fall of mankind into a tree that clearly was associated with her, they sent a clear warning.

---

134 Often associated with great mother goddesses, the tree is an archetype used in many religions symbolizing the fertility of the earth and the source of life.

135 Mark S. Smith, "God Male and Female in the Old Testament: Yahweh and His 'Asherah,' "*Theological Studies* 48, no 2 (June 1987):334.

In 1968, an inscription was found in an ancient burial ground west of Hebron at a site called Khirbet el-Qom. The inscription, found on a tombstone, reads:

> Blessed by Uriah by Yahweh,
>
> Yea from his enemies by his Asherah he has saved him
>
> By Oniah
>
> By his Asherah
>
> And by his A(she)rah.

The inscription has been dated to ca 750 BCE and the syntax has the same ambiguity as the inscriptions found at Kuntillet Ajrud. As noted previously, "Yahweh… and his Asherah" was a phrase that may have been fairly common in the area, as 60 or so miles separate Kuntillet Ajrud and Khirbet el-Qom—not an easy jaunt considering the limited transportation options available at the time. Furthermore, the inscription was found at an ancient burial site, signifying the importance of the phrase "Yahweh and his Asherah". As with the findings at Kuntillet Ajrud, scholarship on this finding is divided, though most agree that the text refers to asherah as a cult object.

In her book *Under Every Green Tree: Popular Religion in Sixth-Century Judah*, Susan Ackerman, Professor of Theology and Religious Studies at Villanova University asserts:

> In the ancient Near East, the idol was god. 'Srth at Kuntellet Ajrud or Kh. el -Qom could refer to Asherah's cult object, the stylized tree, or even to some hypostatized aspect of the female side of Yahweh. But what was the stylized tree or the hypostasis of the female side of Yahweh to the average worshiper? Nothing other than Asherah, the goddess.

Anthropomorphically, Asherah is represented many times in various forms scattered throughout the region. The pillar figurines (see Figure 28) from the southern kingdom of Judah are a standout. These figurines first started appearing in the late tenth to ninth century BCE and had become very common from the eighth through the seventh centuries. There is now considerable evidence that these figurines represent Asherah. The term "Images of Asherah" is used often in the Hebrew Bible. It is possible that the "pillar figurines" are what the writers of the Hebrew Bible had in mind. Numbering in the thousands, the figurines have been found in two varieties: one with an elaborately "molded head" and the other with a "pinched nose".

The heads on the "molded head" variety appear to be mass-produced, yet the bodies are hand-made, leading one scholar to suggest that the person for whom the figurine was intended individually crafted the figurine's body. This would help explain the rough manner in which the bodies were assembled. The "pinched nose" variety was likely for those who were unable to acquire a molded head. Plain as the pinched nose figurines are, their being found in large quantities underscores the importance that acquiring one of these figurines may have played in the community.

What were these figurines meant to convey, and why were they important to the Judean community, in particular? They are thought to symbolize the nurturing aspect of the mother goddess: the breasts are exaggerated, with the hands more or less supporting them. While her cult objects are in public worship spaces, the pillar figurines are found mostly in private houses, which suggests they may have been used principally by and for women with regard to fertility. The fact that many of them were found in tombs underscores their importance in society. Given that survival was the ultimate concern for the average Israelite or Judean, apprehension about lactation and fertility itself was likely widespread.

Sadly, lactation and fertility problems are indicative of some type of famine for which the region was prone. Life was difficult for the average Judean or Israelite. Surrounded by the resource-rich empires of Egypt and Mesopotamia, Israel and Judah were not only vulnerable to invasion but also lacked natural resources and a friendly climate for agriculture with which to sustain themselves. Religion was intimately linked with survival, and appeasing the deities was of great importance. To the ancient Israelite or Judean, life and religion were likely one and the same. When they were not toiling to support their families, they were engaged in religious and ritualistic practices both in the cultic community and in their individual homes. It is in this context that the figurines should be contemplated.

The pillar figurines have mostly been found in the Judah region, many in the metropolis of Jerusalem itself. Most experts concur that these figurines are small clay counterparts to the sacred wooden asherah poles. Because their elongated base is suggestive of a tree it is easy to visualize how they might look on a pole. As discussed previously, trees were symbolic of the nourishing aspect of the goddess, Asherah. When compared to the sacred wooden asherah poles, these figurines are small clay counterparts.

Based on the Hebrew Bible itself, scholar Hadley asserts that "for several centuries asherah poles stood in the [First] Temple of Jerusalem." In 2 Kings 23, dating from the late seventh century BCE during King Josiah's reforms, biblical writers talk about purging the temple of all the cult regalia of Asherah. This suggests her cult was present in the temple. If that was the case—i.e. her cult regalia was present in the First Temple of Jerusalem—then the Asherah cult was not only revered in the folk religion but incorporated into the state or official religion as well.

Along with the removal of her figurines, the sacred poles had also disappeared—the late seventh-century date would be in line with the biblical timeline mandating the purge of her cult objects from the temple. Because of the perishable nature of wood to date no asherah pole artifacts have been found in any of the excavations from the region.

The fall of Judah (ca 586 BCE) occurred 50-100 years after this period. As mentioned earlier, Asherah artifacts and textual references are, for the most part, restricted to pre-exilic, the period preceding the destruction of Jerusalem and the First Temple of Jerusalem. Scholarship indicates that the Israelites of the post-exilic period were manifestly more monotheistic than their pre-exilic counterparts.

Could Asherah have been Yahweh's consort, as many scholars now believe? Was her worship confined to folk religion only, of which we have ample evidence, or was her influence felt in the official cult, as indicated in the Hebrew Bible itself? Fascinating as it is, examining a topic that dates back three millennia has its difficulties. Now that Asherah has been put back on the map, the academic community promises further scrutiny of her all-importance in the lives of the ancient Israelites and Judeans.

Selected Reading for Asherah

Ackerman, Susan. *Under Every Tree: Popular Religion in the Sixth-Century Judah*, Boston: Harvard Semitic Monographs, 1992.

_____. "Digging Up Deborah," Near Eastern Archaeology 66, no.4 (2003):172-184.

_____. Under Every Green Tree: Popular Religion in Seventh-Century Judah. Atlanta: Scholars Press, 1992.

Armstrong, Karen. A History of God: The 4000-Year Quest of Judaism, Christianity, and Islam. New York: Alfred A. Knopf, 1993. Quoted in Jonathan Kirsch, God Against the Gods. New York: Penguin Books, 2004.

Beck, Pirhiya. "The Drawings From Horvat Teiman (Kuntillet Ajrud), Tel Aviv 9 (1982): 27-31, quoted in John Day, "Asherah in the Hebrew Bible and Northwest Semitic Literature," Journal of Biblical Literature 105, no. 3 (1986).

Bloch-Smith, Elizabeth M. Judahite Burial Practices and Beliefs About the Dead. Quoted in Judith M. Hadley The Cult of Asherah in Ancient Israel and Judah, Cambridge: Cambridge University Press, 2000.

Cornelius, Izak. The Many Faces of the Goddess. Gottingen: Academic Press Fribourg, 2004.

Davis-Wyer, Caecilla, Early Medieval Art 300-1100: Sources and Documents, Englewood Cliffs, NY: Prentice Hall, 1971, 48. Quoted in Leslie Ross, Art and Architecture of the World's Religions, Vol 2 Santa Barbara, CA: Greenwood Press, 2009.

Day, John. "Asherah in the Hebrew Bible and Northwest Semitic Literature," in *Journal of Biblical Literature* 105, (1986): 392.

_____. Yahweh and the Gods and Goddesses of Canaan. Sheffield, UK: Sheffield Academic Press, 2000.

Dever, William G. Asherah, Consort of Yahweh?" ASOR 16, no. 255 (Summer 1984).http://www.jstor.org/stable/357073.

_____. *Did God Have a Wife?* Grand Rapids, MI: Wm. B. Eerdmans, 2005.

Dijkstra, Meindert. "El, the God of Israel," *Only One God?* Edited by Bob Becking and Meindert Dijkstra, 100-129, New York: Sheffield Academic Press, 2001.

Hadley, Judith. "Yahweh and his Asherah: Archaeological and Textual Evidence." *Ein Gott allein?* Eds. Walter Dietrich and Martin A. Klopfenstein (Gottingen: Vandenhoeck und Ruprecht, 1994), 236.

Smith, Mark S. "God Male and Female in the Old Testament: Yahweh and His Asherah" *Theological Studies* 48, no 2 (June 1987):334.

Stone, Merlin. *When God Was a Woman.* Orlando, Florida: Harcourt, 1976.

Van Der Toorn, Karel. *From her Cradle to her Grave* (Wiltshire: Sheffield Academic Press, 1994, 112.